FOOD LOVERS' SERIES

FOOD LOVERS'
GUIDE TO
SANTA FE, ALBUQUERQUE & TAOS

The Best Restaurants, Markets & Local Culinary Offerings

1st Edition

Andrea Feucht

Guilford, Connecticut

To buy books in quantity for corporate use
or incentives, call **(800) 962-0973**
or e-mail **premiums@GlobePequot.com.**

Editor: Kevin Sirois
Project Editor: Lynn Zelem
Layout Artist: Mary Ballachino
Text Design: Sheryl Kober
Illustrations by Jill Butler with additional art by Carleen Moira Powell and MaryAnn Dubé
Cover photo: Sergio Salvador, salvadorphoto.com
Maps: Alena Joy Pearce © Morris Book Publishing, LLC

ISBN 978-0-7627-8155-3

Printed in the United States of America
10 9 8 7 6 5 4 3 2 1

All the information in this guidebook is subject to change. We recommend that you call ahead to obtain current information before traveling.

Contents

Albuquerque, 103

Appendices, 325

About the Author

Once upon a time, Andrea Feucht woke up to the realization that she was obsessed with food and wasn't such a bad writer either. For nearly a decade she has been writing freelance, crafting tales of food personalities and casting a critical eye on restaurants. Her work is published locally and nationally for outlets including *Edible Communities*, *Albuquerque The Magazine*, *Culture Cheese Magazine*, and *Guest Life*. She augments the writing and eating with technology consulting and trail running in her adopted hometown of Albuquerque. She also heaps love on Santa Fe for its density of amazing eateries, and on unutterably gorgeous Taos for great food and inky coffee.

For him who is fondly referred to as my "dining companion"

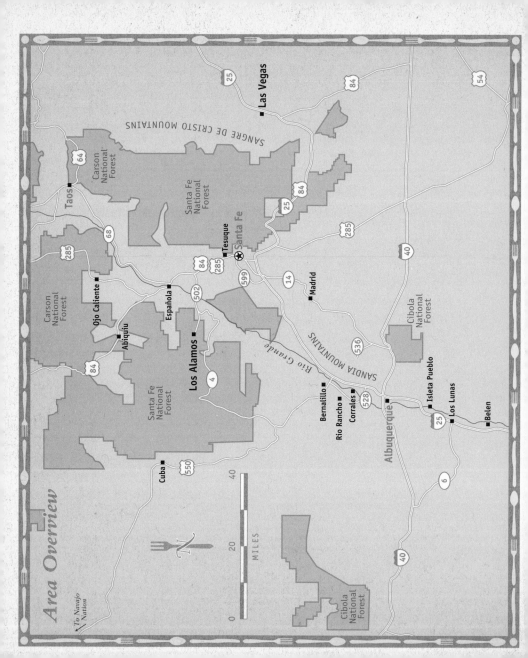

Introduction

The stretch from Albuquerque north to Santa Fe and onward to Taos is rich with culinary treasures—locals adore fancy places just as much as down-home spots that serve almost nothing but chile-smothered platters of comfort food. New Mexico hangs its hat on the devotion to chile seen in every populated place in the state, from farmer to gourmand. Tracing the influence of this fruit (chile is a fruit, not a vegetable) is a journey to what makes New Mexico delicious. It begins with the name *Capsicum annuum,* the genus and species of the Anaheim chile variety that New Mexico calls its own. The heat level famous for turning tourists into chile-heads is highly variable, and that fluctuation has very little to do with the seeds when planted.

You didn't think all chiles from the same species produced the same spice level, did you? (See the sidebar on the hottest chile you can get served in the state, p. 12.) Each chile plant's heat is tightly bound with the growing conditions that season—a harsher climate makes for hotter chiles, as the capsaicin is the protection for the chile fruit against predators. If the environment is relatively nasty, the chiles need more defenses, and your palate is rewarded with a heaping dose of pain. After enough of that pain, endorphins kick in and make everything rosy again. Two other ways to produce this kind of effect are running a marathon and giving birth—eating chiles seems like a perfect compromise.

Consider the question, "Red or green?"

New Mexican chiles are served in two colors: red and green. Each are the same fruit at different levels of ripeness. Green is younger and more vibrant in both taste and texture when fresh; red has been allowed to ripen and mellow to an earthier taste, but the texture has started to soften, so most red chile pods are dried out before use. The famous chile wreaths, called *ristras,* hanging in doorways are simply the best way to dry out chiles for cooking—they happen to be really pretty, too. New Mexican dishes are served with a diner's choice of red or green, or "Christmas"—both colors, one on each side of the plate.

New Mexican Tastes: Fusion Cuisine Before It Was Cool

The origin of New Mexican food can be found in its staples, as reverently spoken of by Natives in their pueblos: beans, corn, and squash. Those are known as the trinity of food—all three ingredients can be grown in New Mexico's climate and provide a complete diet in between hunting seasons (deer, rabbit, and trout) or berry and nut foraging. New Mexico is rather nutty, with an ample history of pecans, pine nuts, pistachios, and walnuts.

Combined with creeping influences from the south (Mexico) and Spanish settlers, the native ingredients fused in new ways to form a basis for a cuisine. The warmer climes provided exotic ingredients such as chile peppers, avocados, and citrus. From Spain came much of the meat we now eat, such as pigs, chickens, and cattle, and the wheat plants necessary for bread. Finally, they brought the one thing that made chocolate tasty to "Westerners": sugarcane. Natives drank the cocoa beverage unsweetened, but Europeans found that unbearable, adding sugar and milk until satisfied. In a way, this foreshadowed what has happened to coffee over the years as well.

Fry Bread & Tex-Mex: Despite Their Popularity, Not New Mexican Foods

There are two categories of "not New Mexican" foods: deep-fried doughy things and Tex-Mex. There's a short story for each, hopefully an illuminating glimpse into the beginnings of local food traditions and the misnomers that came along for the ride.

Fry bread (also spelled *frybread*) was born of ingenuity and hunger and lives on nearly 150 years later. In the 1860s the controlling residents of the territory (namely members of the United States military who had themselves pushed out Spanish, Mexican, and Texan settlers) decided that to keep order after treaty talks went badly, they'd set up a place for the nearby Native tribes to live. By keeping them together and teaching them how to be modern farmers, it was hoped everything would work out, more or less. Almost 9,000 Mescalero Apache and Navajo people were marched in from as far away as northern Arizona to Fort Sumner in eastern New Mexico. Things didn't go well—the native vegetable staples grew poorly, and wildlife harvest was forbidden. Starvation started to take hold. Lard, flour, sugar, and some canned goods were provided in the hope of keeping the peace, but many fled back to their original homes anyway. Those remaining survived by creating a dough, flattened by hand and fried in the lard: Fry bread was born.

Fry bread has been adopted as a cultural icon and declared a traditional food for many Natives from South Dakota to Arizona; it is a staple of roadside vendors and powwows. There is no denying either the deliciousness of fry bread or its dubious health aspects. It remains a hot topic both as a reminder of the horrible conditions endured by the Fort Sumner occupants and a proud symbol of the resolve it took to survive and ultimately move back to federally designated reservations. When your next Indian Taco is chomped by eager teeth, give a moment of pause for the amazing story that brought it to your plate.

Now, Tex-Mex? That's another story altogether, thankfully one with less hardship. Simply put, many "Southwestern" foods such as fajitas, chili with beans, and nachos are foods dreamed up by Texan and Mexican ranchers looking for good eats when the day's work was done. New Mexicans tend to be fond of our local eats and can distinguish between the two states' typical foods, though both are appealing for their own reasons. Here is a dueling list of the two cuisines; keep in mind that neither these relative analogues nor the entire list itself is hard and fast—any item could be found in both states, but the differentiation in menus is still noticeable.

TEX-MEX	NEW MEXICAN
Poblano chiles rellenos	Hatch chiles rellenos
Flour tortillas	Blue corn tortillas
Chips & chile con queso	Chips & salsa
Jalapeños (often pickled)	Hatch green chiles
Cayenne/chili powder	Hatch chiles (pureed)
Fajitas	Carne adovada
Chile con carne	Chile verde or Chile rojo
Breakfast tacos	Breakfast burrito
Chili burger	Green chile cheeseburger
Nopales (cactus)	Calabacitas (zucchini and corn)

Innovation & Modern Sensibilities: The Mark Miller Era

Modern New Mexican cuisine owes nearly everything to Mark Miller, who took local ingredients and started doing strange things with chiles and fruits and meats to wind up with duck and mango tamales and salsas that would raise any Mexican's eyebrows. But he knew what he was doing, and nearly 30 years later the cuisine has been shaped indelibly.

Mark Miller was not alone: Many Santa Fe restaurants incorporated native ingredients into their kitchens to ensure that the stacked blue corn enchilada plate would be forever in our hearts. This uniquely New Mexican platter stacks corn tortillas like pancakes with cheese and/or meat in between each layer, topping the pile with a fried egg and smothering it in chile. That's our comfort food, and it's found at nearly every restaurant that calls itself New Mexican, from the Frontier in Albuquerque to Tecolote Cafe in Santa Fe.

Influences from other continents flow into the local cuisine, and nearly every cafe and fast-food chain offers chile with their food—yes, that includes McDonald's. But rest assured there is no need to visit that burger chain for your meat-chile-cheese fix: Bobcat Bite, Owl Bar & Cafe, Bert's Burger Bowl, or even our small franchise called Blake's Lotaburger will hook you up with the fiery condiment.

The Local Movement: Farm to Restaurant, Local Markets, CSAs

In Santa Fe just a few years ago, a new farming partnership was taking shape. A local organization called the Santa Fe Alliance decided to pair farmers directly with restaurants rather than waiting for the weekly farmers' markets. In a way, this was a restaurant-only CSA. The Farm to Restaurant project was born in 2010 with a modest budget to get the ball rolling and promote the idea. Within months more than a dozen chefs and producers were connected, and the dining front in Santa Fe has benefited ever since, with participants more than tripling in number.

When it comes to farmers' markets, Santa Fe enjoys a vibrant and hopping one year-round. The winter months showcase hardy produce like root vegetables and greens, with meats, cheeses, plants, and storable goods like honey rounding out the offerings. In late spring, however, the full spectrum of produce begins to appear, and while Santa Fe's market goes back into bountiful mode, the summer markets throughout the rest of the state start up again.

Community-supported agriculture (CSA) organizations serve to bring produce directly to consumers, bypassing even the farmers' market. Santa Fe and Albuquerque both have robust options for weekly, biweekly, or longer "food box" subscriptions. An early favorite in Albuquerque was the emergence of Los Poblanos Organics in 2003, not hindered in any way by the fact that the owners were a gorgeous young couple with farming in their blood and a knack for PR. Monte and Amy Skarsgard transformed the way local produce shoppers thought and bought: Now you could pay a few hundred bucks up front and get boxes of produce every week or two for your whole family.

Within a few years, CSAs had sprouted all over the state and have grown like the organic weeds they have to contend with—many have grown from a few dozen subscribers to hundreds or more. There have never been so many ways to get your fresh veggies and fruits, not to mention ranched meats and the seemingly endless supply of delicious goat's milk cheeses.

You can find a larger list of statewide CSAs at farmersmarkets nm.org/Farmers_Markets/CSAs. Following are a few of the many regional farms and CSAs and the primary farmers' market at which to find them:

Beneficial Farm, Santa Fe and Albuquerque; year-round; (505) 453-3360; details@beneficialfarm.com; beneficialfarm.com.

Desert Valley Farms, Albuquerque; mid-May through Sept; (505) 702-6310; desertvalleyfarms@gmail.com.

East Mountain Organic Farms, Santa Fe and Albuquerque; June through Oct; (505) 281-5083; eastmountainorganicfarms.com.

Erda Gardens, Albuquerque; May through Oct; (505) 610-1538; info@erdagardens.org; erdagardens.org.

Pollo Real, Santa Fe and Albuquerque; year-round; (505) 838-0345; polloreal.com.

Red Tractor Farm, Albuquerque; June through Nov; redtractor farm@yahoo.com; redtractorfarm.net.

Skarsgard Farms, Santa Fe and Albuquerque; year-round; (505) 681-4060; skarsgardfarms.com.

Talus Wind Heritage Meats CSA, Santa Fe; year-round; (505) 501-4940; taluswindranch.com.

How to Use This Book

The location-specific chapters begin with Santa Fe as a whole, then head over to Albuquerque in three sections, and finally to Taos. Each area has an overview map.

Final chapters include one on taco trucks and then one on libations, from wine to craft beer to cocktails. To help you create some of the delectable dishes at your own table, the recipe chapter pulls knowledge from the minds of New Mexico's top chefs and brings it out via the printed word, step by tasty step. Appendices follow to help find restaurants and shops by both cuisine and specialties.

Each location chapter organizes restaurants by specific categories, such as favorites or the old-school landmarks, as well as by other features, such as culinary education, noteworthy retail shops, or even road trips. And, of course, there's a price guide so that you'll have a basic expectation for each spot.

Visit foodloversnm.com, the website for this book, for updates on restaurant happenings and maps to all the regions and features.

Foodie Faves

This section covers everything from the hottest chef-driven destinations to the homiest holes in the wall.

Landmarks

Here you will find restaurants that have been around for ages or are reliable legends. Either way, the New Mexican food scene wouldn't be the same without them.

All Chile, All the Time

This section lists restaurants that serve as benchmarks for chile consumption, either for and by locals or lauded for their friendliness to visitors experiencing chile for the first time.

Specialty Stores, Markets & Producers

Helping you navigate the long list of artisan bakeries, local butcher shops, and well-stocked specialty food markets, we give you a list of must-visit shops. Also included are coffee spots for the caffeine-challenged.

Learn to Cook

Hone your cooking skills at these classrooms and establishments.

Price Code

The price guide is based on the average price per entree at each restaurant.

$	**less than $10**
$$	**$10 to $20**
$$$	**$20 to $30**
$$$$	**more than $30**

Keeping Up with Food News

There are a few great resources to stay abreast of what is current on the dining scene, or connect with other food fanatics about where to check out the latest food truck, how to make your own tortillas, or where to find the best source of locally grown poultry.

Print Publications

Edible Santa Fe, ediblesantafe.com. Monthly magazine devoted to food culture, gastronomic personalities, and trends in the tri-city (Santa Fe, Albuquerque, Taos) area.

Local Flavor, localflavor.com. This free monthly publication highlights chefs, recipes, restaurants, and more.

Local IQ, local-iq.com. A biweekly alternative to the *Alibi,* serving up reviews and food-world gossip alongside Albuquerque events and culture.

Santa Fe Reporter, sfreporter.com. A weekly digest of culture and eats for the Santa Fe area, distributed free all over the state. Excellent food writing, with annual guides to dining.

Weekly Alibi, alibi.com. Albuquerque's free weekly available in hundreds of locations, the *Alibi* has been dishing about music, films, and food for nearly two decades. The food section features reviews and articles about edible interests.

CHILE: HOT, HOTTER, HOTTEST

We've got a thing for nearly burning our tongues off around here. While visitors might think this is craziness, locals know that one's heat tolerance can be trained, so in reality the level of "ow ow ow" spiciness experienced is nearly the same for everyone, even at different true heat levels. Those heat levels are referred to as the Scoville scale, named after a chile researcher who wanted to classify the relative heat levels of peppers. Bell peppers are 0, while pepperoncini hit several hundred; jalapeños are several thousand, and those infamous habaneros are 100,000 or more. Our own New Mexican chiles score in the same range as jalapeños, but the heat of each pepper is dependent on both the strain of the plant and the harshness of conditions while growing. Think of it this way: In a tough season with not enough water, the plant needs to take action to protect its seeds from predators so new plants can survive if the bad weather continues. That protection is felt in the heat level, and the chemical is called *capsaicin*.

Now, once the chile is ready to go and be served to your eager mouth, it is good to know which restaurants tend to choose hotter batches and prepare them without extra ingredients that might dull the heat (flour, sugar, et cetera). My strategy for getting all the heat is

Blogs, Websites & Personalities

Chowhound, chowhound.chow.com. First, search for the Southwest message board, then dive in to find opinionated yet experience-backed musings on gastronomic comings and goings all over the state.

to order a "bowl of" whatever color you're seeking. For red, it comes out looking like dark ketchup. Treat it like tomato soup and have a ball. Green is chunkier with chile pieces and sometimes ground meat, but the same eating suggestions apply.

First up in Albuquerque is a longtime favorite, Perea's New Mexican (p. 184). Their green is reliably potent, no matter what you smother it over. They are only open for breakfast and lunch, so you can make a bowl of green your new breakfast of champions. Right next to UNM is the Nob Hill location of Cecilia's Cafe (p. 130), serving the hottest red I have eaten to date. There are spice-loving friends I know who won't go near this bowl of fire. You have been warned—now go for it. Also in Albuquerque you'll find a good and spicy bowl of red or green at Sadie's New Mexican (p. 231; either location). This is notably convenient because many visitors love to try out Sadie's, and the flame-tongues can have their needs met, too.

Finally, Santa Fe: See the details on Horseman's Haven (p. 88) for my story, but suffice it to say that the green is wicked and the "Level 2" green is off my charts. I could eat a few spoonfuls of it but never a bowlful. Shockingly, as the heat level hits the stratosphere, you can still taste the chile and its fresh vegetable flavor—if this is a trick, it's a neat one.

Duke City Fix, dukecityfix.com. Established in 2005, this city blog has been home to many writers and contributors on all things Albuquerque, from where to live to whose tamales are the best.

Duke City Food, dukecityfood.com. Written by a critic for the *Albuquerque Journal,* this blog contains general food musings on the Albuquerque scene and maintains an archive of *Journal*-reviewed restaurants.

Food Lover's Guide to Santa Fe, Albuquerque, and Taos, foodloversnm.com. The website for this very book! You'll find updates on restaurant happenings and maps to all the regions and features—super handy in an ever-changing business world.

Gil's Thrilling (and Filling) Blog, nmgastronome.com. Gil Garduno's long list of evaluations, many complete with photos and notes about number of times visited. One of the most comprehensive restaurant lists for Albuquerque.

Santa Fe Barman, santafebarman.com. A cocktail mixologist's take on the food and beverage scene in Santa Fe; works slinging drinks at the Secreto Bar.

Food & Drink Events

Culinary festivals can be found all over the state of New Mexico, from swanky sponsored soirees to tribe-only harvest celebrations. This collection focuses on the Albuquerque–Santa Fe–Taos corridor, with one famously notable exception in southern New Mexico that no local guide could do without (the Hatch Chile Festival). This is a selection of the most interesting and largest food events, but a more comprehensive schedule is always available on the New Mexico tourism website: newmexico.org/cuisine/food_festivals.

January

Taos Winter Wine Festival, Taos; taoswinterwinefest.com. Nothing is ever small in Taos: The ski area is the largest in the state, the Rio Grande Gorge Bridge is massive and gorgeous (ha!), and this festival of all things food and wine is a phenomenal weekend. Start midweek with featured dinners in the evening, then on to Thursday with a few single vineyard tastings and the Taste of Taos & Reserve Tasting to keep tickling your taste buds. Skiing fanatic? All weekend you can even have booze in your ski boots with Apres Ski Tastings that convene at the bottom of the slopes in the lovely Bavarian Lodge. Friday and Saturday bring more tastings at landmark locations such as the Taos Inn and Lambert's. The crescendo is Saturday night with a Grand Tasting in the Ski Valley Resort with views of white slopes and the sounds of clinking glassware from 30 different wineries.

Souper Bowl, Albuquerque; rrfb.org. **Souper Bowl,** Santa Fe; thefooddepot.org. Every year foodie friends endure a round of questioning about their plans for the Souper Bowl, regardless of their appreciation for the pigskin. Once the meaning is clear—"It's the one with the soup!"—tickets are purchased. Held by the Roadrunner Food Bank and the Food Depot, respectively, these events bring together dozens of soup crafters to each event for competition and gastronomic delight. In Albuquerque the event is held at the food warehouse, a way for the public to see how much their donations really help; in 2011, 251 tons per week were distributed all over the state. Attendees sample as many of the soups as they'd like, vote on their favorites, and finish off with treats from dessert tables dotted among the soups. Restaurants introduce new recipes or bring out their most beloved formulas, hoping for awards from diners and critics. Chowders do well with the attendees, but the critics often gravitate toward the inventive, like Mushroom White Chocolate Cappuccino.

February

ARTFeast, Santa Fe; artfeast.com. ARTFeast is an annual festival devoted to Santa Fe artists, showcasing their new works in galleries all over town. The events go on all weekend, but the focus for food lovers is the Friday-evening Edible Art Tour, an all-you-can-stroll buffet of galleries, each one pairing with a local restaurant or chef. An inexpensive ticket buys an admission button and a map to the treasures, which include bite-size nibbles from each chef's personal trove of recipes. Some foods are the chef's "greatest hits," like the paella on hand nearly every year from El Farol. Others are being tested for inclusion in future menus, or are one-of-a-kind treats just for this event. I've sampled delicate chocolate-dipped fresh herbs from a local chocolatier, sipped award-winning African peanut soup from Jambo Cafe, and quaffed margaritas of one's dreams from Maria's New Mexican Kitchen. The galleries stretch over a mile from end to end, and late-winter temperatures can be chilly, so my advice is stroll as fast as you can—or catch one of the event's shuttle vans to get from one area to another.

March

Santa Fe Restaurant Week, Santa Fe; santafe.nmrestaurant week.com. **Albuquerque Restaurant Week,** Albuquerque; albuquerque.nmrestaurantweek.com. **Taos Restaurant Week,** Taos; taos.nmrestaurantweek.com. Santa Fe is the first slot in the monthlong New Mexico Restaurant Week events all over the state. This relatively small town has embraced the festivities with open arms by showcasing more restaurants than any other city on the roster—even Albuquerque—proving that Santa Feans really, really dig their local culinary talent. The special prices and showy menus draw thousands out of their routine to try eateries on their "to do" list, from eclectic to showy. Most restaurants offer both lunch and dinner menus, giving diners a myriad of options from the frugal ($25 for two) to over the top ($40-plus per person). Other offerings range from wine tastings and cooking demonstrations to discounts on lodging. That means if you are itching for a

New Mexican Food Terms Glossary

Albondigas. A clear-brothed meatball soup, found in down-home cafes.

Biscochito. The state cookie; a shortbread-like round spiced with anise.

Blue corn. Native corn kernels that make for pale blue tortillas.

Bowl of red, and bowl of green. Chopped or pureed chile served as a soup with whole pinto beans and (optionally) meat.

Breakfast burrito. Eggs, hash browns, cheese, and chile nestled in a flour tortilla.

Calabacitas. Zucchini and corn sautéed together, served as a side dish.

Capirotada. Lenten bread pudding studded with raisins.

Carne adovada. Pork stewed in red chile until tender, served alone or as the meat in any New Mexican dish.

Chicharrones. Fried pork skins, with or without a dusting of chile powder.

Chiles. *Capsicum annuum.* Varieties include Hatch in the south, Chimayó in the north, and many others at individual farms.

Chiles rellenos. Green chiles filled (usually with cheese), battered, and fried.

Cilantro. Culinary herb used as garnish or a salsa ingredient.

Empanada. Pocket pie made from pastry dough, filled with spiced fruit.

Enchiladas. Stacked layers of corn tortillas and cheese or meat, topped with chile, with or without fried egg.

Flan. Caramel custard.

Frijoles. Pinto beans, often refried (then called *refritos*).

Green chile stew. Chopped chiles, pork, and potatoes stewed until tender in a rich broth.

Horno. Native clay or brick oven used to bake breads or simmer stews.

Huevos rancheros. Corn tortillas topped with eggs and chile sauce (beans are optional).

Level 2. Infamous "off the menu" chile at Horseman's Haven; only fire-eaters should try.

Natilla. Rice pudding, mildly sweetened and served for dessert.

Posole. Similar to green chile stew, with white hominy instead of potatoes; meat is optional in this traditional holiday soup.

Sopaipillas. Small pillows of fry bread served with New Mexican meals, eaten with honey or syrup.

Tamal. Corn dough (called *masa*) filled with meat or vegetables and then steamed until cooked and tender; traditional holiday dish; also spelled *tamale*.

Tortilla. Unleavened circle of bread, made from wheat flour or cornmeal, the starchy component to many New Mexican meals.

really long vacation, you could tour the entire state, week by delicious week.

Here's a strategy tip: Perhaps your favorite New Mexican spot knows your order by heart (chicken enchiladas with green, no garnish), and your favorite table has scuff marks from the way your water glass is thunked down. During Restaurant Week choose the *other* thing on the featured list—the tamales or the chiles rellenos or whatever—and let your taste buds decide. Make it your goal to choose at least two restaurants: a regular spot like the one just mentioned, and another place that you've meant to visit but haven't made the time. You might end up a happy regular.

National Fiery Foods & Barbecue Show, Albuquerque; fiery foodsshow.com. There are few better places than New Mexico to hold an event dedicated to piquancy of all kinds. Whether "hot, hotter, hottest" is a rallying call or your tastes run more toward edibles with "just a little kick," everyone will find spicy joy at this massive festival. The show spans three days, with hundreds of exhibitors and aisle after aisle of vendors offering up their concoctions for sale—with samples to whet your appetite. Producers that were talented enough to win a current-year Scovie Award will be sure to brag, loud and proud, that they emerged victorious from the previous fall's judging. Many companies win year after year—proof that they know the ins and outs of their category, from "Fresh Salsa" to "Sweet Heat." Barbecue fans and vendors are abundant, trading smoking secrets or talking about the best new rub they've found on the show floor. In the crowded rows, just as many folks cannot wait to sample treats like ultra-spicy Bloody Mary mix or eat a chocolate-dipped habanero on a dare. I love to shop, especially when the company is a local favorite. You can bring home delights like hunks of Chile-Pecan Brittle from C. G. Higgins Artisan Chocolates in Santa Fe or a tub of Holy Chipotle Chevre from the Old Windmill Dairy east of Albuquerque. Both are Scovie winners, and for good reason—for the many small companies featured at the event, their love comes through in that chile burn.

Southwest Chocolate & Coffee Fest, Albuquerque; chocolate andcoffeefest.com. Just a few years old, this tribute to everyone's two favorite brown fermented foods is hard to resist. That's right, coffee and chocolate are both plants that have been through a necessary fermentation step to develop the flavors we love so much. Simply wallowing in the fare is plenty for most attendees, with vendors both sampling and selling their finest in java and cacao. Others will get inspired by cooking demonstrations, chocolate-eating contests (what, no espresso-drinking contest?), coffee and tea seminars, and, of course, a gigantic chocolate fountain. Enterprising bakers can enter a chocolate dessert contest open to the public. Can you say "homemade chile brownies"? Willy Wonka is said to be one of the featured guests, but I'm betting we won't see Gene Wilder or Johnny Depp in character—what a shame. The grown-ups' consolation prize is a Friday-night after-hours party with funky bands and dance performances—put the heels on and leave the kids at home. With ample caffeine and sweet chocolate on hand (and in mouth), attendees' energy should be unstoppable.

May

New Mexico Wine Festival, Bernalillo; newmexicowinefestival .com. Baby, it's *HOT* outside: How about a stroll around the park with a few thousand of your closest friends, drinking wine from a souvenir glass? It took many years for me to head over to this Memorial Day party, partly due to reports of long lines and ridiculous temperatures. In fairness, the New Mexico Wine Festival is a far better event than rumored; bring both water and sunscreen and things will go very well. Walking from vendor to vendor on the cool grass to sample dozens of wines makes one overly enthusiastic after about the tenth sip. Keep your credit card handy to purchase the wines you really adore—some are limited batches or specially priced for the weekend. Just make sure you step over to the "express buy" line when your tongue gets inspired—coming back later might mean an even longer wait and a frustrated stomping away before you make that purchase. Sample some of the edibles while you're at it, listen to live music, and catch up with the friends you last saw earlier in the spring, promising to "do lunch soon." The logistics are not bad: Shuttle buses help with the spread-out parking situation, and the designated driver in your group gets free admission and a gift in lieu of a tasting glass.

July

New Mexico Pork & Brew Barbeque Championship, Rio Rancho; rioranchonm.org. Since 2004 this festival has drawn serious BBQ talent into a vortex of smoke rings and down-home goodness in a state that used to lag behind the curve in general barbecue appreciation. Thankfully, we're catching up, in part because of this event—over 50 com‐ petitors warm up their smokers and get to busi‐ ness each summer under the fully sanctioned eye of the Kansas City Barbeque Society, who say it is one of the top 10 competitions in the country. Local superstars like  Mad Max's, Porky's Pride, and the Smoke Ring have all won awards in categories from straight-up brisket to chicken and sausage, along with the necessary accoutrements like coleslaw and desserts. The atmosphere is not unlike a county fair, with rides, carnival games, food-on-a-stick, and frozen beverages to curtail the scorching sun (or spicy sauce!). And like that county fair, it can seem a little too country, but just wait for the piglet races and you'll forget every‐ thing else and start squealing along with the rest of the crowd.

August

Santa Fe Indian Market, Santa Fe; swaia.org. Technically this is not a food-centered event, but the sheer depth of culture and sampling of Native foods are both worth investigation. The largest Native arts market in the world is also Santa Fe's largest event of any kind, bringing $100 million into the local economy. While the entire event spans a week, the draw for the food lover is on Saturday, when the Plaza and surrounding streets become home to nearly a thousand white open-sided tents, each one shielding a table from the summer sun. Even if you have no interest in buying art, you can get a taste of Native culture with authentic cuisine that you may have not encountered before. Sure, there's fry bread—an untraditional treat that has become beloved despite its history. Few have the power to resist the smell of freshly fried dough, judging by the lines at the fry bread vendors and the smiles on faces as the first bite is taken. The heart of the food offerings, however, comes with items like mutton-chile stew, Navajo blue corn pancakes, Hopi piki bread, bowls of red or green chile, and roasted sweet corn on the cob. These foods are the source on which all modern interpretations depend—taste them as made by generations of Native cooks, and you'll see New Mexican cuisine in a whole new light.

September

Hatch Chile Festival, Hatch; hatchchilefest.com. What's a four-hour drive when the destination is the eponymous celebration of the best-known New Mexican food? Saddle up the gas tank and head south to Hatch for Labor Day's tribute to all things capsicum. The late-summer weather will be hot with a chance of afternoon thunderstorms—it's the best way to take the edge off the temperature and the glare out of the sun. Set up at the edge of town and looking just like a county fair, the chile festival will load you up with at least two things: sacks of freshly roasted chile and all the "fair" food you can handle. An oversize tent holds some of the smaller exhibits like local baked goods, chile lore and literature, and the featured live entertainment. For those in the chile industry, this is a holiday party of sorts—kicking up the heels near the end of harvest and showing off the heat levels of the year's crop. I keep my eyes peeled for a green chile ice-cream truck, but so far it has stayed in my dreams. One can hope.

Santa Fe Wine & Chile Fiesta, Santa Fe; santafewineandchile .org. Food events in New Mexico get no fancier than the Wine & Chile Fiesta. The sandals and T-shirts come off and the cowboy boots and turquoise are put on; everyone gets decked out for this star-studded gala. Tickets start at $50 for low-key classes and tastings and venture north of $150 for lavish prix-fixe meals that combine the talents of the best chefs in town and wine experts from all over the country. Previous fiestas have offered a jaw-dropping tour of Georgia O'Keeffe's home in Abiquiu followed by lunch back in Santa Fe at her eponymous restaurant. For those who like wine and gourmet food but find the intensive seminars daunting, Saturday's the day to take in everything at once, a nibble at a time, under one enormous roof at the Grand Food & Wine Tasting. While the north-of-$100 ticket price may seem steep, you can immerse yourself in the best bites from 75 restaurants and 90 wineries, held on the gorgeous grounds of the Santa Fe Opera just north of town. Think of it this way: It's a pricey meal, but likely the only one you'll need all day.

Santa Fe

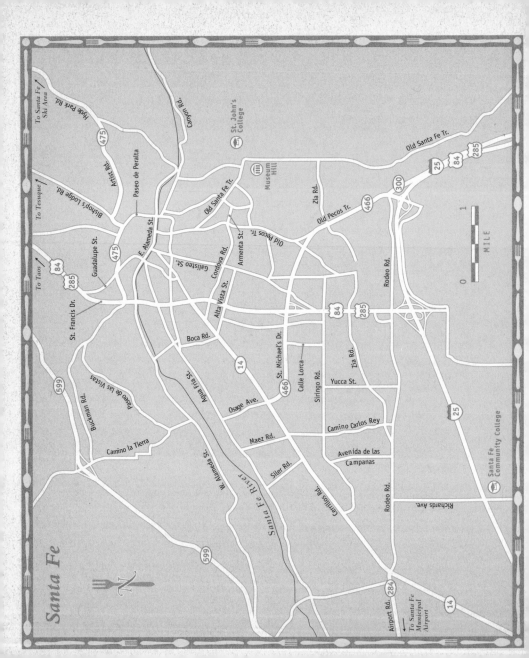

Santa Fe

Tipping the atmospheric scales at 7,000 feet above sea level, the Santa Fe air is crisp and the winters are nothing to take lightly—it is the place to go when Albuquerque seems too big or too warm, and is a wonderful getaway for residents and vacationers alike. Visitors find oodles of history in the winding central streets, carved out long before any type of large transport was used, from buggies to wagons to cars. These are foot and horse streets by design, and drivers are reminded of it when they try to find parking or pass along a narrow lane.

Mixed in with that settler culture is a rich territorial history: This is the state capital, home to earnest politicians, intrepid journalists, and the longest-occupied public building in the nation—the Palace of the Governors. From that 1610 landmark it is an easy stroll to the public History Museum and on from there to more museums than you thought possible in such a small town. Spend just a little while in Santa Fe, and any notions of this being a cowboy town stuck in the past evaporate as you take in art galleries and architecture that anyone would call modern marvels.

Adding to those modern marvels are the innovative dishes being plated at restaurants all over town. Starting with a base of local ingredients and traditional foods such as chiles, corn, and beans, chefs have brought their creativity to bear on their customers' plates. Mark Miller's Coyote Cafe was among the first to expose the world to modern New Mexican, taking the tamale and applying unheard-of fusion ingredients like jerk-spiced shrimp or even foie gras to the flavor profile. This was both ludicrous and delicious, and the snowball was rolling. One of the most common new-wave border foods is duck in everything—duck confit tacos and duck enchiladas are normal these days.

Ultimately, there's a reason Santa Fe is front and center on a New Mexican foodie's radar: The best and brightest talents all congregate in this "City Different," where the money seems to flow in good times and lean. It makes for a competitive (often cutthroat) market where the best chefs and dishes survive and the barely passable are not invited to the party. Perfectly great restaurants close all the time, to the chagrin of their fans, but inevitably a new spot will pop up with the same staff or with a chef transplanted from another kitchen or city. In recent years the legendary Palace Restaurant was closed for a long renovation, reopening to much anticipation with Joseph Wrede, one of Taos's most beloved chefs, at the helm. Another foodie favorite, Torino's @ Home, closed in Santa Fe, only to reopen in Albuquerque.

Dynamism will always be with the restaurant business, for better or for worse. The benefit of the western mindset is that an hour's drive to get somewhere delicious is not daunting, making the 60-mile trip from Santa Fe to either Taos or Albuquerque a nonissue.

Getting Around

Santa Fe is laid out in a west-fanning triangle shape, with rough edges of I-25 on the south (which has an unusual east–west section here), NM 599 on the west, and the Old Santa Fe Trail to the east. Driving most places in town will involve the north–south St. Francis Drive, leading from the interstate to the Plaza area and onward. Paseo de Peralta forms a U all the way around downtown and the Plaza, joining with St. Francis in two locations; once you can visualize that layout in your head, it's easy. Cerrillos spans southwest from the Plaza in a long stretch of commerce and retail all the way to the airport. Near the Plaza you should walk—parking is not easy and the streets are narrow—but for other spots in town, it is handy to have a vehicle.

Travel between Santa Fe and Albuquerque is wondrously easy thanks to the Rail Runner (nmrailrunner.com). About a half-dozen trains per day take the 90-minute ride from downtown Santa Fe to downtown Albuquerque or vice versa, with free Wi-Fi to boot.

Aldana's Restaurant, 3875 Cerrillos Rd., Santa Fe, NM 87507; (505) 471-0271; Mexican/New Mexican; $. A pleasant mishmash of perfectly done American and New Mexican favorites with a breakfast buffet you won't run away from screaming in overcooked egg horror. Aldana's is located in a most convenient place—near shopping and chain restaurants, which makes this homey destination practically an oasis in the culinary desert that surrounds it. *Chilaquiles* are a welcome breakfast dish—that inspired border concoction of eggs and old tortillas—but this diner-oriented place also serves up chicken-fried steak for the truck-stop fans out there. A few surprises liven up the menu, like the rarely seen chile relleno omelet: Picture a fluffy blanket of egg wrapped around even more layers—crispy batter, green chile, and, finally, cheese. Try it here and at the **Plaza Cafe** (p. 82), then compare notes if you're up for a food challenge.

Andiamo!, 322 Garfield St., Santa Fe, NM 87501; (505) 995-9595; andiamosantafe.com; Italian; $$. Any doubts about the authenticity of this Italian spot should be quashed by what I saw the first time I strolled by on a late evening. It was several stunning ladies in full "I just flew in from Rome" regalia leaving the restaurant, chatting a mile a minute with accents as thick as béchamel. Now that you have been enticed through the doors, have a seat and start salivating at the starters: pan-seared polenta with Gorgonzola sauce, risotto fritters, piles of crispy calamari. I beg of you to order that polenta, even if it takes a big bite out of your appetite—it is heavenly, each and every tender and rich bite. Assuming you do eventually jump over to entrees, the classics await: Marsala, Bolognese, Scaloppini, and beyond. Finishing with tiramisu is advised—the small portion is perfectly balanced with the decadence that comes from layering cake with mascarpone cheese. Most locals have a top 3 Italian list in Santa Fe, and invariably Andiamo! is on that list: unpretentious and always there for your pasta and polenta desires.

Atrisco Cafe & Bar, 193 Paseo de Peralta, Santa Fe, NM 87501; (505) 983-7401; atriscocafe.com; New Mexican; $$. Don't have visions of cute little lambs in your head. Instead, have the sensation on your tongue of a rich bowl of red chile, studded with tender brisket carrying the strong flavor of the wild. OK, yes, that's the lamb, but it's humdinger good. You can have it as described or tucked into a burrito, again draped in red chile and nothing else—additional cheese or leafy condiments would interfere with that primal flavor. Beyond this specialty you'll find a nice array of classic New Mexican, from enchiladas to *carne adovada* to green chile cheeseburgers, made with grass-fed local beef. Chile in sauces or bowls is nice and hot, leading me to want to only order it by the bowl—my favorite comfort food since the chile bug bit me ages ago. Specialty margaritas from their full bar are a big help to wash down any excess spice. After all that, I still salivate over a slice of homemade banana cream pie—once you get a look, you will, too.

Azur, 428 Agua Fria St., Santa Fe, NM 87501; (505) 992-2897; azursantafe.com; Mediterranean/Spanish; $$$. Secure the love of your grumbling tummy when you step off the Rail Runner train and head 1 block north to this corner bistro offering dishes plucked right out of Europe's coasts. A reasonable wine list offers up pairings for the likes of piquillo peppers stuffed with pork belly (light and fruity, possibly Prosecco), and that's just getting started. The massive starters list could build a meal for me in small plates, one sautéed calamari or chickpea fritter at a time. Early in the evening as the tables are filling up, you can chat with the staff about their favorite dishes: I was steered toward a lamb shoulder tagine gently braised with dried fruit and spices, but instead my eyes wandered over to the Foie de Veau Provençale, calf liver with a tangy mélange of capers, black olives, and tomatoes. This is the kind of cooking you could eat every day—warm comfort without excess richness, like putting on a fleece instead of a parka.

Baja Tacos, 2621 Cerrillos Rd., Santa Fe, NM 87505; (505) 471-8762; bajatacos.net; Mexican; $. Not technically a food truck or a restaurant, Baja Tacos is a walk-up stand with an itty-bitty interior and fierce local fans. A mural on the building's wall is a lovely tribute to Santa Fe culture, but it is the *carne adovada* that pays tribute to every local's edible desires. Local favorites dot the menu, from Frito pie to tacos so inexpensive that you order them in bundles and eat them like popcorn—several friends claim that the tacos are actually addictive, but you'll have to try them out to see if you agree. Their second location is at 2754 Agua Fria St., Santa Fe, NM 87507; also (505) 471-8762.

Bobcat Bite, 418 Old Las Vegas Hwy., Santa Fe, NM 87505; (505) 983-5319; bobcatbite.com; Burgers; $. Foodies all over the country have heard of this tiny slice of a burger joint a few miles outside of Santa Fe. In the early days, some of the hand-ground kitchen scraps were fed to neighborhood bobcats after hours, leading to the memorable name. Hamburger obsessives and experts have rained praise on the item Bobcat Bite does best on its short menu: the burger. Most locals will order it as a green chile cheeseburger; frankly, it does not matter how you order it as long as you know what you are getting into: 9 ounces of the beefiest burger you may ever have. All grades of done-ness are slightly undershot, so a medium will be closer to medium-rare—far better to err under rather than overdone. The barely adequate bun holds the inch-thick patty in your two fists, soaking up pink cooking juices while all your helpless brain can register is "Beef. Beef. Beef. Beef." All your face can do is chew, smile, and swoon. After a Bobcat burger I have a hard time facing red meat for a day or two—the body has been overloaded with delicious excess.

Body Cafe, 333 W. Cordova Rd., Santa Fe, NM 87505; (505) 986-0362; bodyofsantafe.com; Vegetarian/Healthy/Organic; $$. **Vegan and raw sprouted pizza. Healthy truffles. Green energy smoothies.** If those phrases induce involuntary shudders and bring visions of one of your hippie exes cooking at home, take another look. The Body Cafe takes those edgy theories about health food and teases them into palatability for many of us and sheer bliss for the already converted. Note that while Body revels in offering truly raw and vegan menu items, they know that all whole foods are healthy, so you can get a two-egg breakfast or a lamb burger. That being said, I recommend you go the freaky route—you're already here, right? The raw pizza is utterly delicious—but it ain't pizza. It's a crunchy and flavorful seed-based cracker with pesto, tomatoes, olives, pine nut cheese, and greens on top. The vegan Thai soup omits nothing you'll miss: The coconut, curry, lemongrass, lime, and cilantro are all here. You will miss out if you don't have something sweet—the truffles are fantastic, but there's also raw carrot cake and home-made cookies galore.

Bumble Bee's Baja Grill, 301 Jefferson St., Santa Fe, NM 87501; (505) 820-2862; bumblebeesbajagrill.com; Mexican/Fast Food; $. Not long after I moved to New Mexico, I lived in Santa Fe, and Bumble Bee's was my first "fancy" burrito, after cutting my teeth on the straightforward breakfast burrito assembly and finding that all I thought I needed. This Santa Fe staple is served as a San Diego-style fat one—big as your forearm and stuffed with combinations of meat, rice, beans, guacamole, salsa, and cheese. Lighter appetites should opt for a taco or two—they're still big for tacos, but pretty tasty when topped with house-made salsas from mild to habanero-hot. The mascot, a plump and happy bee shaking his maracas, puts a smile on everyone's face and starts the visit off on a good note. Energy is abundant in the staff, and owners "Bumble Bee" Bob and BJ Weil don't seem to be slowing down in the slightest. Southern Santa Fe can partake at their more burger-heavy second location at 3777 Cerrillos Rd., Santa Fe, NM 87507; (505) 988-3278.

Chocolate Maven Bakery & Cafe, 821 W. San Mateo Rd., Ste. C, Santa Fe, NM 87505; (505) 982-4400; chocolatemaven.com; Bakery/Cafe; $$. The Maven does dinner? This came as a shock, as they seem to be so naturally into breakfasting and brunches that I figured the rest of the day was needed to fuel up for another morning of delighting every single mouth that came through the warehouse doors. Their ridiculous house-made granola is likely the unhealthiest granola you'll ever have—crunchy and richly studded with nuts. Other grainy options are legend: pancakes with caramel-ized bananas, cheese blintzes, crème brûlée French toast. Or play it on the protein side and have an omelet made with local eggs and goat cheese. People watching is energizing here—everyone seems to be chatty and gracious, eyeing up food as it comes out and planning their next visit. Dinner brings out more of the local ingredients to rellenos, chile-rubbed chicken, and thin-crust pizzas. At the front, watch the bakery churning out pastries to be

Road Trip from Santa Fe: Northwestward to O'Keeffe Country & Hot Springs

The corridor from Santa Fe that runs north and west to Durango is a striking canvas of red and white rocks, wide-open plains, and scrubby pine trees. You'll find the landscape that inspired Georgia O'Keeffe if you venture far enough, but nearer at hand are some time-worthy destinations. Set out from Santa Fe, pass through Española, and head north on US 285, staying on US 84 when 285 turns off to the right.

After another 10 miles, look for the sign for El Rito and turn north on FR 554 (it's paved). In just a few miles is an off-the-beaten-path restaurant with a tiny footprint but a huge reputation: *El Farolito, 1212 Main St., El Rito, NM 87530; (575) 581-9501; New Mexican; $.* You will literally drive past it, even though the speed limit is 25—look up the Google Street View to get an idea of how tiny it actually is. Once inside, grab one of the three tables and get ready for serious eats. Order Frito pie, or tamales, or rellenos—each item seems to be a winner, especially with a sopaipilla on the side. The folks are friendly, and you're fueled up and happy.

sold at retail shops all over the state—the brownies could send you into a (pleasant) chocolate coma.

Clafoutis, 402 N. Guadalupe St., Santa Fe, NM 87501; (505) 988-1809; French/Bakery; $$. Returning to Clafoutis is like a reunion

Now sated, choose your adventure: the direct, 30-minute route to the hot springs, or 3 to 4 hours and 140 miles to see O'Keeffe country first? For the scenic/long route, head south on NM 554 the way you came down to US 84, then turn north/right toward Abiquiu. You'll pass the reservoir and head into the buttes and mesas of gallery paintings galore. Soak it in, take your time, even visit the Ghost Ranch if you'd like. Then head north again and take US 64 east toward Tres Piedras, itself a high road of lovely alpine vegetation. At Tres Piedras head south on US 285 for 30 miles to Ojo Caliente.

To take the short route, continue on NM 554 until it merges headed south with NM 111, then take a south/right turn onto US 285 just 2 miles north of Ojo Caliente for your hot springs date. In Ojo Caliente, stay the night for a true indulgence, or pop up for dinner and head back the same day. The restaurant on-site is The Artesian, *Ojo Caliente Mineral Springs Resort & Spa, 50 Los Baños Rd., Ojo Caliente, NM 87549; (505) 583-2233; ojospa.com; New Mexican/Eclectic/Fine Dining; $$$.* It's best described as modern native, with piñon-apple-cactus salads and Mayan tacos and fancy enchiladas and the like. It could also be accurately described as "oh, wow."

with my old appreciation for baguettes and imported butter; it's also a reunion with Albuquerque's former French Corner bistro, which closed so that owners Anne-Laure and Philippe Ligier could have some time off. They couldn't stay away, however, and opened in Santa Fe as Clafoutis with nearly the same menu—French Corner

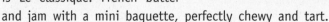

fans couldn't be happier. The breakfast I adored so much is Le Classique: French butter and jam with a mini baguette, perfectly chewy and tart. Paired with a bowl (yes, a bowl!) of café au lait, and you're sated for 6 bucks. French country is the decor; painted wood beams and bric-a-brac shelves provide the backdrop for intimate tables and friendly conversations. Croissants sell like the treasures they are, so you might need to console yourself with a slice of quiche or a *croque monsieur,* or perhaps a tasty crepe with ham and cheese or Nutella. The best lunches are assorted French plates with pâté, pickles, bread, and cheeses—the effect is especially transporting if Francophiles are seated nearby.

The Compound Restaurant, 653 Canyon Rd., #A, Santa Fe, NM 87501; (505) 982-4353; compoundrestaurant.com; French/Fine Dining; $$$$. Mark Kiffin transitioned from working with Mark Miller into ownership of this established destination, reopening after an overhaul in 2000. The national awards began piling up, from *Gourmet*'s Best American Restaurants to recognition by the *New York Times*. The ultra-snooty service had disappeared, but creative modern food remained; lunch hours will satisfy gourmet cravings with a lobster salad or perfectly composed soups made to order— the winter cauliflower with duck bacon is amazing. There are a few cracks in the armor, evident when a burger came out overdone—if it were correct, the quality would be worth the $14. At lunch the service seems downgraded to match the prices, and daylight lets the wear in the upholstery show a bit much. There is still a lot of good going on here, but perhaps a little polishing will bring back the shine that won the accolades.

Cowgirl BBQ, 319 S. Guadalupe St., Santa Fe, NM 87501; (505) 982-2565; cowgirlsantafe.com; American/Barbecue/Cajun; $$. It can get loud in the Cowgirl, but raucous diners are nothing to fear and the energy level is undeniable when you combine fresh drinks, hearty food, and the best live-music lineup in the city. Everyone plays here, from local to nationwide tours, while the folks gathered inside and out just sit back and enjoy (having a conversation can be tough if the music's flowing). Favorite entrees include chicken-fried chicken and the Cajun classics jambalaya and crawfish étouffée— this state could always serve more crawfish, in my opinion. The Cowgirl is a huge relief effort in that regard, especially with the unusual and addicting Dave's Famous Rellenos—chiles rellenos draped in crawfish étouffée . . . magical. New Mexico's location is actually the second: The first Cowgirl Hall of Fame restaurant opened in New York in 1988 (five years prior to Santa Fe) and lives on to this day, with both locations satisfying the hungry cowgirl in everyone. When any festive occasion comes around, it is often the Cowgirl throwing the best shindig, keeping folks up late in a city that can be a bit light on the late-night options.

Del Charro, 101 W. Alameda St., Santa Fe, NM 87501; (505) 954-0320; delcharro.com; Pub/American/Burgers; $. Locals might not want this paragraph written, but you can't always keep quiet about finds, lest they wither away from lack of word of mouth. Del Charro, with its doors right on the street corner, is a treasured hole-in-the-curb that seems never to attract overflow from the Plaza despite being a block away. Their food is simple, delicious, and ridiculously cheap. Read down the menu and you'll rub your eyes before checking again: burger, $6; grilled cheese and soup, $4; stuffed poblano, $7. Even better are the weekly specials where a mere 5 bucks will score a burrito or a chicken-fried steak or blue corn enchiladas. Whew. Even the house margarita is 6 bucks, or try a unique Texas Irish Coffee with Tia Maria and brandy. I treasure the day I was introduced to this friendly spot and hope that many other folks can enjoy it, too.

El Parasol, 1833 Cerrillos Rd., Santa Fe, NM 87505; (505) 995-8015; elparasol.com; Mexican; $. It was one of the first places pointed out to me as I learned my way around being "into food"—the umbrella sign out in front of a burrito place that looked a bit, well, like a shack. A falling-down shack. Now, I was being harsh with the perceived condition of the building, but I was also about to get a lesson in unpretentious tasty food: Find the dives. El Parasol has served a loyal clientele since 1958 in Española, when a mom and two boys set up their big umbrella in the summer and sold tacos and tamales to drivers, running the orders from umbrella to car as the drivers lined up. Now the region has six locations: two each in Santa Fe and Española, one in Pojoaque, and one in Los Alamos. The menu is straight-up burrito joint with tamales ($2!), tacos, and Frito pies as a bonus, with locals coming back year after year for the burritos they grew up on. A fancier sit-down restaurant called **El Paragua** is the refined companion to the El Parasol locations and is located on the way to Taos: 603 Santa Cruz Rd., Española, NM 87532; (505) 753-3211; elparagua.com.

El Tesoro, 500 Montezuma Ave. (Sanbusco Market Center), Santa Fe, NM 87501; (505) 988-3886; sanbusco.com/stores/food/el-tesoro; Cafe/South American; $. Breakfast rules at this walk-up counter in the overly touristy Sanbusco Market Center—you'll come away wondering how a spot like this can be so good. El Tesoro means "the treasure," and this jewel box of an ordering counter and small dining area is a find for South American treats. Unassuming soft corn street tacos overfilled with chicken or fish pack a punch of flavor; sides of rich black beans and Mexican rice are optional. My first pick are *pupusas,* those stuffed masa cakes served with fragrant pickled slaw called *curtido*—look for them on the "lighter side" section of the menu along with the tender Salvadoran tamal with chicken filling and salsa. Little places like this make mall shopping actually tolerable.

Epazote, 416 Agua Fria St., Santa Fe, NM 87501; (505) 988-5991; epazotesantafe.com; Mexican; $$$. Now that Mexican cooking is well established in the minds of Americans, many diners have heard of mole, but the first thing that leaps to mind is a chocolate-brown sauce called *mole poblano,* just one of the seven moles of Oaxaca and one of dozens all over the diverse country of Mexico. Ranging in colors from orange to green, you can experience some of that diversity at Epazote, which features a rotating array of daily moles. A recent visit showcased that chocolate-tinged mole poblano along with a fiery green mole with jalapeños and pumpkin seeds and Chef Fernando Olea's creation: **New Mexican Mole,** with red chile, pecans, and piñon nuts providing the dominant flavors (see the recipe on p. 310). Moles are paired with featured meat dishes, or choose delicate lamb roasted in banana leaves or shrimp enchiladas with an unusual zucchini-blossom poblano sauce. Appetizers are fun when you take a walk on the ancient side and order the Taquitos de Chapulines, tiny tortillas with guacamole and spicy grasshoppers with a fantastic popcorn-like crunch—a far cry and a welcome diversion from New Mexican cuisine.

Harry's Roadhouse, 96 Old Las Vegas Hwy., #B, Santa Fe, NM 87505; (505) 989-4629; harrysroadhousesantafe.com; Diner/American; $$. Everybody loves Harry's. The only people that might hold a slight grudge or pitter of annoyance are those who must wait until their table is ready, stomach growling and happy folks leaving all aglow. It's breakfast, loud and boisterous, with buckwheat blueberry pancakes and maple syrup and black black black coffee. It's lunch, with locals lingering over a local buffalo burger, blue corn turkey enchiladas, and their don't-wanna-go-back-to-work woes. The patio beckons beginning in spring for all meals of the day, especially with the full bar's libations. It's dinnertime, bringing the same crowd, or a different crowd, but they're really all the same: They love Harry's. Tucking into a skirt steak or baked mac and cheese or sultry Guinness stew, the day's cares melt away easily, just like the creamy filling in the best darn ice-cream sandwich you've ever had. Harry's loves you back.

Il Piatto, 95 W. Marcy St., Santa Fe, NM 87501; (505) 984-1091; ilpiattosantafe.com; Italian; $$$. See those three dollar signs to the left? Those are horribly misleading symbols for the best bargain in perfectly executed Italian in town. It is actually hard to adequately describe this place when nearly every plate is a delight and the prices are blink-worthy. Let's consider the dinner prix-fixe option: For about $33, you choose an entree (with prices in the $20s) and any two items from the rest of the menu—appetizers, salads, or desserts. Who would do such a thing? Chef Yohalem, that's who. Matt Yohalem landed here in Santa Fe after cooking with some of the best and brightest in New York, New Orleans, and France. He parked this small restaurant near the Plaza and started quietly serving excellent fare. It was not long before word spread, and local polls put him at the top of Italian cuisine for the last several years. Stop in and see just how comforting a well-prepared dish can be when you don't leave with a skinny wallet.

Jambo Cafe, 2010 Cerrillos Rd., Santa Fe, NM 87505; (505) 473-1269; jambocafe.net; African/Eclectic; $$. In the guidebook called *How to Create an Awesome Restaurant with Happy Customers,* chapter 1 is titled "Case Study: Jambo Cafe." The buzz that surrounds this spot matches the buzz that emanates from the diners within and their mood after leaving—owner and chef Ahmed Obo has made fans out of everyone with his Kenyan cuisine tinged with Arabic and Indian flavors. Take a gander at this appetizer and try to keep from drooling: stuffed phyllo with spinach, Moroccan olives, organic feta, roasted red peppers, and chickpeas with pomegranate sauce. Your only gripe will be that it is so delicious and filling, it threatens to dampen your appetite for the wonders to come: coconut peanut chicken stew (voted best soup in all of Santa Fe for three years running), Moroccan lamb stew over curried couscous, or roasted vegetable salad with goat cheese. Understandably Jambo is busy, so a short wait might be in the cards—take a stroll or just absorb the colorful decor and the boisterous energy of staff and diners alike.

Joe's, 2801 Rodeo Rd., Santa Fe, NM 87507; (505) 471-3800; joes dining.com; Local/Diner; $$. Despite the name, Roland Richter is the proprietor of this upscale diner and a relentless proponent of local ingredients: He was one of the first champions of the Santa Fe farmers' market and continues to spend more dollars on local ingredients than any other restaurant in town. The cheese is local or handmade, and even the meat is grass-fed until the end—a rarity in the grass-fed, grain-finished world. With all those intentions, how is the food? It's good—really good when you let those local ingredients shine, from marinara pizza sauce made with organic tomatoes to grilled farmers' market veggies and in-house mozzarella cheese. Roland puts out a chatty and addictive newsletter every few weeks full of nuggets about upcoming specials, what's been happening with his suppliers, and even his musings on food and community.

Kohnami Japanese Restaurant, 313 S. Guadalupe St., Santa Fe, NM 87501; (505) 984-2002; kohnamirestaurant.com; Japanese/ Sushi; $$$. One of the dueling duo of Santa Fe sushi dominance, Kohnami reigns supreme in the minds of many. Why? The extensive menu spans noodles, sushi, and smaller plates of delights and includes lunch specials in a relaxed atmosphere. It's a respite from the heavy and spicy New Mexican that floods the town, a place where you should take your time and enjoy the mellow yet competent service. The trickling fountain will either be relaxing or a reminder not to drink too much tea, and hanging screens divide the space as well as cut noise levels appreciably. Bento boxes are treasures for lunch, or go the opposite way and have all of those colorful morsels piled on top of rice in a bowl: The *dolsotbob* entrees have the additional attraction of being a lot of food for the money. If you've brought anti-sushi guests, steer them toward those noodles, or perhaps some *katsu*—breaded cutlets of meat served with sauce both salty and spicy. I liken it to a combination of shrimp cocktail sauce and oyster sauce, but still its own delight.

La Boca, 72 W. Marcy St., Santa Fe, NM 87501; (505) 982-3433; labocasf.com; Spanish/Tapas; $$$$. James Campbell Caruso didn't just fall into the tapas game with La Boca; he's honed his skill in town at **El Farol** (p. 78), learning the subtleties of delicately preserved meats and cheeses and how to present them so that the diminutive size is no impediment to the diner's enjoyment. Crunchy fried Marcona almonds are a bridge from one small plate to the next, or merely the accompaniment to a colorful glass of sangria as food is plated. Finger-size anchovies snowed with lemon zest banish all memories of bad pizzas from one's youth, and a creamy cup of roasted squash with cheese is so much better than any artichoke dip. Heavier and pricier options abound on up to paella and skirt steak, both in the $20s, but due to the quality execution of the food and the small plates, you'll spend a fair amount here, or come during happy hour in the midafternoon for a short list of half-price tapas. I still long for the fig tart—a lemony and seed-popping adult Fig Newton, in the best possible way.

La Casa Sena, 125 E. Palace Ave., Santa Fe, NM 87501; (505) 988-9232; lacasasena.com; New Mexican/Eclectic/Fine Dining; $$$. Located in this wonderful little alcove of space off the Plaza, Casa Sena is a common place in town for diners to have their first upper-end experience with modern New Mexican. Under the tutelage of Chef Patrick Gharrity, diners will be taken immediately to northern New Mexico with blue corn and chile muffins in the bread basket, and that's about as boring as the menu gets. Tamales are composed of quinoa instead of corn, and a palate-cleanser granita pairs watermelon and red chile. Those weirdly local beginnings leap forward with my favorite dinner entree: trout baked in adobe clay, every bit as tender as airtight steaming implies. Don't forget lunch at this garden oasis, either—you might just have the best burger within a mile of the Plaza, a grass-fed wonder with smoked ketchup and thick fries. Just like a good diner, this institution has something for everyone.

La Cocina de Doña Clara, 4350 Airport Rd., Santa Fe, NM 87507; (505) 473-1081; lacocinadedonaclara.com; Mexican; $. Birria, birria, wherefore art thou, birria? Oh, there you are, weekends only at this adorably divey Mexican joint down on Airport Road. I can see why you like it here—kept warm in an earthen bowl and served to only the folks who really appreciate such a savory delicacy. If goat isn't your thing, Doña Clara still has you covered: The tacos are tongue-tying, the burritos are properly smothered, and sopesitas are cute little masa shoes. All of this at street-food prices, or at least prices that are refreshingly nonlocal. Like any good Mexican taco shop, the salsa bar is fresh and complimentary, the tacos are four-bite wonders and inexpensive, and the gorditas are properly crispy. Gordita, you say? That's right, a real gordita: a thick, fried masa cake split and filled with anything you'd find in a taco—meat, beans, veggies, and more.

Lan's Vietnamese Cuisine, 2430 Cerrillos Rd., Santa Fe, NM 87505; (505) 986-1636; Vietnamese; $$. **Does the phrase**

Vietnamese carpaccio strike a note of fear in your heart? It only strikes pangs of hunger in my belly on behalf of this rarest of Santa Fe specimens: an actual Vietnamese spot. While Albuquerque is practically overrun with three dozen of the joints, Santa Fe is more like three. Despite the relative lack of competition, Lan's hits all the right notes with every dish, and it starts with that carpaccio. Thin like paper, the beef slices are draped in fresh cilantro, onions, lime, and crunchy fried onion strips. Test your chopstick skills by rolling up each slice with some of the toppings and eating it like a tiny sushi roll. Lamb has a prominent role on Lan's menu, with no

intended alliteration (that I know of): dumplings, stewed lamb soup, even a grilled lamb entree—if this is just a continuation of Santa Fe's overall obsession with lamb, I approve. Pho is on the menu, of course, as are noodle dishes both chilled and stir-fried, but it is the salad menu that induces salivation on every visit—the Bo Tron toss-up of sliced beef, pineapple, cucumber, carrots, and about six other veggies almost makes me put off a visit to **Vinaigrette** (p. 72). Almost.

Los Potrillos, 1947 Cerrillos Rd., Santa Fe, NM 87505; (505) 992-0550; Mexican; $. Far from an institution, this real-deal south-of-the-border spot opened in 2006 and quickly became top of the heap in the often-overlooked Mexican Mexican cuisine of our state. The name means "little horses," if you couldn't guess by the mural on the wall and the wonderful horse heads carved out of every wooden chair back. Los Potrillos is the place to try your first real gordita, a cornmeal pita-like circle stuffed with anything from beans to meat. Try scooping grilled meat out of a hot stone bowl called a *molcajete*—the *al pastor* is succulent marinated pork with onions and pineapple and enough tortillas to feed a foodie army. *Chiles en ahogada* hail from the Puebla region of Mexico, stuffing beef, raisins, and spices inside poblanos drenched in a nutty white sauce. The whole contraption is a sweet-savory punch in the palate. But for meat lovers (and game lovers in particular), you absolutely have to order the chile-stewed *cabrito*. The tender shreds of goat meat melt in spoonfuls or in tortilla-wrapped bites with a pungent squeeze of lime. Sigh.

Luminaria, 211 Old Santa Fe Trail, Santa Fe, NM 87501; (505) 984-7915; innatloretto.com/new-mexico-dining/santa-fe-restaurant.php; Fine Dining; $$$. Take the sensibilities of someone who shops at the co-op, is studying yoga, and has a fine palate to boot. Luminaria is that person's restaurant—a place that strives to serve cuisine in the Ayurvedic tradition of balancing out the tendencies or swings that are too weak or too strong. It makes sense, right? If one leg is stronger than the other, you'd just walk in circles until you bulked up the weak one or stopped working the strong one so hard. While I don't follow the Ayurvedic diet, that's a really rough rundown of the theory. It can mean some restrictions on foods, but at Luminaria your balancing wishes will come true, mostly in the form of seasonally appropriate dishes balanced in their flavor profiles. Each dish isn't marked by its properties, but the spirit of whole foods and complementary tastes is taken seriously, like a "normal" grilled salmon ripe with richness, here paired with a bitter orange sauce and astringent vegetables. What seems to be Ayurvedic is also just good cooking, as it turns out, and Chef Matt Ostrander satisfies on all accounts.

Mariscos "La Playa," 537 W. Cordova Rd., Santa Fe, NM 87505; (505) 982-2790; mariscoslaplaya.com; Mexican/Seafood; $$. You know that feeling when you put your face up close to an aquarium, with tropical fish darting around in their vibrant colors, fake plants waving in the current? That's how it feels to step into Mariscos "La Playa," a cool duck of your head under the ocean to see the stuff that awaits you on your fishing trip. The light and unassuming starters are best as cool ceviche or a cocktail heavy on the tomato juice and chunks of seafood, from shrimp to octopus. A large cocktail is a favorite meal of mine, with or without crackers to soak up that brothy liquid. Warmer plates are, of course, ready for your fork to dive into, starting with the famous 7 Seas Soup with seven kinds of seafood (though two of them are shrimp) in a nice and hefty portion. Sure, there's the typical spicy shrimp dish with habanero chiles called *camarones al diablo,* but the real treasure is a name familiar to New Mexicans: *pescado relleno.* It is not a chile relleno with fish, but rather a fish stuffed with other fish and cheese, then wrapped up and baked to a gooey mess. This dish teeters on unctuous but maintains a level of decorum amid the rich bundle of warmth. Desserts? Yes, of course. *Tres leches* cake should be something you experience at least once in your life, a treat that, like tiramisu, seems light when a bite hits your mouth, but after several the sweetness and joy hit you like a tugboat.

Mu Du Noodles, 1494 Cerrillos Rd., Santa Fe, NM 87505; (505) 983-1411; mudunoodles.com; Asian/Eclectic; $$. Too many Santa Feans told me this was their favorite comfort restaurant in town over too many years. So I went. Finally, I saw what they meant. This is a short-menu mash-up of Thailand, Vietnam, Japan, China, and more when you can start with potstickers dunked in millionaire sauce before moving on to pad thai or lemongrass soup right out of Saigon. None of the menu items is particularly strange—it's seeing them all together, and then tasting each one prepared so well you'd think it was all they made all day long. Hours are short at Mu Du, so securing a reservation is strongly advised, but once you are seated, it is all hushed contemplation over the specials and a strong stare at the wine and sake list. The latter is both accessible and affordable and worth pairing with the whole meal. Just have a ride lined up in case your gustatory bliss comes with a blood alcohol level.

Museum Hill Cafe, 710 Camino Lejo, Santa Fe, NM 87505; (505) 984-8900; museumhillcafe.net; Cafe; $$. This out-of-the-way spot pays off with a nice view of the city and the Jemez Mountains, while the cafe fare is simple and creative. Duck flautas are listed next to Texas chili, but the Nachos Fabuloso sounds like a must-try, doesn't it? Regardless of the decadent nachos, I appreciate the wide salad menu, including Cobb and Greek, and my companion made a beeline for the grass-fed burger (if this is a trend, I like it). Those weary of navigating the Plaza area with their rental car will find ample parking to go with their artwork and tasty meal. If you plan to hang out a bit, there's even Wi-Fi for your working or surfing pleasure.

New York Deli, 420 Catron St., Santa Fe, NM 87501; (505) 982-8900; nydelisf.com; Deli/Sandwiches; $. Repeat after me: There's no pastrami like New York pastrami. Katz's towering sandwiches are a necessary foodie experience, both for the novelty and the quality of preparation. But this isn't New York, and you're going to have to make do with the New York Deli—a spot doing enough of the classics right that most of us won't miss much. Take that pastrami, for example. Shaved razor thin and piled on rye with mustard, it requires fortitude and trust to hand it over if a friend wants a bite. Bagel fans should also recall that this spot used to be called Bagelmania, boiling up chewy toroid shapes in requisite varieties like pumpernickel and onion. Despite the lure of sandwich fillings like chopped liver, burger fans will enjoy grass-fed yumminess in hand-formed 8-ounce patties and topping combinations that could land one right back in California cuisine. Owners Jeffrey and Gary Schwartzberg learned the bagel and bialy skills over a generation ago, earning the respect of any local who has experience with the Big Apple.

Palace Restaurant & Saloon, 142 W. Palace Ave., Santa Fe, NM 87501; (505) 428-0690; palacesantafe.com; Fine Dining/Eclectic; $$$. It is Joseph Wrede's time to shine all over again in this newly renovated icon of fine Santa Fe dining. Taos sharpened Wrede's skills, netting him a Top 10 Chefs in America by *Food & Wine* magazine in 2000. Now he brings the experience to the Palace in old favorites like duck fat fries and a love of kale you thought only possible for a vegan or raw foodist. They might say the menu is Italian, but it is really a strange and mostly successful hybrid with New Mexican eclectic, from stacked enchiladas to seared foie gras with sweet mole to, yes, chopped Caesar salad and polenta fries. The bar menu goes deeper into Italy with pastas and panini-style burgers, and is the way to experience the more lusty, brothel-oriented days of the Palace's history under low lighting and deep-red-flecked wallpaper. Quiet dinners can be had in the updated dining room, with white tablecloths punctuating the space between each table and diners curious to see what this Taos name has brought to the City Different.

Pizza Centro, 418 Cerrillos Rd., Santa Fe, NM 87501; (505) 988-8828; pizzacentronys.com; Pizza; $. New York–style pizza hits Santa Fe from this duo of brothers, serving up drapey slices at the expected price level ($3 or so). From those beginnings you can have whole pies formed from fresh dough daily, topped with combinations named after Manhattan neighborhoods: the Central Park does spinach, tomato, basil, garlic, and ricotta; the Chelsea piles on sausage, meatballs, bacon, onion, and green peppers; the lust-worthy Hell's Kitchen overloads on sausage, fried eggplant, green chile, jalapeño, red pepper, and feta. There are sandwiches, but that's beside the point, and cannoli, too, for those requiring some sweetness after their cheese. You'll find good pizza spots in Santa Fe, but for a real-deal big honkin' slice place, Pizza Centro does the job.

Pyramid Cafe, 505 W. Cordova Rd., Santa Fe, NM 87505; (505) 989-1378; pyramidcafesf.com; African/Mediterranean/Greek; $$. A town with a light selection of Middle Eastern spots like Santa Fe embraces a place like Pyramid as a moussaka-tagine-hummus refuge—it's a good thing the food is quite delicious as well. Pyramid tries to do a lot, and the resulting menu can be daunting, but if you know you like meaty salads, you can head right to the leg of lamb salad, smoky with harissa. Vegetarians go wild with carrot salad, hummus, a charred chile salad (whoa!), and even moussaka filled with eggplant, zucchini, and bell peppers. It's going to take me a bunch of visits to work through this globe-snacking menu, and forgive me if I skip over the chicken Florentine for the more interesting Mediterranean delights. Take spices and ingredients home from the owner's market called **Ziggy's International** (p. 99) just a few blocks away.

Raaga Fine Indian Dining, 544 Agua Fria St., Santa Fe, NM 87501; (505) 820-6440; raagacuisine.com; Indian; $$. **Paddy**

Rawal added another level of Indian cuisine to this area, already in love with spices and vegetarian-friendly dining but thin on Indian restaurants. He runs another spot in East Lansing, a region replete with Eastern cuisines where competition is fierce, and hit the ground running with Raaga. While dinner is moderately pricey for Indian, the lunch buffet is a steal at around $10—budgeters, rejoice! You've never seen such a rainbow of vegetarian and vegan options as the menu at Raaga, outnumbering the meat entrees and luring in the sworn carnivores with the likes of *chole amritsari* (garbanzos and potatoes with chilies, pomegranate, and ginger) or a standard yet memorable *paneer palak* (spinach and cheese). I hardly care that the curried fish is good or the chicken tikka is expertly done—give me more veggies!

The Ranch House, 2571 Cristos Rd., Santa Fe, NM 87507; (505) 424-8900; theranchhousesantafe.com; Barbecue/American; $$. Local favorite Josh's BBQ closed up shop so that this expanded location could spread some culinary wings, mostly in the genre of "upscale manly food." So the digs are larger but also fancier, and the menu retains a few genuine BBQ items while adding highfalutin crab cakes, flatbreads, and local burgers. The decor is somewhere between a BBQ barn and a modern, upscale, rustic dining destination—if that makes sense. My favorite table accessories are the napkin holders crafted from old whiskey boxes, but some might say it's the squeeze bottle of BBQ sauce. Everyone who tries both the smoked chicken taquitos and the tater tots comes away a convert, and if anything, it could be that the menu is too ambitious and disjointed. Discombobulation aside (along with some sporadic service issues), the green chile slaw came over from Josh's and it is a wonderfully light (read: hardly any mayo) and piquant side dish to pair with that pulled pork platter. I dare any fan of Southern cuisine to skip the banana bread pudding—two concepts that always belonged together.

Restaurant Martin, 526 Galisteo St., Santa Fe, NM 87501; (505) 820-0919; restaurantmartinsantafe.com; Fine Dining/Modern; $$$$. Martin Rios is the only New Mexican chef to appear on *Iron Chef America*—for this he has won recognition that transcends state lines, showing off his skill set far and wide. Luckily for the patrons of Restaurant Martin, his skills are formidable. It doesn't get more trendy than dishes listed with quotation marks, denoting some kind of deconstruction-gastrowizardry, but Rios scores big with

his "Bacon and Eggs" riff on eggs Benedict, piling lobster hollandaise on poached egg on pork belly on polenta. He could just call it "7 Minutes in Breakfast Heaven." From that far-off place you sail right back to regular gourmet food with an Angus strip loin partnered with potato croquette and spinach with a wine sauce. There is whimsy and flavor genius all over the place, and artistic plating fans will swoon approximately every 3.4 minutes. Picture a carrot cake with a mascarpone parfait and walnut powder—it defies contemplation, yet no matter what you decide, it will surprise you when placed at your table. Go on, try it.

Rio Chama Steakhouse, 414 Old Santa Fe Trail, Santa Fe, NM 87501; riochamasteakhouse.com; Steak; $$$. This highest-end companion to **Chama River Brewing Company** in Albuquerque (p. 288) and **Sleeping Dog Tavern** right off the Plaza (p. 64), the Steakhouse shows off a selection of dry-aged beefy goodness. For better or for worse, prices match the quality, so the New York strip nudges the $40 mark but carries the gift of deep flavor with each tender bite. Bird fans adore the Duck and Duck, where a confit leg meets a slice of duck meat loaf, with greens to cut that decadence. I especially enjoy going downscale at their bar, where the chef has created a gourmet experience for the bar-stool crowd. Even potato skins show up here, with green chile and four cheeses to fancify the humble dish beloved by chain-restaurant patrons of the '80s and '90s. The furthest you can splurge is a prime rib sandwich rubbed with red chile and served open-faced with mushrooms and cheese. Finish up with a relaxing digestif, or a grin-inducing chocolate pot. Or both.

San Marcos Cafe, 3877 NM 14, Santa Fe, NM 87508; (505) 471-9298; sanmarcosfeed.com/cafe.htm; American/Cafe; $. It is easy to drive right by this little place with a yard that looks like a normal residential yard, albeit one that collects small metal knickknacks and a chicken or two. Inside, it is also literally homey, with rustic furniture and a laid-back pace that on occasion will translate into service that is nail-biting. Just relax and think of the serenity of the rural

Beaucoup Breakfast

Santa Fe is a breakfast town. So says a foodie friend, and evidence of it is abundant from breakfast burritos to *huevos rancheros* and pastries on every menu. Find morning nirvana in the sweets department at local favorites like Chocolate Maven Bakery & Cafe (p. 37), Dulce (*1100 Don Diego Ave., Santa Fe, NM 87505; 505-989-9966*), Clafoutis (p. 38), and Tree House Pastry Shop & Cafe (p. 70). I've rarely had a better (or bigger) macaroon than those from Santa Fe Baking Co. (p. 61).

Adding to good pastries and coffee are the larger full-meal establishments serving classic cafe fare: Harry's Roadhouse (p. 44), Cafe Pasqual's (p. 75), Tecolote Cafe (p. 65), Crumpacker's Cafe & Bakeshop (*5 Bisbee Ct. #108, Santa Fe, NM 87508; 505-471-0226*), and Tune-Up Cafe (p. 71). More in the diner and dive category are some of the casual deli and Mexican spots, like La Cocina de Doña Clara (p. 49), New York Deli (p. 54), and Los Amigos (*3904 Rodeo Rd., Santa Fe, NM 87507; 505-438-0600*).

area and your food to come. Pick up that sturdy coffee mug emblazoned with their name, filled with coffee for the caffeine-heads or excellent hot chocolate for the chocoholics, and take a deep, leisurely sip. Assuage a sugar lull by having a famous cinnamon roll, unique for its tall height and nearly croissant-like flakiness—this is no heavy, dense blob of bread. San Marcos does reliable morning food, including fat and tender biscuits with country gravy, and egg specials that might include chile or may be done up like a localized crepe—it is the specials chalkboard you'll want to pay attention to. Ever-changing and almost always the best thing they're serving that day, those specials deserve investigation. It may be a cafe, but they've served coq au vin on at least one occasion.

San Q Japanese Sushi & Tapas, 32 Burro Alley, Santa Fe, NM 87501; (505) 992-0304; sanqrestaurant.com; Sushi/Japanese/ Tapas; $$. It seems that Santa Fe can support another Japanese place, especially if there is "a twist": At San Q the curveball is tapas, otherwise known as *izakaya*. Small plates span the range of typical sushi to grilled yakitori to tempura. The underappreciated gem is grilled rice balls—the perfect pairing for grilled salmon belly. I bet you didn't know that salmon have bellies, too—they're rich and delicious in all the ways that only salmon can be. San Q is owned by the same folks behind **Kohnami** (p. 47), and some menu items appear at both spots, but the decor here feels nice and new, with deep red accents and intimate dining alcoves. The actual dishes are done quite well, with green chile tempura hot enough for locals and a weirdly good noodle dish combining kimchi, pork, and cheese. The tucked-away spot is perfect for walking around town or if you'd like a slight change of scenery from Kohnami.

Santa Fe Baking Co. & Cafe, 504 W. Cordova Rd., Santa Fe, NM 87505; (505) 988-4292; santafebakingcompanycafe.com; Bakery/

Cafe/Coffee; $. Santa Fe Baking has the best macaroons in the state. This homey spot up the road from Trader Joe's also has Wi-Fi, leading to some serious hang-out potential by diners, some of whom come to work and others just to sit and chat over coffee. The ordering protocol is tricky the first time, with hung menu-boards at neck-straining height and so full of stuff it takes 10 minutes to read, let alone decide. The pastry case is so tall, there is a risk of failing to make eye contact with a server at all. But at least you'll be facing down your delicious future: apple strudel or brownies or, yes, those macaroons. Everything you could ever want to eat is available: Cobb salad, vegan veggie platters, green chile pork stew, blue corn piñon pancakes. The latter are faintly blue-gray and earthy like buckwheat, but melt under syrup and an eager fork. Artwork plasters the colorful walls, while live music serenades from the corner as you sail off to your happy place.

Shibumi Ramenya, 26 Chapelle St., Santa Fe, NM 87507; (505) 428-0077; shibumiramen.com; Japanese; $$$$ (cash only). Eric Stapleman opened this alternative to his **Trattoria Nostrani** (p. 69) right next door in late 2010, and the whispers started within weeks: "There's this new ramen place but, like, fancy ramen!" Santa Fe had both sushi shops and places to get noodles, but nothing like Shibumi, a true Japanese *izakaya* with nary a roll nor spicy anything on the menu. Restrained but beautiful dishes, paired with sake, is how to dine; the space matches this idea—small, intimate, and cleanly appointed. Have your dumpling world expanded with pork gyoza, tender inside with a perfectly toothsome wrapper; move along to tangy salads like black seaweed or sesame spinach, sipping sake all the way. Dinner offers grilled items called *yaki,* from salmon to chicken to quivering pork belly. Regarding the ramen, you will have the *tonkotsu* with roasted pork. It doesn't matter if it is all you are ordering or you are starting to feel sated—the cashmere-rich broth, tender pork, and chewy noodles will disappear before you can register anything other than pure delight. See Eric's recipe for **Roasted Pork Belly** on p. 314.

Shohko Cafe, 321 Johnson St., Santa Fe, NM 87501; (505) 982-9708; shohkocafe.com; Japanese/Sushi; $$$$. Shohko has been serving sushi as long as I've been alive—if their motto of "Food for Health" is any indication, they're as fit as a fiddle while approaching 40. I've visited a few times and felt like I was in any big city's favored sushi joint, although this one is housed in a former bordello with adobe walls thicker than James Beard. Luckily the opposite should occur when you order and enjoy such conscientious selections as on offer at Shohko. Evoke the Santa Fe weather with Prawns Blanketed in Snow, crispy mouthfuls dusted in rice flour, or get any one of two dozen tempura options, each executed flawlessly. The special bento box had better be pretty darn special for $35, but after an appetizer or two, it's enough to share. The aficionados should head directly for sashimi to taste perfectly tender morsels of fish, evidence that the chefs' knife skills are on par with the best in the country. Spend some or spend a lot—just sit at the bar for personalized recommendations and the best experience of Japanese dining.

Sleeping Dog Tavern, 114 W. San Francisco St., Santa Fe, NM 87501; (505) 982-4335; sleepingdogtavern.com; Pub/American; $$. To call Sleeping Dog cozy is easy once you enter its near-underground location just off the Plaza and adjust to the low light. A menu lands under your gaze and—first things first—you must order a drink. This is a tavern, after all. Local beers are on tap, but the full bar can craft any traditional or bizarre cocktail you'd like. Back to the menu: The indecisive like me can consider the section called "Smaller Plates" to share many flavors with the whole table. I love the wild boar sausage and local lamb wontons as precursors to a trio of miniature buffalo short-rib burgers—as you can see, their handling of red meats is diverse and delicious. Veggie lovers don't have to freak out—not only are the salads good, but the vegetable plate entree mixes grilled tomatoes and polenta with sweet braised fennel. Stumble back up the stairs to the world, sated and only a little surprised.

Station, 530 S. Guadalupe St., Santa Fe, NM 87501; (505) 988-2470; stationcoffeeandtea.com; Coffee/Cafe; $. Within spitting distance of the Rail Runner train depot, have a seat, some Wi-Fi, and a cup or three of well-crafted coffee to the din of chatting locals and frantic laptop typists. Caffeine and pastries are well and good, but Station offers more significant nosh with quiches, salads, and the occasional savory tart. A recent visit revealed just-dropped-off chile fudge from a friend of the shop. That's the kind of treats you'll never see at a corporate coffee chain, and exactly why owner Clark Le Compte has been keeping customers happy since opening several years ago.

Tecolote Cafe, 1203 Cerrillos Rd., Santa Fe, NM 87505; (505) 988-1362; tecolotecafe.com; Diner; $. Toast is often a throwaway breakfast item—if great, you'll eat it; if not, you still might eat it. Tecolote gets around that by not ever serving toast for 30 years. Founder Bill Jennison is no longer with us to tell the tale, but according to his son-in-law, it goes like this: After Bill had the perfect New Mexican recipes to open his diner, he was asked, why go to the trouble to make authentic local foods when diners would probably just complain about the toast? Bill then decided: no toast = no toast complainers. The policy remains, and it means that there are fantastic home fries on every breakfast plate—almost as thin as potato chips. You can have bread in the form of French toast or pancakes, the latter in a common but welcome blue corn piñon variety and served with hot maple syrup. I admit a fondness for the chicken liver breakfast with salsa and eggs, but the Huevos Yucatecos is another favorite with beans, fried bananas, eggs, feta, and tortillas—it's weirdly awesome, just like the whole place.

New Mexico Green Chile Cheeseburger Trail & Culinary Treasures Trail

Perhaps it's the endemic local pride, the state's centennial in 2012, or just enthusiastic staff at the New Mexico Tourism Department, but I think we have a phenomenal state tourism website. It's chock-full of destinations, summaries of state terms and quirks, and wonderful guides, and has even been a companion along the research portion of this book. But one of the best ideas they have had in recent years is to create state "food trails" that highlight some of the beloved edibles all over the Land of Enchantment.

The first list, the Green Chile Cheeseburger Trail, was released in 2009, consisting of more than 50 green chile cheeseburger havens and way posts, along with a state fair competition champion for best in the state (alas, the winner did not remain open long enough to make the next edition of the list). Readers and state food experts all weighed in on which places should be featured for their history and their tasty burgers. The second edition hit in mid-2011 with a fully revised list and interactive features to give both locals and visitors the information needed to plan their own tour.

In 2010 the Culinary Treasures Trail was released, showcasing restaurants all over the state, from tiny hamlets to locations in

Terra Restaurant at Encantado, 198 NM 592, Santa Fe, NM 87506; (505) 988-9955; encantadoresort.com; Fine Dining/Eclectic; $$$$. What's the term for when fine dining nudges past itself and

downtown Albuquerque, all of which had been in business for a minimum of 40 years, with fewer than two locations in existence. The culinary spectrum is vast, from walk-up counters inside grocery stores to The Compound (p. 40) with James Beard Award–winning chef Mark Kiffin. Other Santa Fe spots include the Pantry Restaurant (p. 81), Bobcat Bite (p. 35),  Bert's Burger Bowl (p. 74), Maria's New Mexican Kitchen (p. 89), El Farol (p. 78), the Plaza Cafe (p. 82), and The Shed Creative Cooking (p. 90). Taos has a good showing with five spots, including Doc Martin's (p. 259).

In the Duke City, entrants are understandably numerous. Several you'll see elsewhere in this book, and they are appreciated for their contributions: Charlie's Front & Back Door (p. 181), Duran's Central Pharmacy (p. 131), El Camino Dining Room (p. 221), El Modelo (p. 226), El Pinto (p. 227), Grandma Warner's K & I Diner (p. 222), Mannies Family Restaurant (p. 155), Mary & Tito's Cafe (p. 230), Mr. Powdrell's Barbeque House (p. 223), Murphy's Mule Barn (p. 207), and the Western View Diner (p. 219).

Plan your tour at the full site: newmexico.org/cuisine/index.php.

becomes the local "ultra fine" spot? In northern New Mexico that term might be Terra and, by way of association, its chef, Charles Dale. All the hallmarks are present—quietly competent service, far-reaching dishes that push boundaries just far enough, and restaurant practices that are cutting edge: I heartily endorse Terra's commitment to sustainable seafood and wish I saw it in more restaurants. Now, let's push some boundaries. Take the salmon-mustard flavor combination and smoke the salmon before pairing it with cauliflower-almond mousse and kale. Interesting, but not outlandish, and, of course, gorgeous from first view to last bite. Chef Dale will host themed dinners as the mood strikes, like a retro Trader Vic's spread with pupu platters and bananas Foster, but his skills are frankly expert no matter what he does—he could be cooking cheese tots (and does) and they're still awesome. Local ingredients are always part of the best dishes: Venison Two Ways as tamale and grilled loin garnished with berry salsa, or winter posole that fires on all cylinders with warmth and local comfort.

315, 315 Old Santa Fe Trail, Santa Fe, NM 87501; (505) 986-9190; 315santafe.com; French/Fine Dining; $$$. The name is short and the restaurant flies under the radar much of the time with quiet excellence in French bistro fare. Chef and owner Louis Moskow used to work at a second kitchen in town, but 315 was always his favored proving ground to show off the best ingredients as soon as the seasons produced them. With only one kitchen to run these days, Moskow can redouble his focus and keep impressing diners who pass over other big-name spots to cozy up in his warmly lit and intimate dining rooms. A love of wine shows in the 17-page list highlighted by Pinot Noirs and Burgundies at all price points (though not a huge selection at the inexpensive end of the range). Finding a pairing for the beet salad or a locally sourced roasted chicken is no trouble for the staff—leaving you to carry on a pleasurable meal.

Tomme, 229 Galisteo St., Santa Fe, NM 87501; (505) 820-2253; tommesf.com; Modern/Eclectic; $$$. After several college-try attempts at pronouncing this restaurant's name, the story was set straight: It's in the middle of *tum* and *tom,* after a regional French cheese born of ripening curds. This modern bistro seems simple enough: The menu sports a burger and French onion soup. But the lineage is all talent, with Brian Rood and Mark Connell both of international training and national acclaim. Just look closer at the "pozole," quotation marks and all: New Mexican comfort served with culinary twists. With a presentation as showy as the flavors, a moat of broth circles a hominy soufflé, topped with shredded pork as rich as Daddy Warbucks. Before you succumb to sweets from a pastry whiz honored by *Food & Wine* magazine, Tomme dares to serve fried chicken that will forever ruin you for pretty much any other fried chicken. Chefs Rood and Connell should be darn proud.

Trattoria Nostrani, 304 Johnson St., Santa Fe, NM 87501; (505) 983-3800; trattorianostrani.com; Italian; $$$. There's a good chance that you've asked someone what the best romantic restaurant in Santa Fe is, and a good chance they've answered, "Well, Nostrani, but . . ." Let's talk about that "but" right away: Don't wear scents—perfume, cologne, lotion, et cetera. The policy is real and inspired by Chef Eric's own keen sense of smell, sensitive enough that in another career he could be a perfumer. On to the food, then, for it deserves your unscented attention. Spring might bring a dandelion soup or artichoke and arugula salads, each augmented by complementary flavors. Small first-course plates allow the chefs to show off their pasta skills: Cocoa ravioli is almost always on hand, with fillings from beet to pumpkin, and fluffy pillows of gnocchi reluctantly give way between your teeth. Chefs Eric and Nelli shine on underappreciated braised octopus as a traditional second course, pairing it with tomatoes and escarole for bite. The Nostrani experience won't sing until you choose liquid pairings from one of the largest wine lists in the state. See Nelli's **Apple Crostata** recipe on p. 320.

Tree House Pastry Shop & Cafe, 1600 Lena St., A2, Santa Fe, NM 87505; (505) 474-5543; treehousepastry.com; Bakery/Organic/ Cafe; $$. Beets enthrall me—I'll be the first to admit it. That's what got me to step inside a spot hailed for its pastries and organic food (not always the best indication of healthy eats, even if well-intentioned) for something called the Birdhouse Burger. Their vegan patty is smooshed from rice, beans, carrots, potatoes, nuts, and, yes, beets. The sweetly savory burger becomes merely vegetarian when on its bun with cheddar cheese that provides needed richness. The owner and cook is CIA-trained (that's Culinary Institute of America) and takes a special interest in providing gluten-free options for those with restrictions, as well as additional vegetarian and vegan specials every day. The cinnamon rolls ought to be a

draw in the hard-to-spot cafe, so once you've tried one and agree that the little round treats are fabulous, send for all your friends so they can try the *chilaquiles* and house-made granola and marvel at this find.

Tune-Up Cafe, 1115 Hickox St., Santa Fe, NM 87505; (505) 983-7060; South American/New Mexican/Diner; $$. Locals had to adjust to the catchy yet unfamiliar name for a place that had been known under a different sign for too many years to count. Once they embraced the new name and a delectable South American–tinted menu, the crowds were flowing in like waves to the shore. Start with Salvadoran *pupusas* stuffed with veggies or steak, or experience a tamale like no other, steamed in a banana leaf with chicken inside and pickled veggies on the side called *curtido*. New Mexican fans will find a chile relleno, but Yucatan fish tacos might prove persuasive—hey, you can get rellenos or enchiladas everywhere in this city! Tune-Up has been busier than ever since featured on a popular food television show, and that means some deserved fame for a wonderful breakfast dish: Huevos El Salvadoreños, which piles up scrambled eggs, refried beans, pan-fried banana, cream, and a fresh corn tortilla. The sweet-savory combination is extraordinary and worth the trip; if there's a wait, take a seat at the community table and make some new friends.

Upper Crust Pizza, 329 Old Santa Fe Trail, Santa Fe, NM 87501; (505) 982-0000; uppercrustpizza.com; Pizza; $$. Include yourself in the legions of Upper Crust patrons first lured in by the heavenly smells emanating from the kitchen, wafting down the street a good hundred meters. The siren smell of baking bread pulled me in, and the rest was crusty history. Warmish evenings will pack the wood-sheltered front patio with diners sharing their pizza aromas with the world, but cooler weather is pleasantly spent in the historic home's small rooms. Upper Crust's menu is simple: pizzas, calzones, a handful of salads—nothing overly distracting from the crust, the best part of these pies. I don't always eat my "pizza bones," for many pizzerias' crusts are boring—not so here, where every inch of each slice is devoured. Their fans are numerous and fiercely loyal, even if this critic or that says better pizza could be had elsewhere or more cheaply. Upper Crust gets lodged in the sweet memories of your taste buds, and you'll be back.

Vinaigrette, 709 Don Cubero Alley, Santa Fe, NM 87505; (505) 820-9205; vinaigretteonline.com; Organic/Local/Cafe; $$. **OK,** yeah—it really is a salad bistro. Erin Wade used her own garden north of town to supply her 2009 opening of Vinaigrette, creating two situations: the most expensive salads in town and a cult following. Apparently there is a market for expertly crafted piles of veggies with great dressings and local organic protein. A restaurant like this in Aspen or Berkeley would be a no-brainer, but here in

Santa Fe, it is wonderful. It's modern-rustic with wooden tables and a hard-to-find front entrance (the *Alley* in the address is no joke), but once seated, you can contemplate your imminent nirvana. I first had the arugula duck: Duck fans need to leap on the peppery arugula, goat cheese, pear, and duck confit. Classic salads appear as well—Cobb and frisée and so on—but my next object of affection might be the apple-cheddar chop, complete with fennel and pork tenderloin. Regarding the pricing, most non-meat salads are $10 to $12, while meaty ones are $15 to $17, and any salad can have meat added for $5 to $7—with the sourcing of ingredients, it's actually not so bad. Oh, and since you've had salad, feel free to partake in the out-of-this-world pies. If that's a marketing strategy, Erin is a genius.

Zia Diner, 326 S. Guadalupe St., Santa Fe, NM 87501; (505) 988-7008; ziadiner.com; Cafe/American; $$. Every eater goes through phases—cravings for whole categories of food like greens or cheese or bread—and each phase leads to the next, as we compensate or make up for lost time. Zia Diner satisfied my deepest, darkest cheese cravings with their quiche-on-steroids called Asiago Pie that contains enough green chile to remind you this is New Mexico, after all. Over time Zia fulfills many cravings with their extensive menu—that cheese pie is only the beginning. Liver and onions work on old-school diner patrons, while the Zia black bean flauta caters to lighter appetites. Who eats at Zia? Frankly, it takes all kinds, from visitors right off the train to locals who stubbornly avoid anything new and trendy because they know that Zia is always there for them—being open 14-plus hours a day helps a bit, too. Keep in mind that even if you walk in famished, Zia's pastries and desserts are worth an extra couple of bouts of stair sprints—and with the sugar rush, you might feel compelled to do those sooner rather than later.

Landmarks

Bert's Burger Bowl, 235 N. Guadalupe St., Santa Fe, NM 87501; (505) 982-0215; Burgers; $. Not content with being a darn-good burger joint open for nearly 60 years in the heart of Santa Fe, Bert's has to mix things up just a little bit. They offer burgers in the additional configurations of bison, lamb, ostrich, and pork, or simply beef topped with chile and cheese or BBQ. Basic burgers are inexpensive; all are made carefully after you order—the sign clearly states (or warns) that the wait time averages 12 minutes. Whether you watch the sizzle on the grill or head outside to the tables (Bert's offers no interior seating), it's a maddening 12 minutes of smelling all manner of deliciousness, wondering if your burger is next. Skip the usually soggy crinkle fries and opt for breaded onion rings, or go full tilt and order a Frito pie on the side for maximum crunch, salt, and chile. Bert's owners also manage **Epazote** (p. 43), a fine-dining experience of Mexican cuisine that enables them to whet the appetite of anyone in town.

The Bull Ring, 150 Washington Ave., Santa Fe, NM 87501; (505) 983-3328; santafebullring.com; Steak; $$$$. More than 40 years in, Harry Georgeades's homage to all things beef is still bringing back regulars from the entire area. Sure, visitors go for the prime steaks and to have schmooze-worthy meetings, but locals are the mainstay of the traffic here. They all start out by ordering calamari or possibly some fried shrimp before settling into the dark ambiance and the feeling that this is all very familiar. It is familiar like those steak places you were dragged to as a kid, but it is also familiar because the Bull Ring is very good and you were here just last month. Enjoy a hand-cut steak but be prepared for the bill—great meat is never inexpensive. Thankfully the rest of the menu is reasonable, whether you need a break from beef itself (try the huge Cobb salad) or just the big-check numbers (take on the daily multicourse special and get everything covered for one price). Tip a drink and sink into the most comfortable dining room chairs in the city—Georgeades and his staff have you covered.

Cafe Pasqual's, 121 Don Gaspar Ave., Santa Fe, NM 87501; (505) 983-9340; pasquals.com; Eclectic/New Mexican; $$$. Katharine Kagel had just moved to Santa Fe when a business opportunity came up—opening a restaurant in a corner location a block off the Plaza. She jumped, and in 1974 an icon was born: Cafe Pasqual's. From the beginning this was to be a forward-thinking concept, using as many local ingredients and as many local suppliers as possible, and as much love as could be mustered by each and every cook. I don't ascribe magical or spiritual qualities to food, but there is something to be said for the enjoyment of the cook manifesting in a better plate of food. Katharine's specialties are widely revered, from her three-chile red sauce and smoked trout hash to her family's chocolate fudge cookies. The first two recipes and dozens more are in the cafe's two cookbooks, but the latter is one of the few recipes that will never be revealed. All the more reason to take a seat at the community table, order up some banana-leaf roasted pork, and smile, because on the way out you'll have one of those heavenly cookies.

Coyote Cafe, 132 W. Water St., Santa Fe, NM 87501; (505) 983-1615; coyotecafe.com; New Mexican/Eclectic; $$$$. You can't begin to learn about modern New Mexican cuisine without hearing the name Mark Miller (see the introduction, p. 5) and his devotion to all things chile. The name Coyote Cafe was built on his culinary derring-do, and it lingers even as he has passed operations over to Eric DiStefano of **Geronimo** (p. 78). The two minds created a menu with all of their best ideas on display. I've fallen in love with Surf & Turf Tartare, which is pretty much how it sounds: a duo of raw salmon and avocado with a traditional beef tartare, egg yolk and all. As this gorgeous dish arrives, I'm usually sipping from their cocktail menu, something swanky like the cherry-bourbon-based Smoking

Mark Miller & New Mexican Cuisine

A famous poster decorates college dorms and modern kitchens alike: "The Great Chile Poster," published nearly 20 years ago by Mark Miller in his drive to demystify the chile in all its variations and spice levels. It was a companion piece to his book of the same name, and both are still beloved by anyone learning to love that vitamin C powerhouse we like to call "sunshine."

Santa Fe is home to Mark Miller's culinary child, the Coyote Cafe (p. 76). It opened in 1987 and immediately changed the game of Southwestern cuisine, starting by putting those two words together as one harmonious goal. Miller took chiles and did very strange things to them—draping wild mushroom tamales with creamy chile sauce, stuffing enchiladas with lobster, baking rabbit and apples with chile in a wonderfully bizarre potpie. This was strange and new, yet utterly delectable; within a few years the "new Southwestern" had won Miller awards from the James Beard Foundation and *Esquire* magazine.

The state still feels the effect of Mark Miller in any modern or fusion New Mexican recipe. You can see that put to good use at Tomme (p. 69) or Geronimo (p. 78), to name just two. We love those new twists, as long as the old favorites stay around, too.

Jacket with just enough cherry bitters to cut the sweet vermouth. After that I'm off to bigger foods (spine-tingling roasted chicken is a must) with bigger price tags—Coyote is no bargain meal, even among peers. If budget really is an issue, the Cantina upstairs serves some of the best bar food in town. Never had a BBQ duck quesadilla? You will.

El Farol, 808 Canyon Rd., Santa Fe, NM 87501; (505) 983-9912; elfarolsf.com; Spanish/Tapas; $$$. The origin of tapas still makes me smile—an empty, tiny plate on top of one's glass in taverns in the muggy south of Spain to keep out bugs. That's it. As competing bars wanted to win customers, they took that plate real estate and put food on it, gradually outdoing each other (just like some American bars serve pretzels, while others have house-roasted spiced nuts) until we arrive at "modern" tapas as its own cuisine. I only think of El Farol in that context of tapas, not their abbreviated but tasty entree list. That's perfectly fine—tapas are what made this spot famous and they do the small-plate treatment well, even if one cannot do a proper bar crawl on the isolation of Canyon Road. Cool plates include classics galore: *jamón serrano*, *boquerones* (marinated anchovies), fried Marcona almonds just to whet your palate. With sangria in hand, stop for a bit in the embrace of the old adobe walls to enjoy this tucked-away refuge. Take a breath and go for the warm plates: grilled chorizo, calamari, fried avocado— everything is more than a few bites of pleasure and certainly enough to share when ordering with abandon. The Spanish wouldn't want it any other way.

Geronimo, 724 Canyon Rd., Santa Fe, NM 87501; (505) 982-1500; geronimorestaurant.com; French/Asian/Fine Dining; $$$$. This is the biggie, the heavyweight, the "Honey, I have something to ask you" place in Santa Fe, and it's been that way for more than two decades. In my pre-foodie days, Geronimo was even the source of horror when I heard that a better-off friend dropped $300 on his dinner for four—egads! People change, of course, and I've been happy to spend almost that much on an over-the-top dinner for two at this legendary destination. Eric DiStefano built his menu with precision and technique, then applied locally unheard-of service standards to the experience. The results? Water glasses refilled without even spotting a server, conversations that are never interrupted, and solemn presentation of the most lovely and expensive food in the city. If you've never had elk, have Eric sear a tenderloin for you—it's one of his signature dishes and worth every dollar. Other staples include a pear salad with blue cheese and arugula, and blue crab cakes that might make you think you're in a cowboy-boot-clad Boston. Of course, there are wines from reasonable to "whoa!" and desserts portioned in balance with their decadence. Find a reason to go, for this is an experience worth having.

The Mine Shaft Tavern, 2846 NM 14, Madrid, NM 87010; (505) 473-0743; themineshafttavern.com; Pub; $$. The Turquoise Trail is the common way to get from Albuquerque to Santa Fe, both for East Mountain residents and for others desiring a winding two-lane road and rural scenery. Halfway, more or less, is the artists' town of Madrid, serving two very important needs to through-travelers: coffee and road food. The coffee's at Java Junction (2855 NM 14, Madrid, NM 87010; 505-438-2772; java-junction.com), but the road food and the local color come with ease at the Mine Shaft, the hard-earned result of decades of patronage through good times and bad for Madrid and its residents. Live music, burgers, waitstaff that have likely been doing this for quite some time, and probably even a local pooch or two out on the front porch—it's a pub, and a small-town pub at that. The soup is not "of the day" and it comes with crackers; the appetizers include nachos and chicken wings. But it's comfortable like those jeans you can't throw away, the ones with thin spots and fraying. The Mine Shaft is the place you "put on" when nothing else fits; an American beer—or a locally brewed pint—and a charred burger make everything look right again.

Ore House at Milagro, 139 W. San Francisco St., Santa Fe, NM 87501; (505) 995-0139; orehouse-santafe.com; Steak/New Mexican; $$$. Santa Fe old-timers will go looking for the Ore House only to face confusion until it is learned that the classic steak house teamed up with Milagro 139 and moved a block down the street into the tree-garnished two-story atrium of the popular night hangout. Rest assured that the menu moved as well, and you can still have your Plazamole Fresco (their take on guacamole) or the green chile stew with hunks of pork and oodles of chile. Regulars of the old Milagro now swoon over the Ore House's chef and the new skill set of simple items like burgers and Caesar salad. But steaks are what I've always had at the Ore House, and steaks I will continue to have. The prime rib is horseradish's daydream in either 6- or 10-ounce cuts. A perfect pairing with the beef is the off-menu sautéed spinach with huitlacoche mushrooms (a black and earthy delicacy from a fungus that grows on corn—don't google it, trust me on that). You won't need to go anywhere at all after dinner—live music and hip parties are what Milagro is known for, and their events schedule seems to be full every weekend.

Pantry Restaurant, 1820 Cerrillos Rd., Santa Fe, NM 87505; (505) 986-0022; pantrysantafe.com; Diner; $$. The late 1940s saw an immense boom of business and entrepreneurship all over the country—this is why "landmark" businesses often have similar start dates, like a good dozen restaurants in Santa Fe, and the Pantry in 1948 is in that group. I didn't try the beloved little hole-in-the-wall until several years after moving here, and then proceeded to have the best tuna melt of my life. Even at the time, I realized part of the reason it was good was unholy amounts of butter when griddling the sandwich—they don't call a greasy spoon that name for no reason, after all. The Singley family is the seventh set of owners over the Pantry's history, but each new transition doesn't bring a heck of a lot of change, and locals love it that way. Diners must serve corned beef hash from scratch, lest they be derided by all with a shred of food appreciation in their body. The Pantry's hash is indeed within specifications: chunks of corned beef seared just a bit on top of cubed home fries. Breakfast freaks will also have to try the biscuits, treading the perfect middle ground between tender and flaky—I still don't get how a "dry" powder biscuit has that melt-in-your-mouth texture, but it is magical. Lest you think breakfast ends the fun, the Pantry does lunch and dinner, too—come back the same day if you don't mind double-dipping.

The Pink Adobe, 406 Old Santa Fe Trail, Santa Fe, NM 87501; (505) 983-7712; thepinkadobe.com; Steak/American; $$$. Founder Rosalea Murphy made her traditional French onion soup a local treasure, beloved for 60 years. Ownership changes brought about menu "upgrades" several years back, but the clamoring for the decadent soup ensured its quick return, and it is back to stay. The ownership change didn't stick either, bringing the menu back to the foods that made the Pink Adobe famous. Don't miss the Steak Dunigan, a New York strip seared with steak house skill and draped in mushrooms and green chile, or the gypsy stew with a molten bomb of jack cheese like treasure at the bottom. Feeling spendy? Order the lobster salad—you'll feel like a Vegas high roller when this artistic plate arrives. Before leaving, order another famous dish, the apple pie with rum hard sauce, and you'll know that "The Pink" is back to what it does best. Next door in the Pink Adobe's **Dragon Room Bar** (p. 281) you can find your hipster vibe and eat variations on the main menu, like duck nachos piled high with flying abandon. At either location, burger fanatics rejoice in the Pink Adobe Burger: Cheese, bacon, sauce, and green chiles deliver a genuine two-fisted mess of umami pleasure.

Plaza Cafe, 54 Lincoln Ave., Santa Fe, NM 87501; (505) 982-1664; thefamousplazacafe.com; Greek/New Mexican/Cafe; $$. Things don't normally go well for restaurants that want to achieve "be-all, end-all" status—they do too much, the cooking starts to slip, the service can be overwhelmed, and just like that, you're a Denny's. But hold on a minute. The Plaza Cafe has been frantically busy with their Greek and New Mexican fare for almost 100 years (since 1918), yet never have I felt constrained by the weight of that history. The eclectic menu draws in an unusual mash-up of locals and tourists—the latter because they hear it's good, the former because they know it's great. The Razatos family has innovated the menu (quinoa fritters, moussaka, apple *cajeta* pie, halibut ceviche? yes!) during their ownership since 1947, with third-generation Andy running the show these days. The original Plaza location just went through a tough few years with a kitchen fire that sparked a total renovation, with the planned reopening in late 2012. The Southside spot has been operating for over five years—first they were an outlet for Southsiders but had to take up a lot of the downtown location's overflow. Things should be back to normal soon, a big relief for every fan in town. Now, diner or not, this is Santa Fe, so there are few bargains on the menu—you won't leave with a belly-busting $5.99 special. That being said, nothing is far above the $10 mark, including the favorite anchiote pork plate with Yucatecan spices and *calabacitas*. My longtime standby bowl of chile comes with *carnitas* or *carne asada* and is still affordable.

Leave a little room for that famous apple pie, or red velvet cake of the gods. The Southside location is convenient at 3466 Zafarano Dr., Santa Fe, NM 87507; (505) 424-0755; plazacafesouthside.com.

Santacafé, 231 Washington Ave., Santa Fe, NM 87501; (505) 984-1788; santacafe.com; Modern/Fine Dining; $$$. I'll admit that this is one of the most simple and clever restaurant names in town, evoking locality with casual flair. Way back when, Santacafé's kitchen was under the creative helm of Ming Tsai, who left a few marks on the current menu—"classics" like the shiitake and cactus spring rolls. The rest of the menu is innovative without adhering to one cuisine. Chicken confit enchiladas share space with a green chile cheeseburger and the house niçoise salad. Sitting in this 19th-century house with gorgeous styling, you'll enjoy dinners that are elegant and a bit upscale with rack of lamb or seared scallops. I think the poblano relleno is fantastic for a light entree, with or without a starter of their famous simple greens salad. The current owners, Judith and Robert, keep this classic destination running for the love of the craft, offering daily specials and deals to entice repeat customers over and over again. We all hope that continues for the long-term future.

Steaksmith at El Gancho, 104-B Old Las Vegas Hwy., Santa Fe, NM 87505; (505) 988-3333; santafesteaksmith.com; Steak; $$$. It is almost easy to write off this spot on the edge of town as a has-been, not as interesting as other things that have come along in the 40 years since its inception. But that would ignore the fact that year after year the readers' survey in the *Santa Fe Reporter* awards

Steaksmith the top steak honor. Someone is actually eating the steak here rather than assuming the worst. For 40 years old, well, it looks it—but in the "I run marathons!" kind of way rather than "I watch TV." Chairs are deeply upholstered with indented cushions, but no tattering is evident, and the dark wood tables look like they were made to hold platters of shrimp cocktail and onion rings. Order those if you'd like, but keep your eyes on the prize and choose your cut of meat. The doneness is important—medium-rare for filet, medium (maybe) for rib eye or strip—because a lean steak cooked quickly (like they are here) will toughen once pinkness is achieved and then passed. Correspondingly fattier cuts can handle a little more cooking and still taste good if the fat is not trimmed away completely. Now that you've had your little steak lesson, savor the perfectly portioned filet here, eat your baked potato and sides, or simply save room for a bit of old-style steak house dessert. Bread pudding, anyone?

All Chile, All the Time

Casa Chimayó, 409 W. Water St., Santa Fe, NM 87501; (505) 428-0391; casachimayosantafe.com; New Mexican; $. **Roberto Cordova** is finally home: The home built by his grandfather in 1938 is now the building for his restaurant, where he can prepare and serve *comidas de las abuelitas*—the food of our grandmothers. Northern

CHILE ON EVERYTHING!

So, we all love our New Mexico chile. This much should be abundantly clear. An unofficial state motto is "A day without chile is like a day without sunshine," and thanks to the weather patterns, it is rare to have a day without either one of them.

Chile can be found on menus all over the state, from enchilada dens to cafes with the now-standard "Albuquerque turkey" sandwich (the basic assembly is turkey, cheese, avocado, and green chile—other condiments optional). Green chile in particular shows up in places that seem unusual to the visitor: chain restaurants. It is so much a part of the cuisine that a number of national chains incorporate it, just for our addicted palates. You can get green chile on your burger at McDonald's, Burger King, or Wendy's, or you can add it to a Pizza Hut pizza. And that's just the beginning of our infiltration . . .

It is a fair-game ingredient in desserts, breads, even beverages. For visitors this can be discombobulating, but it soon becomes part of the background: Of course we can put chile on that! Even if "that" is your ice cream, or your salad dressing. Most non-chain restaurants also offer some kind of chile dish—Italian spots will often feature a green chile Alfredo, while Mexican restaurants offer green and red chile sauces right alongside their normal salsas and jalapeño-based spicy foods.

New Mexico chile is a menu mainstay, a bright and fruity red sauce as hot as most locals can handle, available by the cup, bowl, or as a side. Breakfast includes the recently trendy but locally welcomed

This isn't just silly obsessiveness—chiles are actually addictive in addition to being really darn good for you. The capsicum in the peppers (the chemical that makes your taste buds register "heat") can promote the release of endorphins if you eat just above your current tolerance level. The next time, your tolerance will go up a little, and over time that good feeling from the heat coupled with a high threshold means a mild addiction. But with insane amounts of vitamin C and antioxidants, there are few better things to be addicted to. Even nonresidents can heed the call: I am able to find New Mexico salsa in my tiny Midwestern hometown's grocery store, including El Pinto's fantastic blends.

Some of the most amazing and unique chile dishes or chile-accentuated foods I've tried in my years of residence: Level 2 at Horseman's Haven Cafe (p. 88), red chile in the town of Chimayó, Chocolate Cartel's chile truffles (p. 187), The Candy Lady's red chile fudge (p. 132), "atomic hot" green chile pistachio brittle from McGinn's Pistachio Tree Ranch (7320 Hwy. 54/70, Alamogordo, NM, 575-437-0602; pistachiotreeranch.com), southern New Mexico's obsession with putting chiles rellenos on hamburgers, my own homemade green chile ice cream, New Mexican apple-piñon-chile pie from the Good Pie Cafe in Pie Town (p. 119), and the crazy hot red chile sauce from Cecilia's Cafe in Nob Hill (p. 130).

blue corn piñon pancakes—here made with fresh masa instead of flour—and, of course, huevos in lots of configurations. Hearty soups are traditional New Mexican, warming the soul with red chile posole

handed down from Roberto's grandmother Tita (see
the recipe for **Grandma Tita's Red Posole** on
p. 312). While more on the Mexican side of cuisine, the *chile en nogada* (poblano chile draped
in white sauce) is from the Zacatecas culinary
heritage, also tied to Cordova's history in this
state; it is both lovely and delectable. Or you
can stick with the true local classics like *calabacitas* in blue corn
enchiladas—that's New Mexican through and through.

Horseman's Haven Cafe, 4354 Cerrillos Rd., Santa Fe, NM 87507;
(505) 471-5420; New Mexican; $. For locals getting their chile
wings, it is a required step to dine at Horseman's Haven, the place
that everyone knows has the hottest green chile around. My first
visit was not long after moving to the state: A friend who wanted
to either show off his chile prowess or just torment my taste buds
hauled me down to this little dive of a place in a converted gas
station on Cerrillos Road. We sat at a cramped table and I ate my
burger like a tourist—chile on the side. That first time it was necessary, for even small dabs of the green was like lava on my tongue.
They source the chiles from several different farms, blending to
achieve lofty levels of both heat and flavor. Once acclimated, you'll
knock back smothered burgers or one of the best carb-laden meals
in town: home fries done up in perfect crusty brown, drowned in
fiery green chile. Ready to graduate? Ask for "Level 2" and prepare
to feel like a tourist all over again.

La Choza, 905 Alarid St., Santa Fe, NM 87505; (505) 982-0909; New Mexican; $$. Sister restaurant to **The Shed Creative Cooking** (p. 90), this tucked-away spot is a good pinch hitter when everything around the Plaza is utterly packed. The space is smaller and more intimate, and the dishes are different enough to satisfy your urge for something new. Plates of local comfort foods span posole, burritos, rellenos, and the like, but of particular note are the enchiladas, tender and flavorful in a city (and state) brimming with enchilada plates. *Carne adovada* fans should try either of La Choza's versions: the original with pork or chicken *adovada*, chunks of marinated white meat doused in their fiery red chile sauce. Despite the off-the-path location, this is still a well-known spot—make a dinner reservation or get there early for lunch to avoid a long wait. Even in the warmer months when the patio is in full swing, this place is beloved for more than just their from-scratch margaritas.

Maria's New Mexican Kitchen, 555 W. Cordova Rd., Santa Fe, NM 87505; (505) 983-7929; marias-santafe.com; New Mexican; $$. Maria Lopez and her take-out kitchen began wooing diners in 1952 (just one year before the Shed opened) with New Mexican cuisine, including the now-popular green chile cheeseburgers. One day she ran out of buns; as a result, we have Maria to thank for the delicious fusion of the Tortilla Burger—a flour tortilla folded over a burger patty, with or without a smothering of chile. After several ownership changes, local boy and Maria's fan Al Lucero became the owner in 1985 and added what has become Maria's claim to fame:

hundreds of margarita combinations, with an underpinning tequila selection in the dozens. He even wrote a tome called *The Great Margarita Book,* which details how to make wonderful margaritas and includes some of the Maria's recipes so that you can create the full experience. It is worth noting that Al also restored much of the menu to higher quality, with fresh tortillas and *carne adovada* that uses whole chiles, seeds and all, to impart piquancy.

The Shed Creative Cooking, 113½ E. Palace Ave., Santa Fe, NM 87501; (505) 982-9030; sfshed.com; New Mexican; $$. On your first trip to Santa Fe, or your triumphant return, or whenever, this mainstay of local cuisine is a must-visit. Due to its proximity to the Plaza, making a reservation is strongly recommended—without it, waits can be long. My admiration for the Shed lies in their refusal to tinker with their own traditions; for example, meals are served with buttered French bread, not sopaipillas, because that's what original diners back in the '50s requested. Every corn tortilla in the establishment (as far as I can tell) is blue corn, an inky indigo rich with tradition in northern New Mexican home cooking, best savored in a smothered enchilada plate with their *carne adovada* and a splash of red. The chile can be hot, but it varies day to day; many locals will order whichever chile is hotter that day—a strategy I both practice and endorse.

Tomasita's, 500 S. Guadalupe St., Santa Fe, NM 87501; (505) 983-5721; New Mexican, $$. This longtime Santa Fe destination has a few things going for it: proximity to the train station and farmers' market, and fast turnaround of New Mexican comfort food. Many who have been coming here for decades to partake in platters smothered with house-made red and green chile say that things are not what they used to be. My visits were memorable for incredibly fast service and chile that was nice and hot. It's worth a visit for the wonderfully fluffy sopaipillas that conclude each meal and a trip down memory lane when you, too, were a newbie to this cuisine.

Specialty Stores, Markets & Producers

Betterday Coffee, 905 W. Alameda St., Santa Fe, NM 87501; (505) 780-8059; betterdaycoffee.com; Coffee. The well-appreciated local co-op **La Montañita** (p. 96) decided to bring another great coffee shop to town, appointing it with Wi-Fi, breakfast treats and burritos, and beans shipped in from the "third-wave" coffee mecca of the Pacific Northwest. Owner Tom Frost used to manage **Second Street Brewery** (p. 291), but a trip to that coffee-lovin' region convinced him that Santa Fe deserved better. Welcome!

ChocolateSmith, 851 Cerrillos Rd., Santa Fe, NM 87505; (505) 473-2111; chocolatesmith.com; Chocolate. It all started with a guy who liked chocolate and hiking but didn't want a mess after a few days on the trail. Clif Perry was his name, and he started dipping bars of chocolate in wax and tossing them in his pack. It worked, and it was the start of a business model that expanded to confections and barks and distribution all over the state. Clif sold the retail shop, but when you stop in, you'll get nothing but sweetness from current owners Kari and Jeff Keenan. The bark I cannot resist is white chocolate with almonds, lemon, and lavender. Coming from someone who is pretty neutral on white chocolate and lavender, that's a vote of confidence. Prices are tolerable, but prepare for sticker shock if you order up one of everything that looks good—it *all* looks good, and tastes even better.

Cocopelli Chocolatier, 3482 Zafarano Dr., Ste. A, Santa Fe NM, 87507; (505) 438-2626; cocosantafe.com; Chocolate. Lauren is the name behind this recent emergence in the local chocolate scene, and she's a welcome presence. Fresh out of the gates in 2012, she started offering not only chocolate creations in iterations to please the pickiest customers, but also classes on chocolate technique, from tempering to bean-to-bar production. She's confident that not everyone will run right out and start making  handmade chocolate, so her store is in no jeopardy anytime soon.

Salted, vegan, bitter, fruity, toasted, or sweet, Cocopelli has every-thing in the chocolate world.

Ecco Espresso & Gelato, 105 E. Marcy St., Santa Fe, NM 87501; (505) 986-9778; eccogelato.com; Coffee/Frozen. **Many locals got their first taste of Italian-style gelato at this spot right off the Plaza; we were quickly familiarized with *stracciatella* and *giandula*, never getting enough of the teeny cups and relatively strong fla-vors. To many, Ecco is only known as the place to get gelato, but their best product on slightly chilly evenings is a double shot of espresso, on its own or poured *affogato*-style over a scoop of gelato. In an *affogato,* vanilla tends to be the default flavor, but coffee gelato doubles your pleasure. Ecco still does well, especially given that they stay open later than any other coffee vendor around.**

Holy Spirit Espresso, 225 W. San Francisco St., Santa Fe, NM 87501; (505) 920-3664; holyspiritespresso.com; Coffee. **Bill Deutsch is Holy Spirit Espresso; he is the heart, the soul, and the foamy bonus at the top of each macchiato. I don't mean to say that the place isn't the same when he is not working—there is no "he is not working." His shop is literally 10 feet square (maybe less), filled with a tall countertop, room for him to stand, and room for you to stand. Decor is his tacked-up collection of postcards from all over the world, every single one catalogued and numbered. Bill doesn't just pull a fantastic shot—he does it with a grin and then asks for less money than the green-logoed lady up the street. You gotta love this place. I do.**

Santa Fe Invented the Frito Pie— Maybe?

Good and long Internet searches will reveal the possibly shocking allegation that the Frito pie was not created in Santa Fe at the Woolworth's food counter, but that it could possibly be the brainchild of . . . the folks connected to Fritos? Say it ain't so! Admittedly it might have been the Fritos inventor's mother, which makes it sound a little better than being some corporate scheme.

OK, the problem seems to be that the stories about Frito pie, the bag of Fritos with chili and cheese on top, do go back to the 1930s, not long after Fritos were invented. However, any documentation of the original is missing. We do know, of course, that in the 1960s a woman named Teresa Hernandez served Frito pies to patrons at the Woolworth's lunch counter in Santa Fe. The structure of a Frito pie is a bag's worth of original Fritos corn chips, topped with chili con carne (not New Mexican chile sauce, but of course that would be quite good) and optional onions and cheese. It's warm, messy, and tasty.

As for the Woolworth's, there is now a different store in the original location on the Plaza, the Five & Dime (*58 E. San Francisco St., Santa Fe, NM 87501; 505-992-1800; fiveanddimegs .com*). Tourists and locals alike find themselves browsing the aisles and wondering if a Kokopelli shot glass would really be all that bad . . . The lunch counter is wonderfully still there and still serving what New Mexico has taken on as our own local treat: the Frito pie.

Kakawa Chocolates, 1050 E. Paseo de Peralta, Santa Fe, NM 87501; (505) 982-0388; kakawachocolates.com; Chocolate/Sweets. There is always room for dessert when you are walking all over such a gorgeous city. Tucked just blocks away from the Plaza, here the focus is everything cacao, from ancient drinking elixirs to truffles and cakes. Cheese even makes its way into the aromatic concoctions. If you're lucky, the other fanatics haven't eaten the last of the goat cheese chile truffles in the lineup. Even if they have, that's all the better reason to plan a return trip once the deep cocoa afterglow has worn off.

Kaune's Neighborhood Market, 511 Old Santa Fe Trail, Santa Fe, NM 87505; (505) 982-2629; kaunes.com; Grocery. There's much to love besides the cheese at Kaune's, the local go-to spot for ingredients when the mega-mart has lost all interest. The back of the store is focused on two animal products: the meat counter, and the stretch of chilly shelves for all the cheeses on offer. My personal favorite, blue cheese, seems to be well represented with at least a dozen varieties from all over the world, while local products are always available. Produce and natural foods are always on hand, many from nearby companies, so you can keep your money local.

Kokoman Fine Wine & Liquor, 34 Cities of Gold Rd., Santa Fe, NM 87506; (505) 455-2219; kokomanliquors.com; Alcohol. Just north of Santa Fe in the small hamlet called Pojoaque is this destination shop for all things drink-related. Everyone from Santa Fe to Española to Taos makes the drive because nearly everything within easy distance is wanting. I've even heard recommendations "way down" in Albuquerque to head to Kokoman for a specialty item.

La Montañita Co-op, 913 W. Alameda, Santa Fe, NM 87501; (505) 984-2853; lamontanita.coop; Grocery. A favorite store in both Santa Fe and Albuquerque for local products and produce, La Montañita has been open for just about as long as any chain grocery store—kudos for that. They stock meats, local products, organic veggies, bulk foods, and cheeses from all over the world. I love their "tiny bin" of 1- to 2-ounce cheese portions for trying something new, and the periodic produce markdowns that make any budget-shopper's day.

Ohori's Coffee, 1098 S. St. Francis Dr., Santa Fe, NM 87505; (505) 982-9692; ohoriscoffee.com; Coffee. My stint at trying to be a Santa Fean coincided with my early years as a coffee drinker, and when introduced to the ultra-dark roasts of Ohori's, I was *Ohorrified*. Years later the "black mud" I couldn't handle would be my mainstay roast, both in Santa Fe and from Ohori's original roast master in Albuquerque. Additional location at 507 Old Santa Fe Trail, Santa Fe, NM 87501; (505) 982-9262.

The Spanish Table, 109 N. Guadalupe St., Santa Fe, NM 87501; (505) 986-0243; spanishtable.com; World Market/Spices. Patrons of the excellent tapas restaurants in Santa Fe will soon wonder how to do the same style at their next party: The solution is a long visit to the Spanish Table (and probably a big bill). Everything looks wonderful, from paella pans to jarred sardines and, of course, almonds in every variety and state of preservation.

The Spice Lady, 509 W. Cordova Rd., Santa Fe, NM 87505; (505) 471-3833; thespiceladysantafe.com; Spices. Midwesterners move to New Mexico in droves—the reasons are varied, but some of the things missed from home include Chicago-style pizza and Penzey's Spices. Barbara Nass created her store to supply locals with all of the whole and powdered flavor bombs you might possibly need. Last time I visited, I walked out with flavored salts, curry, and smoked paprika, with plans hatching for the next trip back.

Susan's Fine Wine & Spirits, 1005 S. St. Francis Dr., Santa Fe, NM 87505; (505) 984-1582; sfwineandspirits.com; Alcohol. Personalized service is how local businesses can survive; Susan's exemplifies that, fulfilling orders for both locals and inquiring callers from all over the country. The selection of wine and beer is huge, including (possibly heretical) gluten-free beer, and there is a comprehensive hard spirits list as well. Right on St. Francis, it's easy to spot and pull right in. This is the destination of choice for local beverage and supplies acquisition—it is the one retail shop in town where you can buy Bitter End Bitters, the indispensable cocktail ingredient created locally by Bill York.

Todos Santos, 125 E. Palace Ave., #31, Santa Fe, NM 87501; (505) 982-3855; Chocolate. If the phrase *jewel box* is overused to describe cutesy little shops or cafes, I apologize and reassign all previous usage solely to Todos Santos, the most adorned sweets shop I've set foot in, ever. Enough space to browse is all you'll get in Hayward Simoneaux's shop with stacked presentations of imported confections, chocolates, and his own molded candies. Pricey but still a treasure.

Whoo's Donuts, 851-B Cerrillos Rd., Santa Fe, NM 87505; (505) 629-1678; whoosdonuts.com; Donuts. You have to admire a place that does one thing really, really well and nothing else. No pastries, no sandwiches, just donuts (and coffee to wash it down). Whoo's owners are behind the local favorite **ChocolateSmith** (p. 91), allowing for some ingredient crossover. Ask any of the perpetually perky staff for a recommendation, and they'll steer you toward one of their originals: a lemon cake with frosting and pistachios. The nearly dripping frosting and pound-cake density make this decadent almost to a fault, but that doesn't mean you won't enjoy it. They also carry the trendy maple-bacon combo. If you've never put those two flavors together, it is worth trying at least once, with or without the local addition of chile sugar. Hanging around in the shop carries the danger of inducing second helpings, especially if they're browning butter in the back and that cloud of unutterably wonderful nuttiness wafts to your nose.

Ziggy's International Market, 1005 Pen Rd., Santa Fe, NM 87505; (505) 986-5054; World Market/Grocery. Near **Susan's Fine Wine & Spirits** (p. 97), you can stock up on anything international you might need for that fancy dinner party—Britain to South America to India and beyond are all represented, at prices that locals will appreciate. The owners also run a Middle Eastern restaurant called **Pyramid Cafe** (p. 56), so they know their spices well.

Learn to Cook

Las Cosas Kitchen Shoppe & Cooking School, 181 Paseo de Peralta (DeVargas Shopping Center), Santa Fe, NM 87501; (877) 229-7184; lascosascooking.com; info@lascosascooking.com. Chef Johnny "Vee" Vollertsen is a local mainstay in food writing, menu consulting, and all-around foodie-ness. Cooking gigs in Australia and New York and travels to Phoenix and all over the Southwest finally led him to Albuquerque to work with Jane Butel in her cooking school before taking his large skill set up to Santa Fe in

1998. He's parlayed that talent into teaching classes and ultimately becoming Cooking School Director. The class schedule is comprehensive as well as stuffed—at least a dozen classes are held every month in topics from basic knife skills to Thai street food, covering both techniques and cuisines.

Santa Fe Community College, 6401 Richards Ave., Santa Fe, NM 87508; (505) 428-1435; sfcc.edu/programs/culinary_arts. No mere set of cooking classes, this is an associate's degree in the business school at the local college, demanding full-time work for a good two years while you learn food safety, cooking techniques, even the anthropology of food (neat!). I'm relieved to see that the website doesn't mince numbers: They state that sous-chefs in Santa Fe can make $25K to $32K annually, thoroughly removing much of the perceived glamour of this profession, which is more akin to teaching than anything else. It is made up of dedicated and hardworking folks just barely scraping by but doing what they love. That latter part is an overlooked aspect of many working lives. Starting your food career may not be easy, but if it is what you are destined to do, this school is for you.

Santa Fe School of Cooking, 116 W. San Francisco St., Santa Fe, NM 87501; (505) 983-4511; santafeschoolofcooking.com. Just upstairs off the Plaza is this awesome little shop and class area that educates hundreds of students every month, locals and visitors alike. You'll get schooled in rellenos, tamales, basic techniques, or entire cuisines like a series on Mexico. Guest chefs stop in to teach their specialty cuisine or their own featured restaurant dishes. Single-class prices are generally in the $50-to-$80 range and run several hours, with hands-on experience. Other attractions for the school's customers are walking tours of Santa Fe food destinations, giving tastes and talks at three or four restaurants during each itinerary.

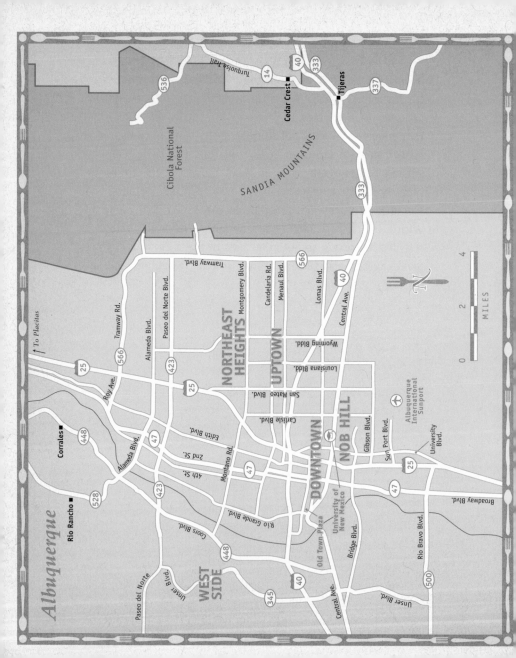

Albuquerque

Albuquerque

Downtown, East Downtown & Old Town

Just after the turn of the millennium, downtown Albuquerque was humming with another attempt at growth and revival—making downtown a fun destination had been pushed in the 1980s, but things kind of puttered out—and this time everyone hoped it would actually "take." A decade later, the verdict is coming back and seems to say, "Yes, this is really happening." New condos (some successes and some still working out the kinks), restaurants, clubs, and street vendors prove that if you make it look fun and pretty, people who want to have fun while looking pretty will come.

Some of the first projects were big, like demolishing a whole city block to build a movie complex with restaurants and condos to start luring folks in, both for entertainment and to live. More restaurants arrived: Sandwich and sushi shops replaced floundering dives, while a fresh coat of paint was literally applied to the whole area in lovely earth tones and art murals. State projects like the Rail

Runner light-rail system added appeal, with commuting to Santa Fe now easy even without a car.

On either side of downtown lies Old Town to the west and East Downtown, or EDo, to the east. Old Town is the shopping and strolling district, full of curio shops, old buildings, a central plaza, and striking old churches. The oldest is San Felipe de Neri, built in 1706 and then again in 1793 after rains destroyed the adobe in 1792. Many visitors will spend time in Old Town and at the nearby biopark and museums—it's good for at least a full day or two.

East Downtown needed a hip name to go with the renovated buildings and gourmet eateries, so a SoHo-inspired moniker was coined: EDo. Home to walking neighborhoods, hospitals, schools, and delectable eats, it is a good place to call home whether you stick nearby or hop on the freeway to commute to a job. EDo sits on an upslope from the railroad tracks downtown, giving a lovely view of the city, especially at night.

Getting Around

Walking is a good option here, especially between downtown and EDo—many folks will prefer to drive to Old Town so they can explore the museums, shop, and not have to lug purchases around. The city runs a free bus service loop downtown on weekdays—just look for the buses that say "D-ride." Transit info for longer trips is on the city website: cabq.gov/transit/getting-around.

This area's boundaries stretch from the river on the west to I-25 on the east. Beyond I-25 are the UNM and Nob

Hill areas, covered later. The northern boundary is I-40, while the southern is approximately Bridge Boulevard, the southern edge of the Barelas neighborhood.

Foodie Faves

Bulldog Burgers, 710 Sixth St. NW, Downtown, Albuquerque, NM 87102; (505) 242-7800; bulldogburgers.net; Burgers; $. With a restrained menu and walk-up service out of a tiny stand-alone building (that also advertises bail bonds—it's just that part of town, nothing unusual), Bulldog is exactly in its niche: downtown lunch patrons on a schedule. A few dedicated parking spots are constantly in rotation as fans pick up their food and head on their way, but a few picnic tables make dining al fresco an option as well. The food is unfailingly fresh—hot, juicy burgers flanked by cool pickles and sides, at unbelievable cheap-as-fast-food prices. Optional green chile on the burger is fiery love for a locally trained tongue. Chips are the side option—no fryer on the premises. But you can add a pastry from Roma Cafe to your order. It's always fantastic to see local businesses helping each other out instead of going for cut-throat competition.

Cafe Cafe, 200 Third St. NW, Downtown, Albuquerque, NM 87102; (505) 843-6203; Bakery/Deli/Sandwiches; $. At first glance this spot is "just another sandwich shop" that caters to downtown workers looking for something locally owned and fast. But scratch the surface to find that these sandwiches are on house-made bread and the early-morning burritos are some of the best you'll find anywhere in walking distance. Those prework hours could only be faster if they had a drive-thru—they batch up on the day's featured burrito to ensure a fast in and out, and piles of homemade muffins await the sweet breakfasters. The expected New Mexican spin is put on their tuna melt with green chile, and daily soups offer another alternative (though for quiche I'd likely go over to the nearby French cafe).

Cafe Lush, 700 Tijeras Ave. NW, Downtown, Albuquerque, NM 87102; (505) 508-0164; cafelushabq.com; Cafe/Eclectic; $. Teeny, tiny spaces have always appealed to the kid in me that would hide under tables and make pillow forts; Cafe Lush is a nubbin of a restaurant but makes use of the sidewalk on most days to expand seating and give patrons their daily dose of vitamin D. The food is eclectic nosh: grilled pizza named after friends ("the Irminator," "the Callan"), fancified salads with beets and sweet potatoes and feta, and house-made ice cream for the post-salad healthful glow. Breakfasts pull in locals from the northern downtown area and parents after schoolchild drop-offs. How could someone toting around a youngster turn down an order of bread pudding masquerading as French toast? Keep your cup of strong coffee black as the perfect counterpoint to that sweet breakfast.

Downtown Brunchie Munchies

Find your late-morning nosh at a number of downtown Albuquerque spots from fancy to frugal, and don't forget—Sundays are dry in the entire state until noon, so keep that in mind if a mimosa was in your wake-up checklist.

The environmentally conscientious hotel patron with a refined palate simply stumbles downstairs from an LEED-certified room to brunch at the Hotel Andaluz's **Lucia** (p. 116) dining room. The rest of us just head to Second Street 1 block north of Central and take a seat, ready for deliciousness, starting with green chile biscuits and turkey gravy—a pairing made in heavenly New Mexico (turkey was the presettlement game bird, and, of course, there's the chile). Heartier appetites meet their match with chicken and waffles or an open-faced burger. Watch the schedule for occasional Jazz Brunches with a fixed plated menu and live entertainment.

Here are three words to ponder when considering downtown brunch: red chile bacon. Did your eyes roll back in your head? Then point your head toward **Gold Street Caffe** (p. 112) just south of Central, where that red-chile-glazed bacon can be all yours, along with a stiff cup of coffee and some of the best scones in town. If pastry is merely a diversion, try the best thing on their morning menu: the Cowboy Breakfast, misnamed in my opinion but still utterly delicious. It takes a green chile biscuit and stuffs it with fluffy scrambled eggs, ham, and mascarpone cheese. I think "cowboy" implies hearty but rough, and this is more Melodious Muffin. If they trademark it, let me know.

Other spots serving good brunch-time eats, even if they don't doll it up with a brunch-bow:

It's good to promote the idea that brunch should be laid-back and yet a step above just rolling out of bed for food (that's what the Frontier is for), so it makes sense the "finer diner" concept at Standard Diner in EDo (p. 121) would deliver a tasty brunch, from burritos to French toast. Open every single non-Monday day of the week (trust me, that has caught me a few times), the Grove Cafe & Market in EDo (p. 113) is the see-and-be-seen brunch spot in town. The Grove is fun, casual, and funky, yet has all the street cred of organic/local ingredients and a talented staff to cook it all for you. Oh, and the coffee (from Intelligentsia) is the best-brewed joe in town. A few blocks south of the downtown farmers' market you'll run into everyone you know at Flying Star Cafe (Silver Avenue location; p. 134), having coffee, gossiping, and eating from the most famously well-stocked pastry case in the city. Their *huevos rancheros* plate is enough for two, or go the Fiesta Sandwich route with eggs, cheddar, and green chile in a chile bun.

Cocina Azul, 1134 Mountain Rd. NW, Downtown, Albuquerque, NM 87102; (505) 503-8009; cocinazul.com; New Mexican; $. Full belly, happy heart. That's the phrase at the top of the menu at Cocina Azul ("blue kitchen"), and they mean it—you'll be satisfied by the love that is cooked into every dish here, from New Mexican to traditional American. Breakfast fare is eggy or chile-soaked, including burritos and a crunchy sweet bread they say is the best combination of waffle and French toast. Later in the day the savory fare dominates, but you must start with their Albondigas Nuevo Mexico: meatballs sauced with red chile. It's so simple, it makes one wonder why no other restaurant has thought of it. You can then move on to the famous *carne adovada* plate with more of that red chile, or venture greenward with a green chile cheeseburger or a rich bowl of green chile stew. My mouth salivates for the next visit when I'll have the specialty burger smeared with guacamole and served on sopaipilla "buns." Yum.

The Daily Grind, 414 E. Central Ave., EDo, Albuquerque, NM 87102; (505) 883-8310; dailygrindabq.com; Coffee/Cafe; $. A hop and step from both downtown and the university district, the Daily Grind is a calm oasis that defies its position right on Central Avenue. The back patio with shady trees is even lovelier in the summer, but small semiprivate areas in the main building offer nearly as much comfort and seclusion. Espresso drinks are done very well here, as are pastries to nibble or dunk—the scones are some of the best in town. A small breakfast and lunch menu is handy for those with hunger pangs or needing to get some quick takeout for lunch at the office. Owner Nancy Rodgers keeps things simple and smiling from the moment you walk in the door.

Farina Pizzeria, 510 E. Central Ave., EDo, Albuquerque, NM 87102; (505) 243-0130; farinapizzeria.com; Pizza; $$. From the minds of **Artichoke Cafe** (p. 123) comes what might be the best Naples-style pie in the state. The head oven-master, Stew Dorris, consulted with the legendary Pizzeria Bianco in Phoenix before tossing crusts and packing in diners to the hilt each and every day since opening in 2008. Farina has a short menu, but every item is executed masterfully, from a *pasta e fagioli* soup to balsamic roasted meatballs to the chopped salad. Oh, but those pies! Small, crackling, and charred, they will be topped with simple yet potent items such as Tallegio cheese and thyme or broccolini and hot peppers or a perfect Margherita (basil and fresh mozzarella). Don't even think of leaving without the butterscotch *budino* custard topped with sea salt, even though you'll be back.

Forque Kitchen, 330 Tijeras Ave. NW (in the Hyatt Regency), Downtown, Albuquerque, NM 87102; (505) 843-2700; facebook .com/Forque.Kitchen.Bar; Fine Dining; $$$. Replacing a mediocre hotel restaurant, Forque stormed in with a dining room and kitchen facelift, ready to change people's minds. Swanky booths in a sunken dining pocket with white-shirted waitstaff set the mood and expectations, which the new chef is all too happy to deliver. A mixed clientele of hotel guests—you can spot them by their loosened ties—and couples out for a fancy night all have options ranging from the mixed American menu, like local-topping-adorned flatbread and chicken tortilla soup, all the way up the decadence scale to short ribs. A strong cup of coffee and desserts will end the meal before embarking for either the car or the hotel room. One benefit to the hotel restaurant is the hours—you'll consider coming back for the equally mouthwatering breakfast and lunch menus.

Gold Street Caffe, 218 Gold Ave. SW, Downtown, Albuquerque, NM 87102; (505) 765-1633; goldstreetcaffe.com; American/Cafe; $$. Long before the relative newcomers **Slate Street Cafe** (p. 120) and **Lucia** (p. 116) hopped on the fancy downtown trend, Gold Street Caffe provided high-end eats and wonderful brunches to anyone near downtown or willing to head that way. Through a few chef and ownership changes, the place has kept the doors open and is better than ever (something a diner can always cheer about, especially in slower economic times). Chile-dusted fried calamari is the solid starter choice before moving on to an unusual enchilada rendition with mole instead of chile sauce. Despite the departure from local tradition, these are some pretty amazing enchiladas, worth investigation. They serve a fantastic brunch (see sidebar, p. 108) and maintain a small but lively sidewalk patio for people watching while you dine.

The Grove Cafe & Market, 600 E. Central Ave., Ste. A, EDo, Albuquerque, NM 87102; (505) 248-9800; thegrovecafemarket.com; Cafe/Coffee/Organic/Local; $$. Be ready for breakfast at the Grove with three words: homemade English muffins. I thought so. Add to the mix the best-brewed cup of coffee in town, using beans from Intelligentsia (the only place in Albuquerque to brew the high-quality Chicago beans), local raspberry jam, and cupcakes that will make you forget that trend has jumped the shark, and you have the makings of a sweetly carb-loaded morning. Lunch just keeps getting better: salads based on local produce, sandwiches loaded with house-made cheese and condiments, and a daily soup that always knocks my socks off. The Grove can get crowded and rather noisy, with parties lingering long enough that no available Wi-Fi is a blessing. Even in winter months the outdoor patio stays buzzing with activity, with portable heaters at the ready. It is one of the closest things Albuquerque has to an everyday hipster hangout the likes of which exist by the dozens in places like Los Angeles. We'll take the Grove, and only whimper on Mondays, when it is easy to forget they do close one day a week.

Holy Cow, 700 E. Central Ave., EDo, Albuquerque, NM 87102; (505) 242-2991; Burgers/Organic/Local; $. Holy Cow is Yet Another Burger Joint in a town that has seen a cavalcade of gourmet burger places of late. And yet they live up to the name in nearly every way, serving grass-fed beef on (too dry) buns with well-executed sides. Onion rings that win favor for a light beer batter start out the lineup, and standard sweet potato fries flank Parmesan-crusted zucchini fries. A "no cow" burger is made of roasted eggplant with chickpea aioli for the full-on vegan crowd. Bun-haters find solace in salads that stand in stark defiance to the restaurant's name: roasted beets, seared ahi, Thai chicken, and more. Don't forget to take notice of the mascot perched on the front counter: a speckled heifer, halo and all.

La Crepe Michel, 400 San Felipe NW, Old Town, Albuquerque, NM 87104; (505) 242-1251; lacrepemichel.com; French; $$. Lack of knowledge about La Crepe Michel is only due to the quiet, tucked-away location off a side street in Old Town—not due to lackluster food, for in the realm of home-style French, this mainstay has been pleasing diners for more than 20 years under the masterful management and cooking of Claudie Zamet-Wilcox. House-made pâté is a wake-up call of luscious meatiness, only punctuated by how much grainy mustard is used on the accompanying bread. Crepes and tarts and mussels, oh my! The entire menu is recommended for first-timers, and relaxing while you dine is a must for the rare occasions when the service is slow. Dessert crepes are shareable; otherwise, a long walk will be advised before plopping down on a car seat or your chair.

La Quiche Parisienne Bistro, 401 Copper Ave. NW, Downtown, Albuquerque, NM 87102; (505) 242-2808; laquicheparisienne.com;

French/Bakery; $. Even if this town is dominated by chile shops and "American" restaurants, they still need to have a source for bread, so we have a handful of nice French bakeries around. If a bakery also serves cafe food, all the better. La Quiche does a brisk lunch service right in the middle of downtown in a pedestrian walkway—great for strolling to lunch, not as great for visibility when driving around. Owners Sabine and Bruno make nearly everything in the restaurant from scratch, every day. Bruno's breads are the delicious base for more than a dozen menu sandwiches, from the Jambon Beurre (ham and butter) to a hot Frenchy with roast beef, provolone, and horseradish. The pastry side is run by Sabine and her buttery sweet talent; you owe it to yourself to try one of her croissants so that you can be ruined for any mass-produced crescent pastry—blissfully ruined.

Little Red Hamburger Hut, 1501 Mountain Rd. NW, Old Town, Albuquerque, NM 87104; (505) 304-1819; littleredsburgers.tripod .com; Burgers; $. "Satisfaction *gare-un-teed!*" That's what you'll hear from owner Gene Quintano (directed at folks already ordering food) when you walk into the building festooned with midcentury nostalgic decor from wall to wall. Even the old fireplace has been turned into a Marilyn Monroe shrine, while doo-wop music filters through the air. Here, the recipe is homage to a 1980s local favorite called the "Wimpy burger," fresh ground beef and fresh fixins. They call it the Little Red, and it comes with or without cheese and chile—no price hikes. Sit in one of the vintage fast-food booths that dot the room while you await the ear-splitting call of your order's number by a large-lunged tiny woman, just as happy to serve you as could be. That's the secret here—while the burgers are tasty, it is the people that are the meat of the operation.

Lucia, 125 Second St. NW (in the Hotel Andaluz), Downtown, Albuquerque, NM 87102; (505) 923-9080; hotelandaluz.com/lucia; Fine Dining/Mediterranean; $$$. Long ago in the foodie world, there was a place called Kanome, and lo, it was good. Chef Albert Bilotti won fans, but the doors closed around the turn of the millennium when Bilotti opened a respectable New York–style pizza place downtown. He is also a friend and consulting chef for **Slate Street Cafe** (p. 120). And then along came Lucia, where Bilotti created a Mediterranean menu that dazzled critics and hungry patrons in equal measure. After his departure, other chefs have picked up the reins (recently Michael von Blomberg came over from Seasons Rotisserie), but the menu still retains much of the original focus and Bilotti's talent. Bright flavors zap the tongue in a fig salad, and everyone adores the scallops and sugared shrimp plate with sautéed mushrooms. While the finishing touches are typical (crème brûlée, chocolate torte), they are still skilled examples of their kind, reminding many a diner that downtown Albuquerque is a long way from the days of the old boys' club steak house.

P'tit Louis Bistro, 228 Gold Ave. SW, Downtown, Albuquerque, NM 87102; (505) 314-1111; ptitlouisbistro.com; French; $$. There's a new king in town when it comes to French food, and the royal family is personified by a wiry bundle of energy named Christophe. He manages the front of the house at both locations of P'tit Louis, only having to choose between them when the hours overlap (lunch during the week). Even with his vigor, he can only deliver what his kitchen whips up, of course, and if the special of the day contains nothing against your religion, order it. I don't care if you think frog legs are weird or ratatouille is both unpronounceable and freaky—just order it. (See the recipe for **Frog Legs Provençale** on p. 318.) Yes, the rest of the menu is perfect, from mussels to steak frites, but you can order that stuff on follow-up trips, because there will be follow-up trips. The dining area is shoebox-tiny, but that only adds to the ambiance; bonus points if a Francophile is sitting nearby to further enhance the sensation of being in some exotic non-Albuquerque realm. Lemon tart is a must at the end, with a wicked strong pull of espresso. The second location was recently added (right next to Limonata) at 3218 Silver Ave. SE, Nob Hill, Albuquerque, NM 87106; (505) 314-1110.

Robin's Kitchen at the Harwood, 1114 Seventh St. NW, Downtown, Albuquerque, NM 87102; (505) 350-6558; robinskitchen .net; Healthy/Organic/Local; $. Robin is the idealized lunch-lady

Road Trip:
All the Way South for a Weekend

This is a nice long weekend or 3-day trip of sightseeing on the open New Mexico roads with chile, gourmet meals, and awesome pie. Head south from Albuquerque on I-25, and in little more than an hour, exit signs appear for Socorro. If you need coffee, take Socorro's business route through town, with sights like the fantastic neon sign of the old-school 24-hour El Camino Family Restaurant, a diner's diner since 1963.

Turn right at Manzanares Street and pull into the lot next to the huge coffee mural. Allow M Mountain Coffee *(110 Manzanares St., Socorro, NM 87801; 575-838-0809; Coffee/Cafe; $)* to pull a dark Americano or just a strong cuppa so you can keep rolling.

Onward on I-25 for a stretch of rolling hills and (hopefully) sparse traffic. Take the exit for Hatch, cutting southwest directly toward your lunch destination: B & E Burritos *(303 N. Franklin St., Hatch, NM 87937; 575-267-5191; New Mexican; $).* It is one of the most divey restaurants I have ever fallen in love with. The green chile stew is phenomenal; I can't not order it when I'm in town. A wider menu, green chile cheeseburgers, and kitsch galore are yours at Sparky's *(115 N. Franklin St., Hatch, NM 87937; 575-267-4222; sparkysburgers.com; Burgers/Diner; $$).*

Now, on to Silver City. Head south on Hwy. 26 from Hatch through Deming and then north on 180 to Silver City. You made a reservation for dinner already, right? I'd send a foodie halfway across the state just to eat at The Curious Kumquat *(111 E. College Ave., Silver City, NM 88061; 575-534-0337; curiouskumquat.com; Eclectic;*

$$$). Trust me on that. (See Chef-Owner Rob Connoley's Thai Rice Balls recipe on p. 305.) Find the best gelato in the state at Alotta Gelato (*619 N. Bullard St., Silver City, NM 88061; 575-534-4995; alottagelato.com; Frozen; $*). Other well-regarded dinner options are 1zero6 (*106 N. Texas St., Silver City, NM 88061; 575-313-4418; 1zero6-jake.blogspot.com; Eclectic; $$*), where the menu is fixed and changes every weekend; and the world cuisine of Shevek & Co., (*602 N. Bullard St., Silver City, NM 88061; 575-534-9168; silver-eats.com; Mediterranean; $$$*).

Whet your caffeine whistle at my favorite coffee shop sans Wi-Fi: sit back and talk to people without glowing screens and tappety sounds (and eat both fresh sweets and a light cafe menu): 3 Dogs Coffeehouse & Eatery (*503 N. Bullard St., Silver City, NM 88061; 575-535-4546; Coffee/Cafe; $*).

Head north on US 180 toward Reserve, taking NM 12 all the way along the lovely Gila Wilderness. Take NM 32 north from Apache Creek until you get to US 60. Head east and you'll come upon Pie Town, which you can take literally when you stop at the two—count 'em—two spots that serve pie. First, check out Pie-O-Neer (*US 60, Pie Town, NM 87827; 575-772-2711; pie-o-neer.com; Sweets; $*), for a slice of Kathy's renowned chocolate cream pie. Then, give due to Good Pie Cafe (formerly Daily Pie Cafe) (*US 60, Pie Town, NM 87827; 575-772-2700; goodpie.com; Sweets/Cafe; $*). Enjoy my favorite pie in the state: New Mexican apple with green chile and piñon nuts. Keep going east to pass through an amazing tableau of technology and nature: the Very Large Array of radio telescopes made famous by 1997's movie *Contact*.

US 60 heads east to I-25, finishing your loop. Whew!

for schoolkids at a Montessori school, and she's loved her work for more than a decade. Over time, parents started asking about this wonderful food, and Robin made takeout for them, too. In 2011 she made her creations available to the public, opening up a tiny cafe just outside the prep kitchen, serving the downtown area for breakfast and lunch four days a week. Ridiculously simple is the menu—a breakfast burrito here, a chicken sandwich there. But delicious is the food, especially Robin's flavor-packed salads like black bean, corn, and bell pepper, or her "great grains" composition with wheat berries, sprouted lentils, and barley in a tangy citrus dressing. Eating at Robin's is not unlike hanging out at a domestic diva's house, letting her bring out whatever is cooking that day, from creamy soup to berry pie—and, yes, Robin's pies are also fantastic.

Slate Street Cafe, 515 Slate Ave. NW, Downtown, Albuquerque, NM 87102; (505) 243-2210; slatestreetcafe.com; Cafe/Eclectic; $$. Myra Ghattas has a well-pedigreed place in Albuquerque's dining history: Her family owns the legendary **Duran's Central Pharmacy** (p. 131), beloved by locals. Myra got her management chops by working for Hyatt for many years and is a CIA-trained sommelier. What she's made is an upscale yet friendly joint suited to breakfast business meetings and evening wine events in a swanky loft. Slate Street Cafe nestled itself a few blocks from the major court buildings downtown, and to this day the restaurant's morning customers are a who's who of city politics, from counselors to litigators and beyond. Myra's creations foreshadowed the upscale comfort food movement, with fish-and-chips made from salmon, house-made tater tots, and perfectly decadent and grown-up mac and cheese. Despite being a bit ahead of its time, cuisine-wise, the restaurant has always been busy and well regarded—a fantastic achievement in the last decade of topsy-turvy economic times. Perhaps it helps that Myra provides a little sweetness to balance any sour feelings from the legal system, in the form of the best and earliest entrants to the cupcake scene.

Standard Diner, 320 E. Central Ave., EDo, Albuquerque, NM 87102; (505) 243-1440; standarddiner.com; Cafe/Eclectic; $$. Matt DiGregory and his business partners get to lay claim to one of the first new-generation EDo eateries with his "finer diner" concept (though a few years after Slate Street Cafe tested the market waters, successfully). He fell in love years ago with a worn-down classic-car showroom across the street from the old Albuquerque High in the throes of its loft/condo transition; more than a year and a cool million bucks were spent renovating the space into the comfort-able but showy restaurant, opening to the public in 2006. Lovely curved windows illuminate the goings-on, from bizarrely delicious shakes (Espresso Guinness, anyone?) to tangy sourdough made from a starter first brought to life in the 1800s on the Oregon Trail. The diner gained some notoriety with a segment on *Diners, Drive-ins & Dives* in 2009, but things have thankfully calmed down. After all, if a local cannot get a table to enjoy the chicken-fried tuna or the famous Osee's Tomato Soup, there might be anarchy!

Taqueria Mexico, 415 Lomas Blvd. NE, Downtown, Albuquerque, NM 87102; (505) 242-3445; taqueriamexicoabq.com; Mexican; $. This is the place where downtown Albuquerque comes to eat when what you want is good food at reasonable prices—far more reasonable, in fact, than most fast food. For more than a decade, this walk-up spot with a tiny interior seating area has been doing huge volume every single breakfast and lunch hour. Location-wise, Taqueria Mexico is closer to the state and federal buildings than downtown's central corridor, but it is still refreshing to see the line queued up at the window with an even mix of blue-collar workers and business-suited lawyerly types. Mexican street food is the cuisine, not New Mexican, but of course there are nods to local favorites, such as breakfast burritos with meat ranging from bacon to shredded beef, and most under $4. Other selections include ceviche, tamales, tacos of nearly any meat your mouth desires, and forearm-size burritos. All of this under the warm sunshine, served quickly by a staff that never seems to stop moving or smiling.

Landmarks

Antiquity Restaurant, 112 Romero St. NW, Old Town, Albuquerque, NM 87104; (505) 247-3545; antiquityrestaurant.com; Fine Dining/Steak; $$$. Back before eclectic modern American cuisine seemed to take over fine dining, there was Antiquity for your Valentine's Day, anniversaries, and intimate celebrations. Decidedly old-school is exactly where Antiquity wants to be: chilled shrimp cocktail, oysters on the half shell, steaks and broiled lobster tail with baked potato. It is all that, with a dining area cavernous and cozy—no large open spaces here, just high-backed booths with privacy enough for hand holding or even popping the question if the time is right. But if a throwback meal is all you want, Antiquity is happy to provide: Order the Henry IV filet, served on artichoke hearts with béarnaise, and a delicate dessert called *polyczenta* that stuffs creamy walnuts inside a crepe. The only shocker is a lack of Baked Alaska—it seems like the kind of restaurant that would showcase the underappreciated dessert.

Artichoke Cafe, 424 Central Ave. SE, Downtown, Albuquerque, NM 87102; (505) 243-0200; artichokecafe.com; Fine Dining; $$$. Around as long as Antiquity Restaurant, the folks at Artichoke Cafe have served as a mild counterpoint in the upscale arena—the atmosphere is just as fancy, but the food usually has an inventive twist. Starting with the number one appetizer—a steamed artichoke with dipping sauces—is how many meals begin. Couples in the evening and business partners during lunch will then move on to Pat Keene's specialties with delicate fishes or well-portioned meats. Where other places might lob a 16-ounce steak your way, Artichoke serves an 8-ounce cut so well seasoned and seared that anything larger would seem frightful, and pairs it with tender couscous or braised greens. With Pat at the helm for so many years, her talents continue to

TREATS ON THE TROLLEY:
TOURS FOR FOODIES

Local boys Jesse Herron and Michael Silva started up a tour company a few years back and have blazed a new path in zany, irreverent Albuquerque touristing. They bought and loaded up an open-air trolley bus and then started hosting 90-minute tours from Old Town, catching sights such as haunted mansions downtown and key fixtures from the TV show *Breaking Bad*.

They found that it was a nice break to stop once or twice each tour for a small treat, such as tastes of custard at **Chillz** (p. 187) or pastries from **Flying Star** (pp. 134, 150). This seemed like a new concept ready to hatch, so after two years of making the rounds, they added edible-themed tours called the Foodie Tours, starting with a microbrew-themed Ale Trail. Real noshables followed, with the Burque Burger Tour, a Pizza Tour, and even a Dessert Tour, taking participants on a wild ride of gastronomic or hoppy delights. Each season brings new ideas to the company; repeats of old themes with new spots added are likely, and entirely original tours are in the works. I suggest a "crazy chile" tour with the weirdest chile products, or a "crazy capsicum" tour, with stupid hot chile dishes that require chocolate milk shooters in between each stop. I'd sign up—wouldn't you? Find out everything you need: **ABQ Trolley Co.**, *boarding at 208 San Felipe St. NW, Old Town, Albuquerque; (505) 240-8000; abqtrolley.com.*

sharpen, even as sous-chefs have come and gone (some on to other acclaim around town, as it is in the business).

Golden Crown Panaderia, 1103 Mountain Rd. NW, Downtown, Albuquerque, NM 87102; (505) 243-2424; goldencrown.biz; Pizza/ Bakery; $. Without Golden Crown and the youthful enthusiasm of owner Pratt Morales, you'd never have the opportunity to order a turkey-shaped loaf of green chile bread for Thanksgiving dinner, and that's just one of his many "tricks." Morales knows that once you are in the door soaking in the friendliness, you'll be hooked on the flour-based goodies he bakes every day with his son, Chris. Shaped breads are just the beginning (and those can be ordered to your specifications—past sculptures include castles, Greek goddesses, and a full-size trombone), as the shop is known for cookies, empanadas, and pizzas you can enjoy while lounging in the patio area. If you're lucky, the website's "bread cam" will be online to stoke your cravings. Four decades in, business is brisk even at the off-the-downtown-track location on Mountain at the cusp of Old Town. My favorites are the barely soft pig-shaped molasses cookies called *marranitos*—cute, but not too cute to eat.

High Noon Restaurant & Saloon, 425 San Felipe St. NW, Downtown, Albuquerque, NM 87104; (505) 765-1455; highnoon restaurant.com; Steak; $$$. Admit it—you have a soft spot for restaurants that were founded in the year of your birth. We all do—it gives a nice personal touch to think that a business has been serving up food and making bellies happy for as long as you've been crawling around in the world. High Noon works for me that way, in addition to being an unassuming steak joint in the middle of touristy food-land that actually serves great food with enough creativity to keep foodies interested. I've had the steak, of course, but I've also enjoyed buffalo burgers, meat loaf sandwiches, and an ancho chile chocolate cake. That will put a warm glow in anyone's belly. The building is something to behold, with the original structure set in place in 1784, long before statehood was a twinkle in anyone's eye—the settlers were just trying to dig their heels in at that point. Dig your fork into this gem, and then you can wander back over to the shops—they'll still be there.

Seasons Rotisserie & Grill, 2031 Mountain Rd. NW, Old Town, Albuquerque, NM 87104; (505) 766-5100; seasonsabq.com; American; $$$. When thinking about the classic torch-bearers in the Albuquerque dining scene, it is shamefully easy to forget about Seasons, simply because they do what they do very well and with little fanfare. After many visits over the years to this landmark, that fanfare ought to be bumped up a few notches. Start with the rooftop patio, a rare and wondrous thing in this city of low-slung buildings (there is a legally mandated limit of 23 stories on building height—yes, really), offering a respite from the wandering crowds in Old Town and a way to hold up a glass in salute to another gorgeous sunset. The scene is intentionally busy: Have some drinks and a few appetizers, and hobnob with friends that also love this place. Formalized dinners can also be had, or experience the chef wizardry up close by taking a seat at the counter of the open kitchen. You'll be reminded of the word *rotisserie* when torn between a roast chicken or bone-in pork chops, paired for enjoyment with California wines and a well-dressed salad.

All Chile, All the Time

Barelas Coffee House, 1502 Fourth St. SW, Downtown, Albuquerque, NM 87102; (505) 843-7577; New Mexican; $. This is classic family-friendly Albuquerque to a fault—waitresses who love what they are doing, lines of customers waiting for tables while others linger over weak diner coffee, huge tables with all of the relatives having breakfast late on a Saturday morning. They are famous for their red chile, and smothering it all over a plate of *huevos rancheros* is a great way to punctuate your day—breakfast or lunch. Barelas Coffee House takes its name from the neighborhood, an enclave of midcentury houses nestled perfectly between downtown and the South Valley that has yet to experience the benefits and/or drawbacks of gentrification. What that means is Barelas Coffee House is a comfortable and well-worn dive of a place—you'll have good food served by loyal employees, taking in the scene of regulars all the while.

Road Trip:
Green Chile Cheeseburger History

This is a quick southward road trip taking about 75 minutes to a gosh-darned good burger (or two) and then back to Albuquerque, perfect for a lazy Saturday.

Head south from Albuquerque on I-25, passing through a few hamlets like Los Lunas and Belen, and just keep going. The scrubby terrain opens up, and in little more than an hour, exit signs appear for Socorro. Keep going, and just 8 miles farther is the exit for US 380 East and the town of San Antonio. You have one or two stops to make, depending on who's open (call ahead—hours have been known to be sporadic).

The first is Owl Bar & Cafe *(79 Main St., San Antonio, NM 87832; 575-835-9946; socorro-nm.com/owlbar.htm; Burgers; $)*, the very place where our beloved green chile cheeseburger was invented. It goes like this: During the Manhattan Project, scientists were spending weeks at the Trinity Site and weekends back at home in Los Alamos, passing through the Owl Bar for a drink at the end of their workweek (or at the end of workdays). Owner Jose Miera didn't

Ben Michael's Cafe, 2404 Pueblo Bonito Ct. NW, Old Town, Albuquerque, NM 87104; (505) 224-2817; New Mexican; $$. It's a lovely building and something not easy to miss—three tiered stories, strangely narrow despite the height—yet the cafe Ben Michael seems hard to find when you actually intend to go there: Is it 2

serve food, and the physicists asked him to cook something so they'd not be hungry all the way home. Jose starting grinding burgers fresh, putting local chile on top, and that was that. The Owl, currently owned by Miera's daughter Rowena, is a treasured place in New Mexico's culinary history—you owe it to yourself to try the original.

Literally across the street is another legend for deliciousness, even if they weren't the first: Buckhorn Tavern (*68 Main St., San Antonio, NM 87832; 575-835-4423; socorro-nm.com/buckhorn.htm; Burgers; $*). Owner Bobby Olguin cares about his burgers, enough that they won't come out in a flash from the kitchen, especially when busy. That just makes the first bite of the patty, cheese, chile, and condiments all the more rewarding—and I'm making an exception in Buckhorn's case to say to order the burger "with everything" instead of just chile and cheese. This is a burger more than the sum of its parts and worthy of a head-to-head with that place across the street. Try them both—you might have to be sneaky if you're thinking about bringing one joint's burger into the other's dining room.

Finish this little trip with a stop at the San Antonio General Store (*inside the Fila gas station; 75 Main St., San Antonio, NM 87832; 575-835-4594; Sweets; $*): homemade fudge to knock the fillings right outta your head. Enjoy in moderation, but still, enjoy.

blocks north of Central, or 4, and where is that darn cross street? Just north of Mountain on the west side of the Rio Grande is where you'll find it; inside you'll find the owner, Ben Michael Barreras, presiding over a modest dining room and a menu full of chile-laced favorites. His *huevos rancheros* are highly recommended, or you could take a slight detour and have tender chiles rellenos, all with sides of flavorful pinto beans. I have found the service and food execution to have some off days, but this is a spot worth investigating as much for the character—hearing Ben Michael tell you about constructing the all-adobe building by hand is fascinating—as it is for the perfection of the cuisine.

Cecilia's Cafe, 230 Sixth St. SW, Downtown, Albuquerque, NM 87102; (505) 243-7070; ceciliascafe.com; New Mexican; $. A few temples to incendiary chile are dotted around the state, for those that like good flavor but also want a little endorphin rush from the painfully capsicum-laced hot stuff. Cecilia's fits that bill. The caveat is that some days the chile is hotter than others—it comes down to batch variations and crops from year to year. That being said, if you have a bowl of red at Cecilia's and finish the whole thing, you probably should have your photo hung on the wall—it is really, really hot, and you'll be warned before ordering. Not just for the fire-eaters, Cecilia's does a brisk trade in deliciousness of all kinds,

 from relleno burritos to enchiladas and, of course, *huevos rancheros*—the king of New Mexican breakfasts. For replenishment of the serious sort, the Fireman's Burrito stuffs *chicharrones* into a bundle the size of a puppy. A second location near UNM recently starting winning over another base of fans, and the red chile here is even hotter, if you can believe it; 2933 Monte Vista Blvd. NE, UNM, Albuquerque, NM 87106; (505) 268-1147.

Duran's Central Pharmacy, 1815 Central Ave. NW, Downtown, Albuquerque, NM 87104; (505) 247-4141; duranscentralpharmacy .com; New Mexican; $. Chances are you've had someone take you by the hand to introduce you to the local fare, from bowls of chile to handmade tortillas, and along that path they darn well better have taken you to Duran's. It really is inside a pharmacy, so get your shopping done at the same time as you feast on red chile so pure it sings to your tongue. In most restaurants I default to corn tortillas (and delight when I find them handmade), but at Duran's it is flour that must be your default, for these thick circles are without compare in Albuquerque. Whether you top them with butter and eat them with abandon or use them to scoop up beans and chile, they are embarrassingly addicting. In a way, this compensates for an unusual side with Duran's entrees—slices of boiled potato unadorned by frying or "hashbrowning." The family that has brought Duran's to your life has been doing this for much of their lives, and it shows.

Specialty Stores, Markets & Producers

Cafe Giuseppe, 222 Gold St. SW, Downtown, Albuquerque, NM 87102; (505) 246-4338; cafegiuseppe.com; Coffee. Best. Espresso. In. Town. Period. This is their second (and only current) location, added to accommodate the downtown working and residential crowd

7 days a week. The space is lovely and narrow like a coffee shop squeezed into a slot in Manhattan, with deeply hued exposed brick. The pastry selection is minimal, but it's all about the espresso, pulled by expert baristas replete in hipster garb.

The Candy Lady, 524 Romero St. NW, Old Town, Albuquerque, NM 87104; (505) 243-6239; thecandylady.com; Sweets. Many first hear about Debbie Ball's confectionery by a tired old controversy: She sells "naughty" stuff. Some folks don't appreciate having chocolate bits in the shape of, um, bits. Within a year of opening in 1980, local groups filed petitions. Debbie stood her ground on the advice of the ACLU. No legal action ensued, but business exploded as a result of the publicity for several years afterwards. She is still famous for the little adult room. But, if that is how you end up wandering in for a look, consider it your lucky day when you spy the dozen varieties of fudge, the largest selection of black licorice I've ever seen, or the brittles and chocolates and candies. Sample some delectable chile fudge or a handmade brandy cherry, and it's clear there is love in her efforts.

Truffles to the Stars: Cocopotamus Chocolates

Cocopotamus is the adorable name of an adorable couple's company that makes the most delightful little chocolate truffles around. The company started out of a New York pastry cafe but moved here just as its fame was accelerating, with owners Max and Ally rolling and dipping little balls of fudge heaven. Their company motto is "Fudge happens. Have a ball."

One of the first popular flavors was Mr. French—a dark fudge truffle with sea salt, pure joy in a foil wrapper. As their flavors grew more numerous, innovative combinations blossomed: Bébé-Lala (green apple salted caramel), Hottie (cinnamon and chili), Kiss Blarney (peppermint and rum), Rosie Posy (rosewater infused), and Sumos Never Sleep (matcha green tea). They have supplied truffles for the gift/schwag bags for the Academy Awards the last few years—quite the boost to visibility! Available in dozens of stores in the state and sold individually (they tempt me every week in the checkout aisle at Whole Foods) or in boxes of five, you don't have to look hard for your next favorite flavor, but see the current list at cocopotamus.com.

Your mouth will know if you've eaten the racy stuff: Those shapes are merely melted and molded chocolate, but Debbie's main creations are her, through and through.

Flying Star Cafe, 723 Silver Ave. SW, Downtown, Albuquerque, NM 87102; (505) 244-8099; flyingstarcafe.com; Cafe/Coffee. Coffee, pastries, entire meals, and free Wi-Fi to boot: Flying Star is one of the hubs of Albuquerque. See their feature sidebar in the Albuquerque East chapter (p. 150) for details.

Java Joe's, 906 Park Ave. SW, Downtown, Albuquerque, NM 87102; (505) 765-1514; downtownjavajoes.com; Coffee/Cafe. My first love at Java Joe's was not the coffee, but rather a curious pancake studded with granola for chewy bits with the syrup and butter. The coffee is still the reason many folks come to this hangout, and it is absolutely a great cup of inky sunshine that you can sip while watching the local ebb and flow. Other breakfasty foods are on hand, and the atmosphere is slouch-chic with comfy chairs and usually a solo guitarist in the corner on weekends. Head here before or after the weekly farmers' market just across the way on Central.

Albuquerque East

UNM, Nob Hill, Uptown, Southeast, Northeast Heights &
East Mountains

Headed eastward from the downtown district through EDo, you'll eventually hop the freeway and cross into the environs of the University of New Mexico, home to 40,000 students and their supporting eateries, from noble to naughty. College students and underpaid faculty are known for their keen sense of value when it comes to restaurants, often forgoing gastronomic delights—it happens to the best of us. Some folks become foodie-aware almost in lockstep with an ascending income, but others find the priority and the resources to visit the culinary legends once in a while. From barbecue (The Cube) to Middle Eastern (Sahara Middle Eastern Eatery), the 1-mile stretch of Central Avenue appeals to all.

Just to the east of the campus is Nob Hill, aspirationally named after the San Francisco district and home to gorgeously maintained lawns and some of the best restaurants in town. This was and is the hip neighborhood long before downtown had the glimmer of revival in its eyes. Nob Hill has a farmers' market, a co-op grocery (La Montañita), and at least a half dozen coffee shops to keep residents fully juiced in between dog walks and baby strolls. Local all-star chefs ply their trade here or have done so on their way to newer digs around town: Jennifer James (formerly at Graze), Todd Lovell (Gecko's), Claus Hjortkjaer (Brasserie La Provence), and many more.

Venturing north and east beyond the immediate Nob Hill area you'll pass through Uptown and the Northeast Heights, which extends all the way to the foothills of the Sandia Mountains. Uptown is the newly adopted name for the business and shopping district near I-40 and Louisiana, with brand-new outdoor shops and a slew of eateries to boot. Ignore the requisite chains and the gems appear, like old favorite Gardunos Mexican Food or the always-convenient caffeine at Satellite Coffee. The Northeast Heights are vast in size but easy to navigate to dining consisting of all cuisines and expense levels.

Albuquerque is home to a surprising number of Vietnamese restaurants; they number more than Thai and Chinese and provide fresh relief to much of the heavy New Mexican dishes. Places designated as Southeast are clustered by Central or just south of it, to differentiate that area from the Northeast Heights. The Southeast is a mother lode of great ethnic eateries, from Vietnamese to Salvadoran.

A quick canyon drive east on I-40 brings you to the East Mountains, a well-populated rural fringe of about 30,000 that is only lightly served by restaurants. Because Albuquerque is so close, eateries are not just competing with each other—they still need to be impressive by city/county standards, and it's a hard business. Places like Pete's Home of the Halfbreed in Sandia Park have survived, but often only after several ownership changes or menu tweaks. Takeout is common for those headed home from work in town, and Trail Rider pizza in Tijeras satisfies that craving for many families each evening. South of Tijeras lies a true destination hole-in-the-wall: Ponderosa Eatery & Saloon, serving up huge "Pondo" burgers and homemade red and green chile with a side of swagger. This area is large but manageable and not all that far from town. For reference, a brisk drive from the post office in Cedar Crest to downtown Albuquerque is all of 25 minutes and just as many miles—locals love the fact that traffic jams are rare, even during rush hour.

Foodie Faves

Bailey's on the Beach, 2929 Monte Vista Blvd. NE, Nob Hill, Albuquerque, NM 87106; (505) 717-2880; baileysonthebeach.com; Cafe/Eclectic; $. Surfer culture is hard to imagine in the high desert of Albuquerque, but here we are with the California-inspired homage to beaches and light fare started by Roy Solomon and named after his daughter. He's been in the local restaurant business for quite some time, but this is a revelation of fish tacos, green smoothies, and cold brewed coffee (with a gorgeous glass brewer in the window and a drip-drip-drip of black nectar percolating down). Without

LEGENDARY HOLE-IN-THE-WALL

The Frontier Restaurant *(2400 E. Central Ave., UNM, Albuquerque, NM 87106; 505-266-0550; frontierrestaurant.com; New Mexican; $).* This is it—the famous Frontier, founded in 1971 by a young Austin couple set on selling hamburgers to college kids. It is the very first place I ate at when I moved to Albuquerque—me the hater of spicy food was hauled on the arm of a friend through the doors. He told me two things about what was about to happen: I would adore the breakfast burrito and be forever hooked on chile, and my Midwestern digestive system might have issues the next day. He was correct on both counts. Chile didn't factor into the Frontier's menu right away, until a dishwasher named Eddie Montoya showed his bosses the light, and after some recipe tinkering, the rest is delicious history.

Almost two generations' worth of UNM students have used the Frontier as their spot for sustenance and study time. On a student's budget the cheapest things on the menu become your friends (grilled cheese with tomato, hash browns with chile), and on spendy days the burgers are darn tasty. The go-to meal is the breakfast burrito, served with coffee or tea. Sludge the burrito with green chile stew from the crock near the silverware and load up the (crappy) coffee with milk and sugar, and you've built a meal that will last most of a day's worth of lectures, all for about 5 bucks. For reference, on my first visit in

pretense, Bailey's food is fresh and accommodating to those who like to paddle around in bikinis—the previously mentioned green smoothie is even called the Tight Bikini Shake. You can spot Roy in

1996 the same order was about 3 bucks, but today it is still worth every penny. Sweet rolls are also the stuff of legend—cheap, tasty, and surely terrible for your diet—enjoy them while you still have a young metabolism.

Even the dining areas are storied—five rooms' worth—each added over time as demand rose. Every wall is covered in local artists' work, and one room is wholly dedicated to art in the theme of John Wayne. The ordering queue often appears long, but the well-designed counter system churns through the line with impressive ease, and an automated number-call display gets food out at record speed. The flour tortilla machine is in full view of the pickup window, spitting out circles for your meal just minutes before you bite into their soft texture.

Until several years ago, the only time the restaurant closed was on Thanksgiving night, Christmas, and New Year's, but nowadays students cramming after UNM library hours need to relocate between 1 and 5 a.m. The Frontier's owners, Dorothy and Larry Rainosek, have been lauded for how they treat their staff, paying employees well and offering health care (part of the reason those menu prices inch up), and even awarding the dozen or more longtime employees Rolexes after 30 years. This probably makes the Frontier the only place in the world you can watch your eggs getting scrambled on a hot griddle by a guy wearing a Rolex.

his off-hours practicing hot yoga at a nearby studio and generally exuding mellowness. Aside from that turbo-caffeinated cold coffee, you'll be mellow after a visit, too.

Blades' Bistro, 221 NM 165, #L, Placitas, NM 87043; (505) 771-0695; bladesbistro.com; Fine Dining; $$$. The village of Placitas is considerably farther than a stone's throw from Albuquerque, but the view from this northeastern perch is phenomenal. There's little better way to enjoy that view than with a glass of wine, a good meal, and a dining companion at Blades' Bistro. Chef and owner Kevin Bladergroen started cooking in Corrales and has traveled the world as a cook and restaurant devotee over the last 30 years, bringing that inspiration back to New Mexico. His recipes are not innovative, but they show attention to flavors and care for how the food will be enjoyed. The full bar is happy to mix cocktails or suggest wines that pair well with courses like roasted beet salad or brined pork chops. Toast the sunset and have a wonderfully relaxing dinner before heading down the hill.

Budai Gourmet Chinese, 6300 San Mateo Blvd. NE, #H1, Northeast Heights, Albuquerque, NM 87109; (505) 797-7898; Chinese; $$. This ain't your American-style buffet-lovin' Chinese, no siree. Check your sugary sweet-and-sour ideas at the door, and hostess and co-owner Elsa will guide you on a journey to what is likely the best Chinese in Albuquerque, from soup (fish and goji berry) to nuts (chicken with cashew). She's originally from Taiwan, and her favorite family foods are here along with Chinese specialties from all of its regions. Three-cup chicken is the stuff of her childhood, when chicken was a rare treat; to use every bit of the chicken's flavor, it was stewed to falling-apart tenderness in a broth of equal parts rice wine, soy sauce, and sesame oil. I recommend diving directly into anything that sounds challenging to your palate, whether that's beef tongue or taro root stew—the preparations are done well enough that you'll come away a stunned new tongue fan. Or use Elsa's knowledge and tell her the things you both like and avoid like the plague, and ask her to suggest something new to you. She has considerable interest in bringing out something delicious, because she'd love to have you return with a smile on your face and an expanded palate.

Calientes Restaurant, 1930 Juan Tabo Blvd. NE, Northeast Heights, Albuquerque, NM 87112; (505) 298-7988; calientesrestaurant .com; New Mexican; $. Everyone has the situation where you need a go-to restaurant for family, visitors, or those who are not yet in the realm of chile addiction. The place will serve good New Mexican food but not try to burn your tongue off (I'm looking at you, Sadie's—with love, of course). That tasty place is Calientes in the Northeast Heights. All the New Mexican favorites you seek are here—enchiladas, stuffed burritos, *huevos rancheros*—plus a couple of surprises like rellenos using poblanos, the mild and dark seductress of the chiles. That relleno is big enough to exist singly on its platter with chopped steak and white cheese inside, under a batter fried well enough to remain crispy under red chile. Tamales get the same mildly spicy red sauce and lots of tender pork tucked into the masa. Serve these dishes to a New Mexican food doubter, and you're one step closer to bringing him or her into the capsaicin fold.

Chopstix, 6001 Lomas Blvd. NE, #L, Northeast Heights, Albuquerque, NM 87110; (505) 268-8777; chopstixabq.com; Chinese; $$. Many Albuquerque Chinese restaurants serve stir-fry that is too sweet, overly sauced meats, or rice that is just OK. Chopstix is not one of those places. Instead of egg rolls, you can have an appetizer of marinated beef, or seaweed salad with cilantro, or obviously hand-pinched dumplings. It pleases me immensely that every single menu item has an accompanying photo on their website—this practice is something that would be handy in all restaurants, but is definitely helpful when you have a hard time picturing Da Lu Noodle. Turn your attention to the specials posted on the wall—these are the more authentic dishes not often requested by Westerners, and they are both fascinating and delicious. Highly recommended is the Szechwan sausage, purple rice, and stewed pork neck. Dine like the "locals," and you'll be rewarded.

Cool Water Fusion, 2010 Wyoming Blvd. NE, Ste. B, Northeast Heights, Albuquerque, NM 87112; (505) 332-2665; coolwaterfusion .com; Eclectic; $$. In a forgettable retail-pad space, this little cafe has made culinary waves for food that you might otherwise expect to find in Nob Hill or some other trendy neighborhood. Chef Glenn Williams brings New Mexican touches to everyday fare, such as his blue-corn-dusted onion rings with green chile ranch, or red chile braised beef over a corn cake topped with a fried egg; both are appetizers but the latter I'd order for a meal in a red meat heartbeat. Osso bucco is done up with turkey instead of veal for a regional (not to mention less cruel) spin on the classic dish. Even the decor is both vibrant and luxurious, with deep blue walls and high-backed black booths. Prices reflect the quality—that is, they're a little spendy for this part of town. Consider it a fair trade for not having to drive to EDo to have food this good.

Cosmo Tapas, 4200 E. Central Ave., Nob Hill, Albuquerque, NM 87108; (505) 232-0535; cosmotapas.com; South American/Tapas; $$. Tapas is a dining style from Spain that became a trend in this country, spreading like wildfire in some regions, but in New Mexico it made a welcome appearance and stayed on with a slow simmer, neither overly hyped nor forgettable. One could debate which was the first "real" Albuquerque tapas shop: **Gecko's Bar & Tapas** (p. 146) came first but also serves standard bar fare. Cosmo's dishes, however, are uniquely tasty thanks to owners who inject their Puerto Rican and Chilean backgrounds with traditional Spanish flavors. Near the top of the menu is the famed *jamón iberico,* a cured and aged ham named for the pig's breed and pedigree, and pricey to match. The menu dips into South America with ceviche and beef empanadas, and back over to Spain for white anchovies, black sausage, and tortilla española—a potato-egg frittata of sorts, not a flour-based flatbread. I adore the Spanish desserts of churros and chocolate as well as Manchego cheese served with quince paste. Given the history of New Mexico, it is surprising that Spanish-influenced cuisine isn't commonplace, but Cosmo will do for now.

The Cube, 1520 E. Central Ave., UNM, Albuquerque, NM 87106; (505) 243-0023; thecuberestaurant.com; Barbecue/American; $$. Smoky whole turkey legs for 8 bucks. If that's not reason enough to at least stick your head in the door at the Cube, I might have to bring out the supporting phrase, *sweet potato pie.* Are you there yet? The Cube suffers from a couple of issues present since inception: a loud and echoing interior, and occasionally long waits for food. In nearly every other way, the Cube is close to perfect. The dry-rub ribs and brisket are among the best in town; the pulled pork is, well, porky and delicious; and the Southern-style sides include no fewer than four potato preparations. They serve hot dogs and salads and stuff, but that's not why you go to the Cube. Trust in their BBQ and do not dare to forget about that sweet potato pie.

Dagmar's Restaurant and Strudel Haus, 2120 Juan Tabo Blvd. NE, Northeast Heights, Albuquerque, NM 87112; (505) 293-1982; German; $$. In New Mexico there are tons of transplants from the Midwest, with Wisconsin and Illinois leading the charge. Despite that, German restaurants are a rarity, and that's a shame. German foods do not get the respect of Italian, despite the German ancestry of one in six Americans. Dagmar's Restaurant and Strudel Haus has been holding its ground for many years (and several locations), showing the way with spaetzle and roulade. Just what is spaetzle, anyway? If you've had fresh eggy pasta or gnocchi with that soft yet toothsome bite, just imagine rough-cut buttery noodles with the same texture. Or, don't imagine and receive them at Dagmar's as the side to your goulash. The goulash fights with roulade as my favorite thing on the menu, goulash's slow-stewed beef versus the bacon-and-onion-stuffed roulade. Both are also served with barely sweet braised red cabbage, a striking purple on the plate (perhaps this was the reason for a colorful side—the dishes can be over-whelmingly brown-hued). On your way out, try not to forget the restaurant's name and have a slice of delicate strudel, or grab a whole pastry to go.

Desert Fish, 4214 E. Central Ave., Nob Hill, Albuquerque, NM 87108; (505) 266-5544; desertfishabq.com; Seafood; $$$. **Seafood** lovers get hassled around here: "Whaddaya mean you want great fish in this landlocked state? I wouldn't trust the fish here!" But the reality of food-shipping technology makes comments like that moot. Desert Fish came into a pretty good restaurant scene and jacked up the standards overnight. Fish fanatics are joyful. The opening chef was the talented Carrie Eagle, who deserves credit for making expensive fish dishes acceptable in this era of inflated entree prices—it's appalling that a mediocre steak could set one back $40, while a fish dish even approaching $30 is viewed as heresy. Good protein is not cheap, no matter from which animal it originates, and treating the seafood well to justify that cost is Desert Fish's strong point. Warm seafood salad sports grilled scallops and bitter greens, while magic is in a huge bowl of cioppino. In late 2011 Chef Josh Gerwin was consulted to overhaul the menu after running his kitchen at Casa Vieja and garnering massive accolades—his twists to the already amazing Desert Fish menu are welcome.

Gecko's Bar & Tapas, 3500 E. Central Ave., Nob Hill, Albuquerque, NM 87106; geckosbar.com; Pub/Tapas; $$. The 1990s saw good business for bars, but mostly the lower-end spots popular with those who just want door-buster happy hour specials. The scene has since vastly improved for beer and cocktail aficionados and those who appreciate food that stands on its own merits. Todd Lovell's menu at Gecko's Bar & Tapas woos diners with tiny plates of flavor, like his dorky and delicious Baba-Fet (baba ghanoush with feta) or red mole sirloin tacos served three to an order. Traditional Spanish small plates appear with lamb Merguez sausage, a hearty portion with new potatoes and jalapeño dipping oil. Gecko's is still a sports bar, but even the sports-ambivalent will come away happy and sated. Find their second, jazzy, art deco–themed location at 5801 Academy Rd. NE, Albuquerque, NM 87109; (505) 821-8291.

Greenside Cafe, 12165 N. NM 14, Cedar Crest, NM 87008; (505) 286-2684; greensidecafe.net; Cafe; $$. Owner Jay Wulf reminds everyone to "take a trip to the green side"—the green side of the

Sandias, that is. On the back slope of the uplifted range in the small community of Cedar Crest, a scant 3 miles north of I-40, you'll find Jay's outpost of darn good eats, his respite from a previous life in some of the more famous restaurants in Albuquerque. He was part of the group that launched the **Range Cafe** (p. 211) and **Standard Diner** (p. 121), and Cedar Crest is glad to have him. The menu is familiar, with a twist. Eggs Benedict is reworked into the Hen Grenade, where a sourdough French toast slab replaces the English muffin. The gravy for your biscuits can be swapped for chile sauce, and his over-the-top *huevos rancheros* replaces the bottom corn tortilla with a chicken-fried steak. Yowza. In later dining hours, you must try the **Romesco** appetizer, a dip made from red peppers, almonds, and lemon (see the recipe on p. 302). All the entrees are well executed, as are Jay's house-made ice creams.

Gregorio's Kitchen, 4200 Wyoming Blvd. NE, Northeast Heights, Albuquerque, NM 87111; (505) 323-7633; gregoriosabq.com; Italian; $$. The slogan for a national chain restaurant says something cloying about being family when dining there, but Matt DiGregory made sure that his restaurant would really give you that "grandma's in the kitchen" feel when supping on simple pasta with Parmesan or sipping a tiny glass of homemade limoncello. The decor is a little bit homey, a little bit cheesy—the family portrait from the '70s near the door, everyone in white, is nostalgic gold. DiGregory has opened places all over town, like the **Range Cafe** (p. 211) and **Standard Diner** (p. 121), but he stifled his Italian cooking memories until now, letting things like *pasta arrabbiata* be a delight to the refugees from that chain place. Stereotypical items are done with panache—the normally greasy artichoke dip of every '80s party is here, but done with lightness and balance and served with house-made bread. They go out on a limb to call an otherwise delectable lemon curd parfait a "citrus tiramisu," but ignore the name and it is the best lemon dessert you'll have in years.

The Grill, 4615 Menaul Blvd. NE, Northeast Heights, Albuquerque, NM 87110; (505) 872-9772; Burgers; $. Phil Chavez is some kind of genius with grilling, having discovered that the biggest problem is controlling the temperature between the heat source and the meat. Sometimes it was too hot, sometimes too cold—but the distance from the meat to the heat is fixed. Or, it was fixed, until Phil built his own swinging crank-operated grill platform. See what I mean? Genius. Now when you order either a burger or a steak at his temple to the grilled arts, he can adjust just how quickly or slowly he wants the protein to cook. Just burgers and one or two steaks form the menu foundation, with sides of beans or fries and occasional home-made cake on a display stand for sweet temptation. Not that you'll need it after one of the best smoky charred patties you'll consume this year, of course. Watch the grill master himself through a picture window, cranking the big black grill with the focus (and smile) of a man in love with his job.

Guava Tree Cafe, 216 Yale Blvd. SE, UNM, Albuquerque, NM 87106; (505) 990-2599; guavatreecafe.com; Central American/ Cafe; $. What a gem this little orange building holds, in the form of casual Costa Rican eats! This restaurant is a shrine to the arepa, a thick corn patty hand-shaped and eaten as bread, often split like a pita and stuffed with delicious fillings. It sounds simple, but each is a skillful layering of flavors, starting with sweet plantains and cheese, then adding combinations of avocado, shredded beef, beans, or roasted veggies. They arrive overflowing and you realize how little you paid—and smile all the more when you bite in, trying to keep the filling under control. Guava Tree offers a Cubano, but pass it up in favor of the Pernil, which combines Caribbean pork with cheese, onions, and homemade garlic sauce. If you must have a Cubano, try its smaller cousin, the Medianoche. It's served on smaller and sweeter eggy bread but otherwise holds to the pork-ham-cheese-mustard-pickle convention. Sweetness ends many meals here—I recommend the guava and cheese turnover, a Caribbean original.

I Love Sushi Teppan Grill, 6001 San Mateo Blvd. NE, #F4, Northeast Heights, Albuquerque, NM 87109; (505) 883-3618; ilovesushiteppangrill.com; Sushi/Japanese; $$. I often forget there is a teppan grill at I Love Sushi until I walk past it on my way to the sushi dining room. There is no problem with the grilling method here—it's just that I love the sushi, which is only fitting. The chefs wield their skills against an unbelievably cheesy backdrop of fake rocks and a stuffed marlin, but once you start ordering, it

FLYING STAR CAFE: HOMEGROWN ROASTERS & PASTRIES EXTRAORDINAIRE

Jean and Michael Bernstein have created a phenomenon in Albuquerque, starting in 1987 with their first Double Rainbow Cafe. They would eventually spread to the rest of the county and Santa Fe. An evident devotion to coffee started with roasting beans just the way they wanted, and they served food with the coffee in that early cafe (at the time, there was a tie to the West Coast ice cream company of the same name). When they shifted frozen treat brands, the restaurants were renamed Flying Star Cafe and new lovely graphics and signs were commissioned. From those moderate beginnings it was a slow and steady process of growth to the current nine locations, the most recent popping up at the edges of Albuquerque and near the Santa Fe Depot in the City Different.

In the many years I have known Jean, she has never been less than wildly enthusiastic about Albuquerque, local products, and serving the best ingredients she can by using her talented staff to execute recipes and serve customers with joy. Flying Star was one of the first local spots to commit to using organic chicken, eggs, soy, and

all just becomes background. Vegetable tempura is done well—lack of grease means correct frying temperature. Rolls start with simple salmon and eel and progress to a bit complicated, like a burrito roll with lobster, avocado, and spicy Sriracha sauce. The New Mexico roll uses chile that is actually hot, not just for color. The chefs here

oatmeal, just for starters. They buy local meats, honey, and tortillas, giving as much business to small companies as they can.

In the last half decade or so, new players have emerged in the same target market as Flying Star (The Grove, p. 113, and Kung Fu Cowboy Tea Cafe, p. 154, come to mind); each has its own strengths and devoted fans. But Flying Star is just always there—it is the place I go when I'm in between Saturday tasks, needing an hour or three to sip coffee and catch up on magazine reading (their magazine selection is broad, appreciated, and always for sale). It's the chosen destination for hundreds of blind and first and continuing dates every single month: Over a milk shake or a noodle bowl, friendships, relationships, and business partnerships bloom and evolve (sometimes devolve).

Head baker and chef Willem Blom is continually evaluating the menu to create new favorites for both old and new patrons, but some of the standards have barely budged: The Rancher's Melt pileup of turkey-cheese-chile is still a favorite more than 15 years after I first discovered this community haven.

See all of their locations, menus, and additional information at flyingstarcafe.com.

always seem to be enjoying themselves, and that's a big part of the atmosphere—sushi is fun, fish are fun, eating is fun!

Japanese Kitchen, 6521 America's Pkwy. NE, Uptown, Albuquerque, NM 87110; (505) 884-8937; japanesekitchen.com; Japanese/Sushi,

$$$. You can choose your level of stimulation at Japanese Kitchen: the refined quiet of the sushi room, or the energetic teppan grill. The teppan grill is well and fine for parties that like to watch a show of their food being cooked. The sushi room, however, is my sanctuary and the business's "better half." Sushi fans can jump immediately into an *omakase* meal and have the chef choose the items, from 5 to 10 courses at a fixed price. Otherwise, let the menu be your guide—Japanese Kitchen does traditional sushi from tuna rolls to complex bento boxes very well. It is refreshing, too, to see modern and whimsical creations, like a Green Earth roll that uses avocado, green chiles, shrimp, and asparagus. Sashimi is generally a solid option—no second-rate fish will be slipped under the radar onto your plate—and I like to let the chef build an array for me with the *chirashizushi*: A bowl of sushi rice topped with the best variety of the day's fish offers a light and perfect meal.

Jennifer James 101, 4615 Menaul Blvd. NE, Northeast Heights, Albuquerque, NM 87110; (505) 884-3860; jenniferjames101.com; Eclectic/Fine Dining; $$$. The virtues of Jennifer James's cooking are not easily condensed, like her bold and innovative flavor constructions. At her restaurant you are likely to try many foods for the very first time—black pepper ice cream, shaved fennel, raw scallops, foie gras, roasted beet soup (see the **Roasted Beet Soup** recipe on p. 304). On the other hand, simple staples are vindicated: Jennifer is the cook who will show you that you don't actually hate lentils, you probably just had them done badly before. This is her third restaurant—the first was fine dining, then a small-plates destination that not enough of Albuquerque was ready for, despite acclaim. Jennifer and her partner, Nelle, are masterminds of the menu, creating community table events on slower nights where you eat like a family, passing dishes around of the best roasted chicken ever, or slicing off pieces of ricotta cheesecake. Foodies all over town hold this rustic yet daring kitchen as their number one in Albuquerque, for great reason.

Kokoro Japanese, 5614 Menaul Blvd. NE, Northeast Heights, Albuquerque, NM 87110; (505) 830-2061; Japanese; $$. Sushi culture has made it as far as the cold deli case in supermarkets, but this is not the only Japanese cuisine, just as "steak" is not the only American food. Kokoro Japanese is a place that refreshingly shows a bit more of the comfortable foods of that lovely Asian country. A Japanese meal is always beautiful to the eye—because sight is a sense, and eating should engage all senses and please them. So first on your order should be seaweed salad, with its black tendrils tangled up in a dainty pile. Then, miso soup: The clear yet cloudy broth delivers umami to your taste buds and fragrant steam to your nose. Crunchy fried pork cutlet is a common add-on to the "just curry" bowl of rice with a rich curry sauce, and you can finally touch your food when the order of potato croquettes arrives, with their comforting pillow-like interior. All five senses, and no sushi, not this time.

Kung Fu Cowboy Tea Cafe, 3107 Eubank Blvd. NE, Northeast Heights, Albuquerque, NM 87111; (505) 292-2832; fb.me/KungFuCowboyTeaCafe; Cafe/Gluten-Free/Tea/Healthy; $. This place has a spunky name to go along with the inventive food and cheerful staff. The tea, sourced via a tea company with the same name, is meticulously chosen, but there is a cafe to behold, too. Owner Brian Clark has assembled a delightfully homey array of dishes to please the healthy and hungry alike. From my first visit I fell in love with the Bowl o' Beans—a pileup of black beans, runny egg, salsa, cilantro, and sour cream—divine comfort food any time of day. Traditionalists can have steel-cut oatmeal or a gluten-free pastry to go with their tea. Of particular note are the half-dozen house-made chai formulas, from fennel to vanilla. Sandwiches and soups are simple and crafted with taste in mind rather than perfect looks. The calming vibe is infectious, even during the low murmurs of local gamers who often hang out to share their favorite of the month. See Brian's **Tea Egg Salad Sandwich** recipe on p. 307.

Lupe's Antojitos & Mexican Food, 8302 Zuni Rd. NE, Southeast, Albuquerque, NM 87108; (505) 255-4082; Mexican; $. The tastiest Mexican foods I have ever had always revolve around corn—tamales, tortillas, posole—that seed that shapes a cuisine. And Lupe's has some of the most flavorful corn dishes on earth: *antojitos* (little snacks) called *sopes* and *huraches*. Basically, thick corn dough is shaped into flat orbs with thick edges to hold in the toppings. Round ones are sopes, long ones are sized and named like the huarache sandals. They're cooked on a dry *comal* or fried until fragrant, then topped with anything: meats, cheeses, cooked vegetables—you name it. The best meats at Lupe's are the *birria de chivo* (roasted goat) and the *barbacoa* lamb; each is delicious stuffed into handmade corn tortillas with a squeeze of lime and a bit of cilantro. One of my trusted sources also says the rellenos, made from poblano peppers and only lightly battered, are the best she's ever had—that's reason for a trip. Also find their Bernalillo location: 1100 S. Camino del Pueblo, Bernalillo, NM 87004; (505) 203-6415.

Mannies Family Restaurant, 2900 E. Central Ave., Nob Hill, Albuquerque, NM 87106; (505) 265-1669; manniesnobhill.com; Diner; $. Repeat after me: Mannies has a waitress named Laverne. I already liked Mannies for their thick pancakes and extra-crispy bacon before I noticed that the server refilling my coffee (diner-quality coffee must be three things: hot, brown, and refilled often) wore a nametag that said Laverne. She called me "Hon" and I was tickled by the whole experience—not because it was kitschy, but because I felt warm fuzzies and believe Mannies is a good place to spend my money. You don't need to know much else: It is close to the university and all of Nob Hill, and the food is solid no-frills diner fare like chicken-fried steak, burgers, and the mandatory liver and onions. Oh, and when you're ready to leave, you run the risk of being confronted at the counter by the largest Rice Krispie treat you've ever seen, all wrapped up and begging you to take it home.

Mr. Sushi, 2400 Juan Tabo Blvd. NE, #G, Northeast Heights, Albuquerque, NM 87112; (505) 298-3081; mrsushiroll.com; Japanese/Sushi; $$. Many restaurants can be assessed by how they do the simplest dishes—are they prepared with care, as you'd expect for their most showy and pricey entrees? At Mr. Sushi, you do this by ordering the Ume & Shiso Roll, which tucks sweet

pickled plum and shiso leaf into a tiny sushi roll, where the rice's flavor is paramount. Once you try this, it might actually be hard to order anything else, but balance is good in dining as well. Outstanding rolls that don't need gimmicks is what they do well: You'll have an excellent rainbow or eel roll—no need to have a super-crunchy-flaming-tempura-saucy monstrosity. Non-sushi-eaters should consider the ramen noodle bowl for something hearty yet delicate; real ramen compared to packaged stuff is akin to filet mignon versus Slim Jims.

Olympia Cafe, 2210 E. Central Ave., UNM, Albuquerque, NM 87106; (505) 266-5222; olympiacafeabq.com; Greek; $$. There are two spots in the UNM area that are beloved to reverence levels by students, faculty, and anyone passing through—the Frontier and Olympia. They have in common food that is tasty and reasonable (but not dirt cheap). The cuisines could not be more different, and that's why both places are adored. Gyros, roasted chicken, massive Greek salads—that's what you order and devour at Olympia. The lines can be long for the counter-ordering system, and the dining room is vast yet cramped—use it for ample chatting opportunities while you listen for your name to be called. When the plate is in your paws, take it to the cutlery station and have at it with the spicy sauces in squeeze bottles, then head back to your table for your feast. The spit-roasted chicken is so good, you could order nothing else, but anything made with lamb is highly recommended, especially if you think you don't like lamb. Baklava is all right for dessert, but *rizogalo* (rice pudding) is the right amount of light sweetness.

Paisano's, 1935 Eubank Blvd. NE, Northeast Heights, Albuquerque, NM 87112; (505) 298-7541; paisanosabq.com; Italian; $$. Whether you've lived in Albuquerque for many years or have just arrived, everyone is shocked at the relative scarcity of Italian restaurants— we have apparently replaced the comfort of spaghetti and meatballs with *carne adovada,* and few are complaining. But when you really want Italian, the search is tricky. Paisano's appears on the possibilities list early because they have won over many local diners, and they all love to recommend the place. Handmade pasta every day, portions that are refreshingly normal instead of "bring me a box along with my entree," and sauces to swoon over—that's Paisano's. They even offer gluten-free versions of nearly everything on the menu; just ask and you shall be transported to happy digestion land. A favorite menu item, when available, is the utterly decadent seafood lasagna—dark pasta layered with four varieties of fish and a rich, creamy sauce. That's a nontraditional take on lasagna but a detour you'll remember. If you feel guilty enough, assuage the shame with Sicilian cannoli. There, all better.

Pho Linh, 5000 E. Central Ave., Southeast, Albuquerque, NM 87108; (505) 266-3368; pholinhabq.com; Vietnamese; $. Pho Linh does a great pho, but they should be equally lauded for other dishes as well. The shrimp salad appetizer is a nice light meal, and the seven courses of beef is red meat luxury for two diners. Only priced for two diners, the seven courses combine several menu beef items (grape leaf beef and others) with a few unlisted creations (cook and assemble your own spring rolls, raw beef tenderloin) to make for a leisurely and filling meal. When I'm eating here I always sip on a salty lemon soda, a refreshing discovery that pairs strangely well with a salty entree like salt-and-pepper-fried shrimp or the spicy lemongrass soup. Finish the meal with drip-at-your-table iced Vietnamese coffee and head back out into the sun.

Pho #1, 414 San Pedro Dr. SE, Southeast, Albuquerque, NM 87108; (505) 268-0488; Vietnamese; $. Sometimes you just really want a bucket of soup. A cup or a bowl won't do, even on a hot day. Vietnamese cuisine is your friend, and the dish called *pho* is everything you desire. Daily workers in Vietnam eat pho for breakfast the way we eat oatmeal or drink an extra-large latte—it's big and sustaining for the morning ahead. The key to good pho is rich beef broth lightly accented by star anise, ginger, cloves, and cinnamon. Served with rice noodles, rare beef, cilantro, and purple basil, it turns into a heavenly meal. Among the dozens of noodle soups around Albuquerque, most will say that Pho #1 lives up to the name. The rest of the menu is fine, but don't even bother with it until you've at least tried the #51, Pho Tai with rare steak. Class dismissed!

Piggy's Hot Dogs & Hamburgers, 4400 Central Ave. SE, Southeast, Albuquerque, NM 87108; (505) 948-1596; on.fb.me/piggys hotdogs; Hot Dogs/Burgers/Fast Food; $. This relative newcomer to the local quick-service lineup already had fans in a matter of days. Why? Because owner Robert Torrez seems to know a thing or two about what people want on the go (the location is drive-thru or walk-up only—no seating whether indoors or out is provided). The building previous hosted one of the local burrito shops, so there could have been some crossover traffic for a while, but the quality of Piggy's is what keeps people coming back. Chile cheese fries are gooey and already beloved, while brats, chicken, and fish round out the sandwich menu—there truly is something for everyone. Even the meat-averse can have a perfectly crispy grilled cheese, seared by Robert and served up by his partner Brandy.

Pinkies Country Cafe, 12129 N. NM 14, Cedar Crest, NM 87008; (505) 286-1175; Deli/Sandwiches/Cafe; $. Yes, there is a woman named Pinkie, and this is her place. She honed a skill for barbecue and wooed many a state fairgoer from her catering truck, until finally it was time to set down roots and open a restaurant. For local residents, Pinkie couldn't have picked a better spot—Cedar Crest has a handful of restaurants, not all of them memorable. The decor is charming and misleading: The pink gingham accents actually dissuaded me from checking out what I thought must be a dainty tea shop or something. Little did I know Pinkies was actually a den of wonderful beef brisket and New Mexican favorites. Her twists on burritos have a state fair touch—the potato component is tater tots instead of hash browns—and they are delicious with or without her brisket inside. Many entrees are available as take 'n' heat from her cooler, a fantastic way to have a good meal at home without too many dishes to wash.

Relish, 8019 Menaul Blvd. NE, Northeast Heights, Albuquerque, NM 87110; (505) 299-0001; relishsandwiches.com; Deli/Sandwiches; $. Gourmet sandwiches and better-than-you-think salads are what have set Relish apart since 2004, when it was founded by a transplanted New Yorker named Johnny Orr with a local partner. The daily fresh mozzarella, the roast beef sandwich, the thin Cubano, and the chopped salad were the stuff of dreams to many who might have been getting foot-longs at some other place for far too long. Over time the ownership shifted and the original team is largely gone, but many of the recipes remain untouched, to the relief of

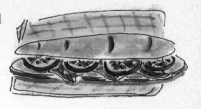

fans. The space has always exuded downtown chic despite being miles away, and the employees are joyful about slinging food your way. May the BLT chicken salad live on with apples and Gorgonzola amid the tomato and bacon—a modern Cobb, in a way. Hungry west-siders can find Relish at 1520 Deborah Rd., Ste. E, Rio Rancho, NM 87124; (505) 702-8962.

Route 66 Malt Shop, 3800 E. Central Ave., Nob Hill, Albuquerque, NM 87108; (505) 242-7866; route66maltshop.com; Diner; $$. First, I was lured in by an award for best homemade root beer in the country. Having been a fan of an "upscale" root beer called Barq's, this was intriguing. What I found was a wife-and-husband team, Diane Avila and Eric Szeman, slinging fresh food and occasional friendly insults at each other while their regular customers enjoyed first-class diner food. Limeades were made from scratch, after you ordered—this made bantering with Eric a must while you waited at the counter. In 2010 the teeny little restaurant finished up with long-term landlord issues and moved to brand-new digs in Nob Hill. In the new space, things are shinier and bigger, but the food seems to still be quality fare, right down to the fantastic meat loaf sandwich, served only on days after it is a plate special. Skip the plate special and get those slices buttered and griddled up—that's where the magic happens.

Sahara Middle Eastern Eatery, 2622 E. Central Ave., UNM, Albuquerque, NM 87106; (505) 255-5400; saharamiddleeastern eatery.com; Middle Eastern; $. Not for the faint-of-kebab, Sahara has been serving up Middle Eastern cuisine in the university area for several years. Jordan is the origin of the Neshewat family and their recipes brightening this and their other restaurant (Times Square Deli Mart) up the road. Swooning is common over the tabouli, a parsley-and-lemon-laden salad much lighter than others I've had that are overrun by the bulgur wheat. Falafel hounds order up the fried orbs like mad, while eggplant aficionados find love in the salad case—not just the ordinary baba ghanoush, but another called Eggplant Delight, a warm stew with olive oil and garlic. Even low-carbers can build a great meal here: Just order a *shawarma* plate without pita bread on top of fattoush salad. Hummus is garlicky enough for devotees and vampire-haters alike.

Sakura Sushi, 4200 Wyoming Blvd. NE, #C2, Northeast Heights, Albuquerque, NM 87111; (505) 294-9696; Sushi/Laotian/Thai; $$. Sakura serves up a curious mix of Asian foods—not mixing recipes, mind you, but serving sushi rolls alongside traditional Laotian fare in a Heights strip mall. Curious, but delicious. Start with the "monkey balls" to experience everything Western about sushi restaurants— deep-fried tuna-stuffed mushrooms with spicy sauce. Then turn the dial back and order Japanese ceviche, a bowl filled with marinated shrimp, tuna, and salmon and topped with greens for crunch. Another dish, another country: The Laotian sausage is ridiculously rich and succulent, while Thailand joins in to offer beef salad and coconut curries. The Laotian-style *laab* is fantastic and one of the best things to share; the lime and rice flavors mingle with pork, and the servings are ample enough for more than one meal. Sakura's real success is that it keeps each cuisine separate—the full list of sushi rolls is inventive yet tasty—and does them all well enough to satisfy any group of Asian cuisine fans.

San Pedro Mart, 4001 San Pedro Dr. NE, Northeast Heights, Albuquerque, NM 87110; (505) 888-2921; Middle Eastern; $$. In that curious-yet-typical occurrence, San Pedro Mart is another example of an utterly fantastic cafe tucked into an ethnic grocery store. Word of mouth is what brings most folks in, because even people who love to eat kebabs and hummus don't often buy the ingredients to make them at home. Once you are inside, the owner-brothers will take care of you, primarily by serving up the best Middle Eastern dishes in town. It's true, the hummus is amazing. The tabouli and baba ghanoush salads are mind-blowing. And lamb shawarma will bring a tear to your eye, while you sop up bites with hot homemade pitas. All of a sudden you contemplate what other holes-in-the-wall you have been overlooking—but then you catch another sniff of the shish kebab platter steaming on your table, and those thoughts are back-burnered. Finish with a tiny cup of sweet and gritty Arabic coffee, and offer thanks to the brilliant brothers.

Savoy Bar & Grill, 10601 Montgomery Blvd. NE, Northeast Heights, Albuquerque, NM 87111; (505) 294-9463; savoyabq.com; Fine Dining; $$$. Roessler brothers Kevin and Keith created their crown jewel of a restaurant with Savoy. They're also behind **Zinc Wine Bar & Bistro** (p. 172) and **Seasons Rotisserie & Grill** (p. 126), but this oasis in the far Northeast Heights is sophistication wrapped up in a creamy leather bow. There is a casual bar area for mingling, but the magic is in the dining room, a swanky eggshell-hued slate to begin your meal. Fresh oysters are a must, and the baked local goat cheese with accompaniments soothes a cranky appetite. The chef adores local lamb and features it on the menu in varying dishes, from braised shanks to loin chops. They take a tragically unhip dish—seared ahi tuna—and make it pleasing by keeping the flavors simple, pairing it with wasabi mashed potatoes and snap peas. Homemade apple strudel is the dessert star, year after year. Make sure you check out the wine-pairing events—they're a bargain and a fun Saturday afternoon.

Talking Drums Restaurant, 1218 San Pedro Dr. SE, Southeast, Albuquerque, NM 87108; (505) 792-3221; talkingdrumsabq.com; African/Caribbean; $$. New residents might be shocked to learn that there were exactly zero African restaurants in Albuquerque until 2012, despite a foodie contingent hankering for Ethiopian delights. An African store, Zenith Market, supplied traditional clothes and hard-to-find ingredients; owner Toyin Oladeji got it in her head that we were ready for Nigerian home cooking and opened Talking

Drums in early 2012. The name refers to the handmade drums that seem to mimic speech, used for long-range communication in West Africa. It is communication that matters, in this case the sharing of a meal, and Toyin is happy to assist by cooking. Order whatever sounds weird, and trust in the experience. Still hesitant? Here's a basic primer to remove doubts: *Fufu* is starch such as potatoes or rice, *moi moi* is steamed savory cake, pepper soup is a rich broth with meat, and jerk chicken is, well, delicious. Take along a sense of adventure, and you'll enjoy this new cuisine.

Thai Tip, 1512 Wyoming Blvd. NE, #E, Northeast Heights, Albuquerque, NM 87112; (505) 323-7447; Thai; $$. Many American diners are exposed to spicy restaurant food through Thai cuisine, typically hotter than Indian and Mexican. At that time the "heat scale" is learned when ordering—"Would you like mild/medium/hot/Thai spice?"—and one chooses to get a little tingle or full-blown pain. Fire-eaters, however, must employ the often-unspoken next level of spice. At Thai Tip this is indicated by the "plus number," as in "plus 2," which is all the hotter I can handle, given that the number is the extra tablespoons of chiles used. Yikes. Thai Tip's food is wonderfully fresh and priced accordingly—the curry might be over $10 but it is really, really good curry. Papaya or seafood salads are vibrant and delicious, as well as the Thai soup with (Tom Kha) or without (Tom Yum) coconut milk. The owner, Tip, is cooking like a dervish in the back, while husband John attends to the dining room, pouring sweetened ginger tea and making recommendations for any spicy craving you can dream up.

Tully's Italian Deli & Meats, 1425A San Mateo Blvd. NE, Northeast Heights, Albuquerque, NM 87110; (505) 255-5370; Deli/Sandwiches/Italian; $$. Lamenting about the relative lack of excellent Italian restaurants in Albuquerque is slightly silly when you consider that Tully's allows you to create the best meals in your own kitchen with the best ingredients for the job. From sausages to pastas to meats and imported tinned foods, you can stock up while asking the advice of the Camuglia family—experts in all things Italian. Taste their expertise with a sandwich for lunch or take-out entrees like lasagna or chicken Marsala for your convenience. The full-service sandwich shop puts together fantastic creations from Sicilian to simple mozzarella with olives and artichoke hearts. Step next door for sweets from the sister bakery at **Saratori's di Tully** (p. 193).

2 Fools Tavern, 3211 E. Central Ave., Nob Hill, Albuquerque, NM 87106; (505) 265-7447; 2foolstavern.com; Pub; $$. Irish pubs can often fall prey to menu clichés and the steady drumbeat of patrons who really just want beer and fried things, but when they rise above with authentic dishes and kitchen talent, you wind up with a place like 2 Fools. The decor is dark and the music can be loud, but few eateries around compete with the food, starting with a delight called the Irish boxty. Imagine a silky beef stew with the aroma of stout folded inside savory potato pancakes nearly the thinness of crepes—that's a boxty. As you'd hope, the fish-and-chips are darn good, but I return again and again to the ploughman's lunch with cheddar, olives, and brown bread. Saving room for at least one boozy dessert is advised, especially once you hear you'll be choosing between things like Scotch ice cream or a Guinness brownie.

2000 Vietnam, 601 San Mateo Blvd. SE, Southeast, Albuquerque, NM 87108; (505) 232-0900; 2000restaurant.com; Vietnamese; $. Holes-in-the-wall are often spots where foodies converge to agree on a particularly fantastic cook or authentic cuisine, but 2000 Vietnam takes this concept to another level by pairing their business in the same building as an auto emissions testing joint. Don't be put off by the looks—the kitchen is all about giving you a fresh and delicious Vietnamese experience, from duck soup to avocado smoothies and beyond. The crowd is always diverse, with hipsters and Native families mingling over steaming bowls of pho and tightly wrapped summer rolls. The scent of star anise and fresh cilantro fills the air, and even for an ethnic spot, the prices are shockingly reasonable. Despite the multitasking possibilities, the food is good enough that you will want to return more than every two years when the car comes due. A newer and slightly more refined second location is at 1405 Juan Tabo Blvd. NE, Northeast Heights, Albuquerque, NM 87112; (505) 298-5888.

Venezia's Pizzeria, 3908 San Mateo Blvd. NE, Northeast Heights, Albuquerque, NM 87110; (505) 883-6000; veneziaspizzeria.com; Pizza/Italian; $. Big, floppy, and chewy: That's how I like my East Coast–style pizza, and that's what I get at Venezia's. Only a few

pizzerias in Albuquerque even claim to do New York–style pizza, so finding one that is darn good is a treat. Slices are under 3 bucks; toppings can add up if you get creative. Simple cheese or Hawaiian are my favorites, but the New Mexico way is pepperoni and green chile for two kinds of spice in each bite. Unless you've just finished a serious workout, one huge slice is plenty—and you can save room for some cheesecake. Specialty pizzas of legend are the Bianca (three cheeses, no sauce) and the Italian Stallion (beef, sausage, pepperoni, Canadian bacon, and green chile). Get a second pizza fix at 1690 Rio Rancho Dr., #E, Rio Rancho, NM 87124; (505) 892-2026; or a third in the Heights: 1331 Juan Tabo Blvd. NE, #2F, Albuquerque, NM 87112; (505) 294-0115. All three locations deliver and have online ordering.

Viet Taste, 5721 Menaul Blvd. NE, Northeast Heights, Albuquerque, NM 87110; (505) 888-0101; Vietnamese; $. The location of this bright-green oasis ought to be noted: It's across the street from the mall, where chain restaurants and big-box food dominate. Diners can find refuge from those mass-produced morsels and enjoy something delightful at Viet Taste. The room is even transporting, with amber walls and bamboo accents as backdrop to your starter of fresh spring rolls or grape-leaf-wrapped beef. The classic Vietnamese/French mash-up food is Bahn Mi, a baguette with grilled pork and both fresh and pickled vegetables. Beat a path to the broken rice combination plate, #80 on the menu. Bits of long-grain rice are topped with a rainbow of tastes from fried egg to steamed pork cake and grilled beef. Soups are a standout—from the cuisine that invented pho noodle soup, they'd better be. The pho is indeed good, but worthy of special attention is #98, vegetables and fish in sweet-and-sour broth. The potent steaming bowl has tender catfish pieces and veggies in that delicious broth; the composition is similar to Japanese *sukiyaki,* another soup with sweet notes.

Zacatecas Tacos & Tequila, 3423 E. Central Ave., Nob Hill, Albuquerque, NM 87106; (505) 255-8226; zacatecastacos.com; Mexican; $$. Few restaurant openings were as hyped in 2012 as the Albuquerque taco spot by the chef-owner of **The Compound** in Santa Fe (p. 40). Mark Kiffin set out to defy history—another Santa Fe venture in the same location had recently closed—with a taco shop flaunting both gourmet quality and prices. Out of the gate, Duke City diners were not wooed by Santa Fe credentials; they just wanted good food without getting gouged. Luckily Zacatecas came together, offering plates of tacos (two double-tortilla engorged tacos or four spread out) for $8 to $10 with meats like braised chicken and chorizo, banana-leaf-roasted pork, or seared cod. Appetizers include lime-heavy guacamole and savory-sweet empanadas with chicken, nuts, and fruit. There are even full entrees of pork ribs or glazed salmon, but the tacos are where it's at. The scene is hopping—cool, trendy, loud, crowded—the house margarita is

SPOTLIGHT ON VIETNAM

It's no secret that there is a large number of Vietnamese families in Albuquerque spread out over several neighborhoods, mostly in the area south of Central around Louisiana Boulevard. It is our city's good fortune that they seem to have a talent for opening restaurants and cooking the food from their home country. (We also have a good number of Chinese, but those restaurants do not seem to appear in quite the same numbers—a puzzle I haven't figured out.) As of mid-2012 there were about three dozen Vietnamese restaurants in town, with little variation in the basic menu features, so something is being done right.

The food of Vietnam is inextricably tied with their daily life; serving the functional equivalent to "sandwiches" in American dining is hot rice noodle soup, and the most famous of those is called *pho* (pronounce it like "fuh" and that's close enough). You should know that pho is served in small and large sizes at most restaurants, with small meaning "bucket" and large meaning "lake." In other words, college guys would find it challenging to finish off a large pho. So order your small pho *tai* (with slices of rare beef), and when the steaming broth arrives, you have some work to do. Take the plate of salad and start tearing it up, then add anything you'd like right into the broth, from basil and cilantro to bean sprouts. This should make the already aromatic soup extra-punchy. The broth is based on beef stock that's had a long simmer with anise, ginger, and other spices; shortly before serving, a nest of rice noodles is dropped in the bowl and they cook by about the time you're eating them. The rare beef cooks in moments as well, and you have just become a slurping and happy pho fanatic.

While pho is something special, it is but the tip of the iceberg of Vietnamese cuisine, which could be considered similar to Thai but without coconut milk, less incendiary heat, and rarer use of stir-frying. Salads based on shrimp and beef and lime are common, as is the use of rice noodles, both cold and hot. They are also fans of beef and like to showcase it in multicourse meals that include their take on carpaccio, washed down with an avocado shake. I am not alone in proclaiming that if I could eat only one cuisine for the rest of my life, this would be it.

By no means comprehensive, here are a few of the go-to Vietnamese spots in town:

Bahn Mi Coda, *230-C Louisiana Blvd. SE, Albuquerque, NM 87108; (505) 232-0085*

Cafe Da Lat, *5615 Central Ave. NE, Albuquerque, NM 87165; (505) 266-5559*

Pho Linh, *5000 Central Ave. SE, Albuquerque, NM 87108; (505) 266-3368*

Pho #1, *414 San Pedro Dr. SE, Albuquerque, NM 87198; (505) 268-0488*

Saigon, *6001 San Mateo Blvd. NE, Albuquerque, NM 87109; (505) 884-0706*

Viet Rice, *1340 Rio Rancho Dr. SE, Rio Rancho, NM 87124; (505) 892-7423*

quite tasty, and a full list of tequilas to sample or mix beckon any agave fan.

Zinc Wine Bar & Bistro, 3009 E. Central Ave., Nob Hill, Albuquerque, NM 87106; (505) 254-9462; zincabq.com; Fine Dining; $$$. Some of the most successful business formulas entail having a handful of locations, each with a different focus (and name!) and target clientele. Zinc Wine Bar is part of a triumvirate of restaurants under one ownership—**Seasons Rotisserie & Grill** (p. 126) and **Savoy Bar & Grill** (p. 164) are the other two—each offering upscale dining with a wine emphasis, but with variations on cuisine and dining style that keep the customers coming to all three. Nob Hill's Zinc often draws me in for its less-formal dining option of weekend brunch. There are other spots nearby that offer brunch in the $10 to $15 range, but they pale in comparison to Zinc's full table service, excellent coffee, and decadent food. Their featured waffle gets no better than when it's the Elvis, slathered with peanut butter, bananas, bacon, and honey. Permanent—and famous—items include duck confit eggrolls, steamed mussels, and steak frites. Formal dining is available on the upper level, where a thrilling view of the whole operation can be had; it's not the best accompaniment to intimate conversation, however, so in that case, choose a private booth downstairs.

Annapurna World Vegetarian Cafe, 2201 Silver Ave. SE, UNM, Albuquerque, NM 87106; (505) 262-2424; chaishoppe.com; Vegetarian/Healthy; $$. Annapurna is often the first place discovered or cited when searching for vegetarian food in both Albuquerque and Santa Fe (thanks to multiple locations); that is the result of 10 years of educated cooking by owner Yashoda Naidoo, who opened the doors in 2002. After spending years cooking Ayurvedic food for herself with no local restaurant options available, she changed the playing field and created a market where none existed before. Simply put, Ayurvedic eating is tailored to a person's health status and is designed to be soothing to your body. Indian foods often meet these goals, so items like *saag paneer* and potato samosas are featured offerings. Yashoda's talent breaks away from all Indian, however, with enormous salads, wraps, and even a rustic pizza on whole-grain crust. Breakfast is a delight with gluten-free cardamom-coconut pancakes, with their potent housemade chai. There is something in the humming energy of this place, even at 9 a.m. on a Saturday. Perhaps it is the addictive date and chocolate balls, or perhaps it is just the buzz of good health. Also at 7520 Fourth St. NW, North Valley, Los Ranchos de Albuquerque, NM 87107; (505) 254-2424.

Burger Boy, 12023 N. NM 14, Cedar Crest, NM 87008; (505) 281-3949; Burgers; $. Jennifer James, the chef who many Duke City residents say is the best of the best in town, calls this her favorite burger. Shall I go on? Start with the incredibly divey digs—a small counter, some plain booths, and an open kitchen with one or two cooks (often owner Kathy Cushing is one of them) slinging patties or flipping pancakes. The banter is entirely rural: "How's the weather?" "Did your kid's team win?" "I hear we're getting snow." The food is prepared with smiles, and the prices, while not inexpensive, are well worth the quality. Topping the recommended list here is the green chile cheeseburger, cooked to order and juicy beyond belief. A milk shake will wash it down with french fries, but frankly, I'd rather just make the burger a double patty and be taken to beefy nirvana. Other burgers are available, like elk and ostrich, and the breakfasts are formidable. Pancakes come out with the perfect edge crust and are served with the all-too-rare pats of real butter. Take the 10-minute drive out of town; you'll have no regrets.

El Norteño, 1431 Wyoming Blvd. NE, Northeast Heights, Albuquerque, NM 87112; (505) 299-2882; elnorteno.com; Mexican; $$. Before every non–Spanish-speaker thought it was no big deal to stroll into a South Valley Mexican taco shop, there was El Norteño. Mexican food seemed different enough from New Mexican to be interesting to locals, and the food was diverse and delicious. Everyone ordered beer in ice-filled buckets—perfect for washing down chips and spicy Camarones a la Diabla. But 2008 was calamitous when a fire caused enough damage to shut the restaurant down. Eventually El Norteño rose from the ashes in a new spot in the Northeast Heights. You can once again have the flaming hot habanero shrimp platter (with a goblet of *horchata* to tame the fire), tender fish tacos done San Diego style, or their famous chicken mole. My recommendation, however, is to push your comfort zone and order the *cabrito* (stewed goat) in rich red chile sauce—it is Mexican comfort food bar none. Before you head back over the border, consider trying the sweet *tres leches* (three milks) cake for one final treat.

Paul's Monterey Inn, 1000 Juan Tabo Blvd. NE, Northeast Heights, Albuquerque, NM 87112; (505) 294-1461; Steak/Supper Club; $$$. Not many places in Albuquerque approach Paul's level of retro authenticity. This is not new hipster nostalgia, but rather it is retro in the we-haven't-touched-a-thing-in-four-decades kind of way. Love it or hate it, Paul's is a 1970s restaurant, and it is where you go when you need a 1970s restaurant. You'll sit at bouncy banquettes and enjoy big pours of inexpensive wine, smearing butter on a warm miniature bread loaf, and wondering if the room looked swankier 10 years ago when you could smoke indoors. No matter, because here comes your shrimp cocktail with potent horseradish sauce, and a pile of onion rings expertly battered and fried. It's a supper club, so expect steaks, fish and lobster, a token chicken dish, and some rather excellent prime rib.

Paul's is a place where you will almost always have the pleasure of seeing a table of a dozen or more celebrating a family anniversary or birthday—that kind of enjoyment is infectious.

Ponderosa Eatery & Saloon, 10676 S. NM 337, East Mountains, Tijeras, NM 87059; (505) 281-8278; ponderosaeateryandsaloon .com; Steak; $$. A saloon in the woods, parking lot full of bikers— just the place for a friendly weekend lunch, right? Indeed, it is. Ponderosa has been doling out steak house food to hikers, bikers, and locals for nearly 40 years, and the menu is diverse enough to offer something for every picky eater in the group. Frankly, the food is perfectly fine, but it is the all-wood-all-the-time decor that is worth the trip. Wobbly tables, a big honkin' bar, and wood paneling all add to the feeling that you're in someone's den— someone who likes to debate current events at the bar with other regulars, then take a break to shoot pool and carve into a big rib eye steak. Come back on Sunday for syrup-sopping pancakes the size of dinner plates.

Scalo Northern Italian Grill, 3500 E. Central Ave., Nob Hill, Albuquerque, NM 87106; (505) 255-8781; scalonobhill.com; Italian; $$$. Is Scalo iconic like a generations-old steak house or pre-freeway-era diner? No. However, when arriving in Albuquerque in the 1990s with a date on your arm or a client to impress, you almost certainly went to Scalo for the white tablecloth treatment. While there are more options nowadays, Scalo has lost none of its consistently great cuisine. Steve Paternoster has manned this Northern Italian ship for more than 20 years, through chefs and dining room overhauls and recessions. Every day he bounces into work on a cloud of enthusiasm for the food, the wine, the special of the day, the new bartender—anything makes this guy bubbly. Like many residents, I had my first real Caesar salad here and still make visits to indulge in award-winning cocktails by Ben Williams or nibble on silky tiramisu. See their **Veal Piccata** recipe on p. 316.

66 Diner, 1405 E. Central Ave., UNM, Albuquerque, NM 87106; (505) 247-1421; 66diner.com; Diner; $$. There are two diners that invoke the name "66" in Albuquerque, and this is the location more themed and more famous to newcomers. The waitstaff is clad in neat blue and white uniforms, the jukebox plays Elvis, and every hour of every day you can sidle up to the counter and order a burger and milk shake. Daily specials keep the diner atmosphere authentic, from meat loaf to liver and onions—yes, really. You can't fault a restaurant for serving up liver and onions to tourists looking for the '50s experience. Their tongues are rewarded no matter what they order, for the 66 Diner's menu is inclusive, from patty melts to pancakes, and includes the locally requisite green chile on many items. Finishing off a belly-expanding meal is tolerably cute with the Itty Bitty Sundae for 99 cents, served in a 2-ounce condiment cup with hot fudge and a cherry. By catering to everyone's memories (or fantasies) of what old-time Americana dining was all about, the 66 Diner is a classic.

Spotlight on Steve Paternoster, Restaurateur Supreme

Many cities have a few restaurant owners who seem to have their hands in everything, from opening new spots to working with local groups and generally being a community presence in all the good aspects. In Albuquerque that guy is Steve Paternoster. His flagship is Scalo Northern Italian Grill, and he also owns Brasserie La Provence just a few blocks up the street. In 2010 the city welcomed a new French spot that brought Paternoster on as an investor (for the first year while they were gaining their stride): **P'tit Louis Bistro** (p. 117), which quickly became known as one of the best spots in town.

He was manager of Scalo for many years, first becoming involved with the restaurant in 1986, before taking a hiatus in 1999 to do work with a national chain concept. That led to six years of moves and turmoil until returning to Albuquerque in 2005 to purchase Scalo outright, bringing it back from the (admittedly) slow decline it had been experiencing. Chefs come and go, even at a place like Scalo, but the restaurant is better than ever—those lost years ought to be forgotten by locals so that they can come back in with fresh expectations.

His hands are full, yet every time I talk with him he is happy, excited, and wants to keep doing what he loves, "jabbering, hugging, and kissing" his friends and clientele. This is one of those guys who believe that doing what you love and surrounding yourself with friends is the only way to survive. He has personal experience with the survival instinct after a family tragedy reaffirmed his desire to keep giving back and being a resource for people in need.

Both of his restaurants earned the New Mexico Restaurant Association's 2010 Restaurant Neighbor award, given to "restaurants that exemplify the industry's philanthropic spirit." As a personal bonus, Steve was chosen as the winner of the Cornerstone Humanitarian Award, which honors exemplary community service activity by an individual in the hospitality industry—meaning, he's an all-around good guy. One of the projects he maintains strong ties with that contributed to the recognition is a local living facility that helps men and women transition from prison life to working productively in society again. That charity and everything else that Paternoster's restaurants contribute back to the community total well over $100K per year.

Stop in at Steve's restaurants for a good meal, or swing by Scalo to say hello in person:

Brasserie La Provence, 3001 E. Central Ave., Albuquerque, NM 87106; (505) 254-7644

Scalo Northern Italian Grill, 3500 E. Central Ave., Albuquerque, NM 87106; (505) 255-8781 (p. 176)

Town House Restaurant, 9018 E. Central Ave., Southeast, Albuquerque, NM 87108; (505) 255-0057; Steak/Supper Club; $$$. Follow the steer to Town House—the mounted fiberglass icon will let you know you've arrived at one of the old gems of Route 66, where Greek and American dinner classics combine. Town House operated for 49 years before a 5-year closure due to lease issues, but had a recent triumphant reopening with original founder George Argyres still making the rounds. True to George's roots, the best appetizer is the combination antipasto with literal piles of imported feta, olives, peppers, and cured meats. Share this one, or your entree's future is in jeopardy. Fish is on hand, but the broiler menu selections are where the magic happens, from tender lamb chops with mint sauce to standard steaks cooked exactly to order. Everything optionally comes with divine Greek potatoes. Antipasto, steak, potatoes—where will it all fit? In a box, that's where, because the 2-inch-thick baklava is a soul-satisfying finish.

All Chile, All the Time

Burrito Lady, 938 Eubank Blvd. NE, Northeast Heights, Albuquerque, NM 87112; (505) 271-2268; New Mexican; $. Despite coffee culture overtaking the breakfast economy, there are a stubborn lot of New Mexicans who opt instead to pick up breakfast burritos rather than get a paper cup full of caffeine, and that's why we love the Burrito Lady. Her name is Consuelo Flores, and she packs a bundle of energy into each morning when the phoned-in orders come in fast and furious, hungry customers standing in line or seated at one of three small tables. Her father was a chile grower; she grew up knowing the importance of chile to the local cuisine and economy. Consuelo worked in other restaurants but wanted to provide her kind of food to a wider audience, and the shop was opened. Far more than burritos are on the menu: There are enchiladas, stuffed sopaipillas, tamales, and *huevos rancheros,* everything with shockingly low prices. She warns customers that her chile is hot, and thankfully it delivers on that promise—this ain't no tourist chile, no siree.

Charlie's Front & Back Door, 8224 Menaul Blvd. NE, Northeast Heights, Albuquerque, NM 87110; (505) 294-3130; New Mexican; $. The curved facade of Hoffmantown shopping center is home to a curiously bipolar restaurant—or pair of restaurants—called Charlie's. The front door leads to a light dining room with calm ambiance, while 25 feet away is the back door to a wholly different dining space with a bar and dark booths. Both are served by the same kitchen and share a menu, so the split is almost a running gag that is observed with seriousness. Also serious is the food and its attention to religious holidays—the annual Lenten season is celebrated with a rarely seen dish of *torta de huevo,* fried eggy disks floating in red chile. It's rich and delicious and I'd order it year-round if I could. Other specials feature local greens called lamb's quarters and

Il Vicino: Homegrown "Chain"

It was the source of many firsts for me when my time in New Mexico was still fresh: first look and taste of an IPA, first strangely topped thin-crust pizza, first place that just seemed reliable no matter what you were in the mood for, from bounteous salads to calzones the size of a newborn. That spot is Il Vicino, where craft beer meets wood-fired pizzas and quick counter-to-table service. You and all your friends have parties, solo lunches, dates, or late-night dessert here, even when it seems crowded and the line to place an order reaches out the door. We do that because the nine Il Vicino restaurants (four in New Mexico, five in Colorado and Kansas) have given us a good experience through thick and thin. And it all started with the Nob Hill location in 1992.

A tour of the menu hits four categories: pizza, pasta, salads, and sandwiches—the latter a relatively recent addition, bringing panini love to diners. It will take you many visits before you leave the pizza menu—if you ever do. Standard pies are about 12 inches of thin and crispy dough, somewhat bland in flavor on its own. Then come the toppings in a dozen specialty combinations. Everyone has a favorite, but the Bianca (ham, mushrooms, onions, goat cheese, Gorgonzola, rosemary) is ordered quite a bit. The daily pie is not on the menu and is typically a buck below average prices; even if you pair it with a beer, your meal is relatively cheap.

When I migrated to the salads it was for one reason alone: the Insalata Il Vicino, a riff on Cobb using blue cheese, walnuts, chicken, tomatoes, egg, and artichoke hearts, all laid out in rows with a tub of dressing on the side. Admire it for just a moment before tossing like mad. There are a good number of popular pastas on the menu, but frankly, I cannot steer away from the pizzas and that salad.

The beers are another story, but of great importance in Il Vicino's success. That IPA a friend was accustomed to quaffing is part of a lineup of suds ranging from red ales up to stiff chocolate porters, crafted by Brady McKeown since the earliest days of Il Vicino. In late 2011 a new outlet opened in Albuquerque called IVB Canteen (p. 289). At this taproom the focus is on the beers, with smaller nosh plates instead of the full menu of the rest of the locations. That's not much of a bother, especially when you realize how awesome it is to eat a freshly baked pretzel with spicy mustard (labeled on the menu as the Beer Sponge) while you sip your pint.

Learn more at ilvicino.com. The Il Vicino New Mexico locations are:

321 W. San Francisco St., Santa Fe, NM 87501; (505) 986-8700

10701 Coors Blvd. NW, Corrales, NM 87114; (505) 899-7500

11225 Montgomery Blvd. NE, Albuquerque, NM 87111; (505) 271-0882

3403 Central Ave. NE, Albuquerque, NM 87106; (505) 266-7855

The IVB Canteen *location is: 2381 Aztec Rd. NE, Albuquerque, NM 87107; (505) 881-2737*

blue corn, making Charlie's a torchbearer in serving native ingredients. At the Back Door, the margaritas are potent and a good foil for the other lauded dish of sour cream enchiladas, equally as rich as it sounds.

El Patio, 142 Harvard Dr. SE, UNM, Albuquerque, NM 87106; (505) 268-4245; elpatiodealbuquerque.com; New Mexican; $$. El Patio is a hangout beloved by UNM students, but it also brings in long-ago graduates who loved the fare when they were younger and find that things don't change. Housed in a residential structure, the rooms are tiny and adorable but accordingly cramped and probably a nightmare for the servers; for fresh air, head for the ample patio, which is heated in cooler temperatures. For health-conscious patrons, El Patio has always been a bastion of vegan (not just vegetarian) options, from omitting cheese all the way down to the beans (no lard) and the chile (no meat stock). Open for nearly a generation, El Patio is now run by siblings Thomas and Christopher Sandoval, creating wonderful meat dishes alongside their vegan counterparts. *Carne adovada* and chicken enchiladas are modestly sized but outrageously flavored. Make sure you've brought cash—El Patio still chooses to not deal with credit cards; usually only newcomers forget and have to find an ATM to (literally) pay homage to their delicious meal.

Perea's New Mexican, 9901 E. Central Ave., Northeast Heights, Albuquerque, NM 87123; (505) 293-0157; New Mexican; $. When green chile is the flavor you crave, Perea's is the place to be, with almost incendiary bowls of roasted green pods studded with ground beef and ample seasonings. This makes Perea's chile anything but simple and far from vegetarian, but as bite after bite makes it to your taste buds, that's the only feedback needed. Fans of both chile colors will like Perea's *carne adovada*, or standards like *huevos rancheros* served with wonderful homemade flour tortillas. Breakfast is my favorite at Perea's; I create crazy combinations like a short stack of their fantastic pancakes topped with eggs over medium, with chile on the side to pour over the whole thing. Until you've tried chile as syrup, don't dismiss it entirely, especially as an alternative to the squeeze-bottle sugary stuff.

Silvano's New Mexican, 5016-B Lomas Blvd. NE, Northeast Heights, Albuquerque, NM 87110; silvanosabq.com; New Mexican; $. Silvano's story is a tantalizing trip into local restaurant lore worth the ride. Silvano's was a beloved New Mexican cafe at this location in the '70s and '80s until being renamed Los Cuates by the owner. Another location went in down the street, and eventually the 5016 restaurant closed. More ownership changes led to the rumor that the Silvano's recipes were not used at Los Cuates anymore, then along comes Silvano's, back in the original location. Nostalgic chile hounds are smiling. If you only ever order one thing at Silvano's, order the chiles rellenos and you'll have the most tender yet perfectly crispy fried chile of your life. It is tragic how many rellenos are soggy and insipid, wilting under their chile sauce. If economy is important, order the bowl of beans with chile for under 5 bucks and enjoy each bite with a thick tortilla or a fresh and crispy sopaipilla. Great frying technique makes all the difference—love, too, but also frying technique.

Specialty Stores, Markets & Producers

Buffett's Candies, 7001 Lomas Blvd. NE, Northeast Heights, Albuquerque, NM 87110; (505) 265-7731; buffettscandies.com; Sweets. George Buffett is pretty much the granddaddy of sweets in Albuquerque. His store is visible from afar by the 20-foot-tall candy cane propped against the bright white and red building on Lomas. In 1956 the store was literally at the eastern edge of town, with a commanding view down the slope toward UNM and downtown. Now it sits merely a third of the way up the long stretch of Lomas to the foothills, but the selection and sweets have not changed a bit. The family's famous for piñon nuts every which way, like brittle, praline, and nougat rolls, and caramel corn made with fresh butter. According to George, no amount of tweaking the recipe for better shelf life made the caramel corn as good as the original, so they kept it fresh—and perishable. "Our candy is made to eat, not to keep!"

Chillz Frozen Custard, 2720 Central Ave. SE, UNM, Albuquerque, NM 87106; (505) 265-5648; chillzcustard.com; Frozen. We've got gelato, yes we do; we've got fro-yo, and ice cream too. We didn't until recently have honest-to-goodness Midwest-style frozen custard. Kurt Nilson, a native New Mexican but addicted to and then trained in the ways of St. Louis custard, usually sums up the distinctive aspects this way: Custard is low in butterfat and high in egg yolk compared to ice cream. (Gelato is typically low in butterfat but sans eggs.) Custard is served at a higher temperature than ice cream, with less air, leaving it creamy and dense, and the yolk imparts decadence beyond compare. Every day Kurt has vanilla, chocolate, and a featured flavor, and the current month's flavor list is on their Facebook page. Think you can handle the Challenge? It's 8 scoops, 8 mini waffles, and 8 toppings in less than 30 minutes. So far the success rate is 5 percent—no surprise when you see the turkey-platter serving tray. The rest of us can get prepacked pints going back a week or so on the flavor list, but nothing lasts long.

Chocolate Cartel, 315 Juan Tabo Blvd. NE, #A, Northeast Heights, Albuquerque, NM 87123; (505) 797-1193; chocolatecartel.com; Chocolate/Frozen. It started in Taos under a harder-to-pronounce name—Xocolatl (shock-e-LOT-el)—but the Van Rixel brothers Scott and Tim eventually moved their chocolate talents to a hard-to-spot haven in the Northeast Heights where the rent is probably a steal and the chocolates can be made with little fanfare. A large room in the back is the factory, fronted by a small retail area where visitors are confronted by bars and truffles and confections. My favorite truffle creations are port-blueberry and honey pollen, but of course there is a red chile flavor as well. A chalkboard reveals the current flavors of their other revered product: gelato. The most popular flavor is salted caramel, but I adore the dark chocolate sorbet and limoncello. While a visit to the shop is an easy way to leave with a lighter wallet, you can purchase bars and gelato in grocery stores all over town, including Whole Foods. Once you have any of the gelati, you'll never go back to Häagen Dazs.

Duke City Donuts, 3005 Eubank Blvd. NE, Northeast Heights, Albuquerque, NM 87111; (505) 294-2470; dukecitydonuts.com; Donuts. Whether you like your fried dough raised or cakey, this shop fills both of those needs on the same visit. Gourmet donuts have not taken hold in Albuquerque like they could, but Duke City Donuts is a great example of moving beyond the chains—the buttermilk glazed are tangy and not overly sweet, with a dark crunchy exterior that satisfies (and holds up well to dunking). Their website features a gallery of "donut porn," so you can salivate even before calling in an order—how else would you explain the run on Coffee Toffee, which looks like a donut dragged through the dirt but tastes like pure bliss? A few available chocolates include barks, fudge, and dipped sweets, but compared to those donuts, they take a distant second place.

Jubilation Wine & Spirits, 3512 Lomas Blvd. NE, Nob Hill, Albuquerque, NM 87106; (505) 255-4404; jubilationwines.com; Alcohol. Three words: monthly wine tastings. Maybe add a fourth if you need convincing: free monthly wine tastings. This spot near Nob Hill may not have the biggest selection in the state, but they are helpful, friendly, reasonable, and oh-so-fun. The store is laid out in sections, with a sunken wine area that hosts the fantastic monthly swirl-and-sip events. I usually buy a couple of bottles, so the marketing is working.

Just a Bite, 7900 San Pedro Dr. NE, Northeast Heights, Albuquerque, NM 87109; (505) 822-5001; justabitebakery.com; Pastries. Amy Markham-Sandoval put her finger on "the problem" with sweet treats—they are often too big to consume without guilt. Many folks who want to keep their belt notches in check or are not sugar fiends still enjoy itty-bitty sweet things, and she makes all kinds at Just a Bite. Mini cupcakes are just the beginning, as the display case shows off an array like little éclairs and cheesecake-stuffed strawberries. They also carry cake pops, but that trend might not last, so it would be back to the basics, and that's OK.

Kelly Liquors, 5850 Eubank Blvd. NE, Northeast Heights, Albuquerque, NM 87111; (505) 291-9914; kellyliquors.com; Alcohol. Kelly is a many-locationed wonder of go-to for your alcohol needs. At most stores there is always someone on staff who can make excellent recommendations and point you to the right product or even another store. Check the website for more locations.

New Mexican Cheeses Got Your Goat

New Mexico is an interesting place to source cheese, yet with the number of goat farms and amazing tangy cheeses, we just might be on the up and up, relative to other states. California and Wisconsin have the history and the dairy herds, but that shouldn't stop you from investigating the wonders of New Mexican cheese. One of the early heralds and educators in the local industry, Sweetwoods, closed up shop in 2011 after decades of wonderful, pioneering work that sadly wasn't fruitful enough. Their soft goat cheese, spreadable or spoonable like peanut butter, won many fans who previously thought of goat's milk as funky or too strange.

A few other companies still carry the torch and will hopefully weather any continuing economic storms. The front-runner in that field is in Estancia, east of Albuquerque by a good hour, the Old Windmill Dairy, *52 Paso Ranch Rd., Estancia, NM 87016; (505) 384-0033; theoldwindmilldairy.com.* They produce not just goat cheeses

Le Paris French Bakery, 1441 Eubank Blvd. NE, Northeast Heights, Albuquerque, NM 87112; (505) 299-4141; leparisfrench bakery.com; Pastries. The white paper baguette sheaths with the iconic Eiffel Tower logo are something you cannot avoid seeing all over town—they appear in grocery stores, on restaurant shelves, and, of course, at their source at the bakery on Eubank. This store is a jewel box of treasures, from "standard" baguettes to layered diplomat pastries, with a small breakfast and lunch menu to boot. Breakfast crepes sound like a great idea, even if your intent was

in wild flavors like caper berry, but also cow's milk cheddar, brie, Asiago, and fresh mozzarella. Old Windmill is featured on many of the top restaurants' menus, and for good reason.

What started as a hobby for owners Donna and Marge turned into South Mountain Dairy, *48 Katzima Dr., Edgewood, NM 87015; (505) 280-5210; southmountaindairy.com.* They grew to a formidable business by treating their "girls" well, and it shows in the cheese. They do goat's milk delicacies like a salted feta and über-creamy Queso Lizette, and sell to farmers' markets and restaurants year-round.

West of Albuquerque, almost to Pie Town, you'll find Coonridge Organic Goat Cheese, *47 Coonridge Dairy, Pie Town, NM 87827; (505) 250-8553; coonridge.com.* Their herd produces organic goat cheese in plain and herb-studded flavors, set with old methods that rely on the heat of the milk when harvested and natural rennet. You can buy the cheese in jars with oil—they keep at room temperature and are the perfect picnic basket stuffer.

only to pick up some bread. They'll do cakes and sweets to order for your special event—what a wonderful way to buy local instead of picking up something from the big grocery store!

Limonata, 3222 Silver Ave. SE, Nob Hill, Albuquerque, NM 87106; Coffee/Cafe. Formerly a Cafe Giuseppe (p. 131) location, this spot changed ownership just as this book went to press—but the owners are from local Italian favorite Torino's @ Home (p. 216) and know how to do great espresso, so I have no worries. Gelato might also be in the works, but time will tell. Operating hours are to include breakfast and lunch Tues through Sat. Stop by to see what fantastic things they've added to the Nob Hill scene!

Michael Thomas Coffee Roasters, 1111 Carlisle Blvd. SE, Southeast, Albuquerque, NM 87106; (505) 255-3330; michael thomascoffee.com; Coffee. Two guys start a coffee roasting shop. Their names are Michael and Thomas. Here we are, tucked in near the Ridgecrest neighborhood with a friendly seating area and regulars chatting it up over their big mugs of joe. The aromatic shop has been open for nearly a decade—longer than most people's experience with that big green coffee chain. Completing the nibble fest are pastries brought over from bakers that know their stuff—I've seen goodies from one of Santa Fe's favorite spots as well as one or two Albuquerque French shops.

Moon's Coffee & Tea, 1605 Juan Tabo Blvd. NE, Suite F, Northeast Heights, Albuquerque, NM 87112; (505) 271-2633; thuntek.net/coffeemoons/moonsite.html; Coffee/Tea. Reminiscent of her tide-creating namesake, Moon runs her business like a benevolent rock. Her smile is infectious, though you'll be smiling already when the cloud of roasted-coffee-bean nectar hits your nostrils as you walk in the door. Nearly every day she roasts beans to a deep oily sheen on many of the varieties, offers her own custom blend (made on the spot instead of prepackaged), and features my favorite African originals like Kenyan AA and Ethiopian. All this *and* Moon has the best prices in town (and that includes the crappy national-brand stuff at the grocery store). Caffeine bliss, I tell ya, and we haven't even started talking about her 50-plus tea varieties. Just go.

Napoli Coffee, 2839 Carlisle Blvd. NE, Northeast Heights, Albuquerque, NM 87110; (505) 884-5454; napolicoffee.com; Coffee. Mike Halcom started this oasis of java in 2002 among a sea of chain stores and retail blandness in the near Northeast Heights. Immediately customers picked up on the scent of lattes in the air and kept the beverages flowing and the pastries flying out the door. One of the regulars by the name of Elizabeth liked it enough to start working as a barista, proving her mettle after several years—she bought the business in 2009 with her new husband, Aaron (she met him at Napoli, of course). The cafe serves not only pastries but also burritos and a heaping dose of free Wi-Fi.

Saratori's di Tully Italian Pastry Shop, 1425C San Mateo Blvd. NE, Northeast Heights, Albuquerque, NM 87110; (505) 268-2627; Pastries. The Camuglia family of **Tully's Italian Deli & Meats** (p. 166) responded to a vacancy in their building by taking over and creating a real Italian pastry shop, the likes of which I hadn't visited since New York's Little Italy. Their daughters, Sara and Tori, provided the name, and family friend Kathleen Cristiani provides the traditional baked goods. Fig cookies, lemon twists, cannoli, biscotti, pignoli, sesame, Venetian tri-layer cookies—everything an Italian grandmother would smile upon.

Satellite Coffee, 3513 Central Ave. NE, Nob Hill, Albuquerque, NM 87106; (505) 256-0345; satcoffee.com; Coffee. Part of the local enterprise under Michael and Jean Bernstein, who also own **Flying Star Cafes** (see sidebar on p. 150), Satellite Coffee is the caffeine source for all of their retail locations across the state—nearly 20 and counting. While the coffee at Flying Star is a useful addition to a bout of people watching and magazine lounging, the brew there can suffer from factors like brewers that over-extract the deeply roasted beans or low carafe turnover. The coffee at Satellite, on the other hand, seems to be perfect nearly all the time. Buy some beans for yourself—the Night Sky Blend is one of the most beloved— and get a sweet bonus of a cup of coffee on the house. Eastern Albuquerque locations at 2301 Central Ave. SE, Albuquerque, NM 87106, (505) 254-3800; 2201 Louisiana Blvd. NE, Albuquerque, NM 87110, (505) 884-0098; 8405 Montgomery Blvd. NE, Albuquerque, NM 87111, (505) 296-7654; and 1131 University Blvd. NE, Albuquerque, NM 87102, (505) 247-0662. See the website for locations in the rest of Albuquerque and surrounding suburbs.

Sergio's La Dolce Vita, 4300 Lomas Blvd. NE, Northeast Heights, Albuquerque, NM 87110; (505) 232-7023; sergiosladolcevitaitalian bakery.com; Pastries. The year 2006 saw the arrival of this unassuming neighborhood bakery that packed a hefty Italian punch, from breads to cookies and cannoli. Items often disappear early in the day, but those that make it to see another dawn are steeply discounted for the bargain hunters. I've seen debates comparing the cannoli at Sergio's and Saratori's, but your taste buds will have to decide on which pastry reigns supreme. Other nations' goodies appear, like Danishes, éclairs, and even donuts. Me, I'll have the sfogliatelle, thanks.

Talin Market, 88 Louisiana Blvd. SE, Southeast, Albuquerque, NM 87108; (505) 268-0206; talinmarket.com; World Market. Since the day I arrived in Albuquerque, Talin has been the place to find the "weird" stuff—the interesting fishes, the spices with unpronounceable names, the containers of things that look delicious but could be dubious, and fresh produce you never knew existed. Moving from a cramped and kind of dingy space to a brand-new building has done much for Talin's business and allowed them to keep serving both old and new customers. The tea selection warrants its own area, as does the bulk rice and dried noodles. But really, I adore Talin for the thin purple Chinese eggplant and fresh ginger at bargain prices.

Learn to Cook

Annapurna's School of Cooking, 2209 Silver Ave. SE, Albuquerque, NM 87106; (505) 440-9502; chaishoppe.com/cooking-school. If you've smiled in delight through a meal at Annapurna, you might wonder how you can replicate the healthy foods in your own kitchen. Or perhaps you'd like to learn the in-depth theories behind Ayurvedic cooking for your own body—this school can serve both goals. Classes are held on Saturday mornings and are timed to let you absorb some healing knowledge, then get on with your day.

Central New Mexico Community College, Culinary Arts Program, School of Business & Information Technology, Smith Brasher Building, 717 University Blvd. SE, Albuquerque, NM 87106; (505) 224-4349; cnm.edu/depts/bit/programs/handt/culinary. **CNM** is a little powerhouse of a school, churning out cooking talent at a rate that leaves local restaurant owners happy. The program is typically two years and can result in an associate's degree or certifications in baking or food service management, any of which can be applied to four-year programs elsewhere if desired. The head chef, Carmine Russo, has won Chef of the Year from the New Mexico Restaurant Association for his contributions. He is proud of every student who comes out of the program, a good number of whom end up at high-end spots all over the country.

DINE WITH THE NEXT ALBUQUERQUE TOP CHEFS: CNM's CULINARY CAFE

A good number of lauded chefs around town actually were trained here, at the well-regarded **CNM Culinary Arts Program**. For a year or two, students are put through the wringer with safety training, knife skills, basic preparations, and culinary theory. Each year the end of the semester marks an opportunity for graduating students to bring together everything they know and put on their best performance for a modestly paying audience: you!

CNM has a periodic "Global Cafe," usually on a few weekends each spring and fall, where the public can reserve a spot at the table and have culinary students prepare a full meal for about $10 to $15. What a bargain! I tasted my first vichyssoise soup at one of these events many years ago, and it was a wonderful opportunity to sample gourmet food at bargain prices. At the meal's end you'll also get to give feedback on all aspects of the experience, from cooking and plating to the service (the waitstaff are hospitality students). You'll get a warm and fuzzy feeling from helping to bring a new crop of chefs into the restaurant world.

For general info, see CNM's program web page: cnm.edu/depts/bit/programs/handt/culinary. For direct inquiries, e-mail Carmine Russo: crusso@cnm.edu.

Rio Grande Corridor & the West Side

Rio Rancho, South Valley, Belen, Los Lunas, North Valley, Los Ranchos, Corrales & Bernalillo

To residents of Albuquerque from downtown to the Northeast Heights, the West Side seems so very far away. Residents of the West Side, however, have a pragmatic worldview—everything they need is nearby (especially restaurants of every variety), and the times they want to go eastward are not that big of a deal. Eating on the West Side is a cornucopia of New Mexican, Asian, and American in equal measure, with slightly more emphasis on Italian and pizza than the rest of the city. Foodies should not be deterred—the best Indian cuisine in the metro area can be found in Rio Rancho, as well as great sushi and more than enough wonderful mom-and-pop places. The North Valley is a culinary darling, with its river proximity fostering farm-to-table enterprises and high-end eateries supported by sprawling estates and the finances they represent.

For our purposes, the region's boundaries are I-25 on the east and Unser Boulevard on the west. Starting from downtown, the North Valley occupies the swath between the freeway and the river, northward through Los Ranchos, until the city runs out at the junction of Roy Avenue and Fourth Street. To the south of downtown, the South Valley begins around Bridge Boulevard and travels south until Broadway intersects I-25. Pockets of interest to the south of Albuquerque include the towns of Los Lunas and Belen (10 and 20 miles south, respectively).

On the other side of the Rio Grande, the West Side region stretches northward along the artery of Coors Boulevard through Taylor Ranch, Eagle Ranch, and Paradise Hills toward the town of Rio Rancho and the village of Corrales to Rio Rancho's east. Even further north is the town of Bernalillo, and that's where we'll call a rough northern boundary.

Rio Rancho, a 1961 development pitched and sold initially to New Yorkers (part of the reason pizza is a big deal), incorporated as a city in 1981. That same year Intel broke ground and transformed the future of the formerly small enclave. By 2010 the population was nearly 90,000, or 10 percent of the metro area and nearly the size of Santa Fe.

Bambino's Pizza, 3301 Southern Blvd. SE, Rio Rancho, NM 87124; (505) 896-7916; Pizza; $. Rio Rancho has an interesting affair with New York pizza; its original Big Apple residents have cultivated more "by the slice" places than the rest of the metro area. Some come and go, but Bambino's has a lot of fans who are doing their best to keep the slices flying. It occupies the same space as two previous slice joints, and through the magic of ownership negotiations and name changes, the pizza formula is nearly the same as the last (and loved) iteration. What that means is you'll get big foldable wedges of cheesy love for a pittance, and little else mars the menu. OK, maybe a sandwich or two, and occasional desserts in the chilled case. But those slices—you pick them up by lifting up the edges of the wide crust and letting it fold, keeping the point from drooping too far. Eat greedily, without a fork, and consider any cheese burns your badge for enjoying the pizza at its freshest.

Corn Maiden at the Hyatt Tamaya, 1300 Tuyuna Trail, Bernalillo, NM 87004; (505) 771-6037; tamaya.hyatt.com; Steaks/ Eclectic; $$$$. The drive to this destination restaurant is just as lovely as the food is delicious. Tucked deep into a resort property that features horseback riding and mountain views, the Corn Maiden oozes special-occasion warmth. Even the servers seem genuinely happy you made the trip, on top of their calm competence. Any of the red meat starters are wonderful, whether it's buffalo carpaccio or lamb skewers; a poultry pocket that unites chicken, brie, and caramelized pears seems too rustic for this place but is tasty nonetheless. Rotisserie is the draw: About $50 will net you three portioned proteins plus salad, au gratin potatoes, and veggies. The Classic is everyone's favorite, with local beef, chile chicken, and spicy chorizo sausage. Even desserts are artful and sized to not overwhelm, making the Corn Maiden the place I'd send anyone with the desire for decadence.

Ezra's Place, 6132 Fourth St. NW, North Valley, Albuquerque, NM 87107; (505) 344-1917; Cafe/Eclectic; $$. In the space that used to house Sadie's, one of Albuquerque's most loved New Mexican cafes, the cooking of Dennis Apodaca sets the tone for the most gourmet meal you'll have while watching pins fall. You see, this is a bowling alley. Inside the Lucky 66 Bowl is a raised dining area, bar, and kitchen where some of the most wildly lauded food in town is being crafted. Ezra's takes **Sophia's Place** (Dennis's first restaurant, just up the street; see p. 212) and one-ups everything—more space, wider menu, cocktails. The fried calamari never leaves the menu, for good reason: It's a whole plate of perfectly crunchy squidful bits. Many people come for the duck; Dennis makes his own duck confit and uses it in tacos, enchiladas, and even full entrees. Weekend brunches tend to get busy, but how many restaurants do you know that make their own butter for the pancakes?

Farm & Table, 8917 Fourth St. NW, North Valley, Albuquerque, NM 87114; (505) 503-7124; farmandtablenm.com; Organic/Local/ Modern; $$$. Every year in every city there are a few "it" restaurants, and 2012 could be the year of Farm & Table. March was the opening, but an early menu induced drools and a deafening buzz before the doors swung open. To every foodie's relief, the place seemed to flow with graceful efficiency from day one. The goal is to serve up-to-the-minute cuisine using local produce from their own fields as well as area farmers—a long-term endeavor that will be fun to watch take root. So here's the gist on the food: It is really good modern cafe fare—seared duck breast, quinoa and roasted veg, grass-fed burgers, pork belly. Brunch is a luxurious affair where the coffee flows freely and the blue corn porridge is strange and comforting. The food's execution alone is operating above the price point, but with the excellent service and local and sustainable ingredients, this place is a feather in Albuquerque's cap.

Federico's, 1590 Deborah Rd. SE, Rio Rancho, NM 87124; (505) 891-7214; federicosmexicanfood.com; Mexican; $. Rare is the restaurant open 24 hours in Albuquerque—this alone makes Federico's stand above the crowd. But even if you never have the burning desire for a burrito at 4 a.m., you can rest assured that the quality of all of Federico's food passes muster at any hour of the day. Let's talk about those burritos: Thin and tough tortillas big enough for a newborn are swaddled around dozens of possible fillings. The tried-and-true breakfast combination of stewed meat (*machaca*) and eggs is probably enough calories for a whole day, but who's counting?

Weekends are enhanced by *menudo* for those morning-after kind of recoveries. For any meal, you can order based on cravings and customize like crazy—I've invented strange burritos after workouts, and Federico's is happy to play along. Also around town for your 24-hour needs: 1109 Juan Tabo Blvd. NE, Northeast Heights, Albuquerque, NM 87112, (505) 271-6499; 5555 Zuni Rd. SE, Southeast, Albuquerque, NM 87108, (505) 255-1094; and 640 Coors Blvd. NW, West Side, Albuquerque, NM 87121, (505) 352-2120.

Green House Bistro & Bakery, 3216 NM 47, Los Lunas, NM 87031; (505) 866-1936; nmagelessliving.com; Cafe/Healthy; $$. This is a restaurant-within-a-place, a destination for conscientious and supported living at any age. OK, I'll play it straight: The Center for Ageless Living is an assisted-living community with a mission of joyful residence and one heck of a fantastic restaurant. Visiting is like strolling a campus where the dining hall is a cozy little European bistro. The menu changes every season and tends to focus on a country's delicacies. Germany brings sultry spaetzle and braised cabbage, while France treats the diner to French onion soup and beef bourguignonne. Chef Ann Sesler creates these menus to connect residents and visitors to the changing seasons while keeping her own creativity piqued. Vegetables grown in the center's garden are used when possible, and when leaving you might feel a couple of clicks on the calendar "lighter."

Underground Dining Clubs

What happens when you have friends who say to you, "You're such a great cook, you should open a restaurant!"? Often the realities of owning a restaurant and making it profitable are way beyond the scope of a normal person's ability to handle stress, so you just keep having dinner parties, wondering "what if?" Then you realize you could keep having those get-togethers, with even more people than usual, even inviting strangers. And you could charge them. Brilliant! Congratulations, you've just started your own private underground restaurant.

In many cities this is a big counterculture—finding the best under-the-table groups and getting on the right mailing lists is almost sport. Albuquerque is just getting into the groove with these nifty social and culinary events. Some pop in and then are gone again. I belonged to one such group that was hosted by a well-known and beloved local chef while she was between restaurants—it seems that people who cook rarely stop, even if not formally employed.

Just a couple of semipublic dining groups can be found in 2012—the not-so-public ones obviously require more digging and/

Harla Mays Fat Boy Grill, 710 Dalies Ave., Belen, NM 87002; (505) 864-2211; harlamays.com; Burgers/Diner; $. Almost worthy of "landmark" status, Harla Mays achieves a balance of great ambiance with tasty food in a converted movie theater. Small-town Belen's Onate Theater opened in the 1930s and operated for several decades before closure and rapid disrepair. The early '90s would have seen

or schmoozing with the folks you meet in the dining scene. In fact, one of the best reasons to join up with these groups is to get to talk "foodie" with everyone and do culinary networking. Here are the two known groups' details and how to find them:

Speakeasy Culinary Club, *speakeasyculinaryclub.com.* Taking from the 1920s speakeasy feel, this group meets about every month for an evening of food and entertainment, from theater groups to salsa lessons, so the meal is not the only item on the agenda. It is recommended for couples bored with normal date night or foodies of all kinds. You can even host an event of your own—just e-mail them with your ideas.

Under the Table—A Culinary Speakeasy, *(505) 620-9555 (or search for them on Facebook).* This group's hostess is nicknamed "Sam Hammich" and is a local chef turned underground cook on the side. Because the group is all about the food, no entertainers are on hand to take away from the plating and execution of Sam's dishes—that's a good thing.

the building torn down were it not for Anthony Baca and his dream of a restaurant. It took a long 10 years to renovate, and the cafe opened in 2004 with pop-culture and movie bric-a-brac adorning the tin and wooden walls. A few token theater seats have been left, as has the screen, now used to project sporting events on weekends rather than films. This menu is all diner, from the dozen burger creations to deep-fried appetizers and thick shakes. A favorite starter is battered green chile strips—a wonderful change of pace from french fries! Get the restaurant's signature burger, the Fat Boy, if you can handle the implications of eating this too often. Two half-pound patties, onion rings, chile, and bacon—yowza. I love the flavors in the Holley's Hawaiian burger—green chile, pineapple, and bacon—but I think it would be even more uniquely Hawaiian with Spam instead of the bacon.

Indigo Crow Cafe, 4515 Corrales Rd., Corrales, NM 87048; (505) 898-7000; indigocrowcafe.com; American/Cafe; $$$. Along the winding Corrales Road, a little bird will appear—the sign of the crow in front of this iconic cafe. Before frou-frou dining took hold in Albuquerque in the last decade, Indigo Crow was a little haven of culinary prowess. The current chef has kept many of the starter standards the regulars love: crab cakes, baked brie, and a riff on Cobb salad with spicy Louie dressing. Steaks and chops are there to appease the must-have-red-meat folks, but there are other delights in store. Most eclectic is the lobster ravioli, an open-faced mess that makes you wonder if it was too difficult to get the lobster inside a pasta pocket. Then you take a bite, and another, swirling up the creamy cheese sauce with pieces of fresh pasta, and sing the praises of open-faced ravioli.

Lumpy's Burgers, 5420 W. Central Ave., West Side, Albuquerque, NM 87105; (505) 833-1300; lumpysburgers.com; Burgers; $. The real estate bust of the last several years left more than a few agents high and dry and wondering about their futures. Jay Kennedy and Jason Mancini were feeling that uncertainty when they jumped on a run-down property on their list to have a go at a recession-proof business: a burger joint. Lumpy's opened in 2010 with only a walk-up window, buckets of potatoes outside, and paper bags to write down your order. Select your burger size (umpy, lumpy, plumpy) and toppings; if you want fries, put a potato (sweet or russet) in the sack and hand it through the window. Gimmicky, but infectious. Your fries are sliced—skrewy-cut is best—and dropped in the oil and the burger is assembled while you pay. Minutes later you'll hear your name and get your food in the same sack. Eat on a picnic table or on your cushy car seat and enjoy the ambiance of happy folks chowing down. The freshness won many fans (whose only grumbles were about undercooked fries—easy to do with fresh potatoes), and a second location followed where Jay and Jason can proudly say, "Now with a roof!" It is located at 10131 Coors Rd. NW, Albuquerque, NM; 87114; (505) 899-0122.

Murphy's Mule Barn, 9700 Second St. NW, North Valley, Albuquerque, NM 87114; (505) 898-7660; Diner; $. When you are in the North Valley and looking for a place that doesn't mind a leisurely visit, sipping constantly refilled coffee and reading the morning paper, Murphy's is your place. In a way, it is kind of like this area's **Mannies** (see p. 155), but even more timeworn by the legions of diners that troop their way in and out every morning. Ample counter space sports the lineup of blue-collar workers having simple egg and hash brown breakfasts, making calls to their day's clients or daydreaming for the last spell before they head to work. Waitstaff patrol the room, coffee carafe in each hand, and the hash brown masters in the kitchen work their magic with the daily specials. Bump up the ticket price just a bit as you pay at the front counter—homemade cookies in plastic baggies are tempting and worthwhile.

Namaste Cuisine of India & Nepal, 1520 Deborah Rd. NE, Rio Rancho, NM 87124; (505) 896-3126; namastenm.com; Indian; $$. There is pretty good Indian food to be found in this county, but let's cut to the chase: Namaste is something special. Even their lunch buffet shows off gleaming hot food with specials like goat and fried spinach leaves, so I am torn between sampling from that spread or just ordering one or two dishes. Start with the best chai in town—neither wimpy nor sweet, it can be sugared up to your taste but floats on its own heady aromas. Because everything on the menu is delightful, my recommendation is to push your boundaries: Order something strange and new, and let the kitchen do its magic. Dark-meat chicken tandoori is broiled over mesquite, and the fiery red goat curry is rich and flavorful from cooking the meat right on the chopped-up bones. You can even try out a new dessert—Namaste does their own version of "carrot cake," *halwa*-style as a butter-and-milk-thickened pile of tender shredded carrot, with nuts for crunch. Decadent but gluten-free, this is a brilliant way to enjoy carrots.

Nicky V's Neighborhood Pizzeria, 9780 Coors Blvd., West Side, Albuquerque, NM 87114; (505) 890-9463; nickyvs.com; Pizza/Italian; $$. Nicole Villareal used to be a contractor (and a darn good one), but in 2010 she and her husband, Greg, found themselves at the receiving end of a sales pitch to take over an empty restaurant space. Apparently someone heard they loved pizza and had traveled in Italy, and Nicky V's was born scant months later. Local ingredients, a limited menu, and well-honed techniques are what made the place immediately besieged by every foodie in town. Soon everyone knew that the Margherita pizza was the real deal, with thin blistered crust and fresh mozzarella, basil, and tomatoes. The delicate crusts can't hold oodles of toppings, so even the local favorite New Mexican gets a light application of both pepperoni and green chile, and those powerful flavors sing together with crunchy garlic on top. Fried ravioli calls out to the St. Louis natives, and even frou-frou salad fans can scarf down a composed beauty with dates, arugula, radicchio, pecans, and Manchego cheese.

Oasis Coffee & Tea, 4940 Corrales Rd., #400, Corrales, NM 87048; (505) 792-4720; oasiscorrales.com; Cafe/Eclectic; $. When you walk into Oasis, you might think the whole premise too crafted: Fountains trickle, pastries and tea displays are surrounded by more potted plants than the nursery down the road. But stick around—you'll find the true nature of this place soon enough. A menu overhaul in early 2012 from simply executed sandwiches and salads (and molten chocolate cake) has led them to a more gourmet stratosphere. This direction had been contemplated for some time, with tasting dinners and special-occasion menus, but now it's time for Oasis to add itself to the culinary map of the North Valley. Hoorah! For the record, once the greenery stops looking so darn weird, it really is relaxing. Sit back and enjoy the fountains and the guitarist in the corner.

Prime, 6855 Fourth St. NW, Los Ranchos, NM 87107; (505) 890-9150; cutofprime.com; Deli/Sandwiches; $$. The folks at **Vernon's Hidden Valley Steakhouse** (p. 218) were getting requests for their steaks—where did they come from, and how can I buy that meat for home? When the next-door restaurant closed up, Vernon's seized the opportunity and opened up Prime to serve lighter lunches and offer a full deli/butcher service to those inquiring customers. As a sandwich shop, it is good, if a bit pricey, with hoagie-stuffed favorites like meatballs or shaved prime rib, but the meat/cheese/wine shop is also worth a trip. Take home an aged New York strip for a little more than half what you'd pay at Vernon's, or stock up on cheeses like Maytag blue to crumble over that steak. Finished meats make your work even less aggravating—buy braised lamb shanks with the juicy cooking liquid included. It remains to be seen how many customers will come for the hearty sandwiches versus how many for the meats, but it is a nice option for the home gourmet chef.

Pupuseria el Salvadoreño, 1701 Bridge Blvd. SW, South Valley, Albuquerque, NM 87105; (505) 243-8194; Central American; $. Excited fervor only begins to describe my mood when I drag friends and strangers alike to this temple of freshly cooked masa. *Pupusas* are like really thick corn tortillas with a filling—a big savory Mexican Pop-Tart, sort of. El Salvador claims these as their favorite street food; there frankly are not nearly enough *pupuserias* in this country. A racquetball-size ball of masa is shaped around beans, cheese, meat, or herbs, then pressed flat and griddled until the masa is cooked. They're served hot with pickled spicy cabbage, called *curtido,* and you hit them with hot sauce and devour. Filling, inexpensive, and oh-so-delicious. Try the *loroco* filling of cheese and flower blossoms to have your mind blown, or even go off the *pupusa* path to order tender roasted chicken or fluffy Salvadoran tamales with chicken and olives. The regular corn tortillas are amazing, but for some reason I've never ordered them to go—I guess I like coming back. Their newer outpost is at 2025 Ridgecrest Dr. SE, Albuquerque, NM 87108; (505) 268-0136.

Range Cafe, 925 S. Camino del Pueblo, Bernalillo, NM 87004; (505) 867-1700; rangecafe.com; New Mexican/Cafe; $$. This spot is beloved by both new residents and locals who can't seem to shake the good feeling they get when dining at Matt DiGregory's homage to

New Mexican cuisine. It is the kind of place that would be lauded in every small town in the country, if chile were as pervasive in Idaho as it is here. A festive entry area festooned with an old stove now covered in local business cards guides you to the bustling dining room; hot coffee is on the way to your morning brain in bright mugs. Lauded breakfast dishes include a riff on eggs Benedict that drenches the plate in *chile con queso* instead of hollandaise. Green chile cheeseburgers start the lunch menu, but things don't end until you have blue corn chiles rellenos or Tom's (legendary) meat loaf. Finish with one of the best desserts in town, called Death by Lemon, with lemon curd and shortbread. Other locations: 2200 Menaul Blvd. NE, #A, Albuquerque, NM 87107, (505) 888-1660; and 4401 Wyoming Blvd. NE, #1, Albuquerque, NM 87109, (505) 293-2633.

Sophia's Place, 6313 Fourth St. NW, Los Ranchos, NM 87107; (505) 345-3935; Eclectic/Cafe; $$. Many picky foodies have a place or two that they hold in the confines of their heart, a place that, if they didn't have this "burden" of needing to try every new chef and every interesting dive, they would be a regular—a real regular of the several-times-a-week variety. Near the top of my short list is Sophia's Place. Dennis Apodaca ran a local burrito chain out of this tiny building before turning it into the cafe named for his daughter. He served the food he liked, which happened to be pancakes, tacos, salads, and big noodle bowls. The strange montage combined with Dennis's cooking skills means that everyone is happy here, all 10 tables in the crowded space. It's hard to get a good read on Dennis: He can seem brusque, but he genuinely loves his work and is likely in the zone while he's working. And work he does—wonderful steak *huevos rancheros,* wild mushroom enchiladas, fish tacos, and coffee oh-so-black and doused with half-and-half. It's a dream of a place, breakfast and lunch. A slight menu refinement and expanded room can be found down the street at **Ezra's Place** (p. 201), Dennis's second restaurant.

Stufy's Takeout, 6100 Coors Blvd. NW, West Side, Albuquerque, NM 87120; (505) 890-7778; stufys.com; Fast Food/New Mexican; $. One of my favorite dishes before fried food started catching up to my belt notches was a pillow of dough, crispy-fried and stuffed with New Mexican goodies: the stuffed sopaipilla. I ate them all over town, comparing and contesting, but then I discovered that if there was a best gourmet version, there also had to be a best "dive" version, and that can be found at Stufy's. The premise is simple: just like a burger joint, only you get smallish stuffed sopaipillas for an affordable price. If they were open 24 hours, this would be the best late-night food ever. And behold, this place doesn't just give its customers bean or meat options—you can get breakfast sopaipillas! What a fantastic idea and a great alternative to the drive-thru "mick muffin" thing or breakfast burrito. Belt notch or not, I'm getting nostalgic. Over the years a few of the Stufy's closed, but two still remain—check out this little treasure of inventive greasy spoon, also at 1107 Candelaria Rd. NW, Albuquerque, NM 87107; (505) 344-1207.

EATING WHILE EXPOSED:
PATIOS & GREAT VIEWS

Who doesn't love a warm afternoon or evening when the sun is staying in the sky for reasonably long hours, sitting on a patio with a cool drink in hand and hot food on the way? Following is a nice selection of spots all over the Albuquerque area that offer al fresco dining, whether it's just a few sidewalk tables or a full-blown rooftop respite:

Apothecary Lounge, *Hotel Parq Central, 806 E. Central Ave., Albuquerque, NM 87102; (505) 242-0040; hotelparqcentral.com* (rooftop dining) (p. 280)

Bailey's on the Beach, *2929 Monte Vista Blvd. NE, Nob Hill, Albuquerque, NM 87106; (505) 717-2880; baileysonthebeach.com* (also has rooftop dining) (p. 137)

Cafe Lush, *700 Tijeras Ave. NW, Downtown, Albuquerque, NM 87102; (505) 508-0164; cafelushabq.com* (p. 107)

The Daily Grind, *414 E. Central Ave., EDo, Albuquerque, NM 87102; (505) 883-8310; dailygrindabq.com* (p. 110)

El Patio, *142 Harvard Dr. SE, UNM, Albuquerque, NM 87106; (505) 268-4245; elpatiodealbuquerque.com* (p. 184)

El Pinto, *10500 Fourth St. NW, North Valley, Albuquerque, NM 87114; (505) 898-1771; elpinto.com* (p. 227)

Flying Star Cafes, *locations all over town, flyingstarcafe.com* (pp. 134, 150)

Gecko's Bar & Tapas, 3500 E. Central Ave., Nob Hill, Albuquerque, NM 87106; 5801 Academy Rd. NE, Albuquerque, NM 87109; (505) 821-8291; geckosbar.com (p. 146)

Gold Street Caffe, 218 Gold Ave. SW, Albuquerque, NM 87102; (505) 765-1633; goldstreetcaffe.com (p. 112)

Greenside Cafe, 12165 N. NM 14, Cedar Crest, NM 87008; (505) 286-2684; greensidecafe.net (p. 146)

The Grove Cafe & Market, 600 E. Central Ave., Ste. A, EDo, Albuquerque, NM 87102; (505) 248-9800; thegrovecafemarket.com (p. 113)

Holy Cow, 700 E. Central Ave., EDo, Albuquerque, NM 87102; (505) 242-2991 (p. 113)

Mannies Family Restaurant, 2900 E. Central Ave., Nob Hill, Albuquerque, NM 87106; (505) 265-1669; manniesnobhill.com (p. 155)

Sandiago's Mexican Grill at the Tram, 38 Tramway Loop NE, Albuquerque, NM 87122; (505) 856-6692; sandiapeakrestaurants.com

Seasons Rotisserie & Grill, 2031 Mountain Rd. NW, Old Town, Albuquerque, NM 87104; (505) 766-5100; seasonsabq.com (also has rooftop dining) (p. 126)

Sophia's Place, 6313 Fourth St. NW, Los Ranchos, NM 87107; (505) 345-3935 (p. 212)

Thai Cuisine, 6200 Coors Blvd. NW, West Side, Albuquerque, NM 87120; (505) 890-3406; thaicuisinenm.com; Thai; $. **Each Thai restaurant in town does dishes just a tiny bit differently, whether that's their coconut curry soup or their papaya salad—I love the variety and finding out whose flavors are balanced and whose are tilted toward either end of the sweet/salty/sour/bitter axis. Thai Cuisine has given me two salads that tilt way over in one direction, but it is my favorite direction—sour. You could be gentler and call it "tangy," for the lime juice and slight fermentation of the fish sauce are delightful to my taste buds. I tend to order them "Thai hot," fully expecting to break a sweat. New patrons to any Thai restaurant should order conservatively until you know each kitchen's tendencies with chile application—this is your only warning. Beyond cool foods, the soups here are also lovely, with potent lemongrass and galangal warming up the broth. Daily lunch specials draw in oodles of college students and office workers alike for a four-component meal: soup, entree, rice, and dessert. Bargains like that are getting harder to find, but Thai Cuisine's second location makes it easier: 4201 E. Central Ave., Nob Hill, Albuquerque, NM 87108; (505) 232-3200.**

Torino's @ Home, 7600 Jefferson St. NE, #21, North Valley, Albuquerque, NM 87109; (505) 797-4491; torinosfoods.com; Italian; $$$. If this guide were to have top 10 lists, Torino's would sail in easily. Originally started in Santa Fe by enterprising catering artists Maxime and Daniela Bouneou, they built up a reputation for exquisite traditional Italian fare cooked with exuberance and love. Then they pulled up stakes and moved the whole business one city to the south: Santa Fe cried, Albuquerque rejoiced. How could you turn down an entree of braised brisket over polenta, or fresh pillowy gnocchi sauced in creamy Gorgonzola, or even their famous duck confit salad that balances the rich meat with tart vinaigrette? This menu has no duds or filler: No matter what speaks to your taste buds, every last thing is probably going to be the best example of the dish you've ever had, right down to the rough-looking tiramisu. Understandably busy after two four-star reviews and gushing accolades from critics and diners, Torino's packs in customers for breakfast, lunch, and weekend dinners. Yet Daniela's smile never fades, even when tsk-tsking a server for not bringing out a parting gift of truffles with your check.

Turtle Mountain Brewing Company, 905 36th Place SE, #C, Rio Rancho, NM 87124; (505) 994-9497; turtlemountainbrewing.com; Pub/Eclectic; $$. Having just crossed the lucky 13th anniversary, this temple to suds and grub is right where it wants to be. Just spot Nico Ortiz, the owner: He seems to always have a smile on his face, pleased that the place named after the Tewa Indian name for Sandia Peak (also his father's Tewa name) is making people happy. Turtle Mountain serves pub food for the foodie crowd—nothing that serves as mere filler for the alcohol. The appetizers are distracting:

handmade pretzels with *queso,* potato skins like you've only dreamed of, wings cooked in beer with habanero stout sauce. Bring a crowd so that you'll have room for the best pizza on the menu, the Adam Bomb, with pepperoni, sausage, chile, spinach, and pine nuts. I could go on, but you see the problem: Turtle Mountain's entire menu is mouth-watering. Commit to a few visits to do a proper tasting tour, and see to all of those craft beers on hand, too.

Vernon's Hidden Valley Steakhouse, 6855 Fourth St. NW, Los Ranchos, NM 87107; (505) 341-0831; yougotta password.com; Steak; $$$$. From day one the way to get into Vernon's was to meander through a wine-selling store-front, then make your way to the back wall and knock on the door. A slide opens and you giggle a little before blurting out the password  (given when you made the reservation), and then your night begins. A darkened room with plush seating near the bar, a piano, and jet-black walls set the tone, but it is the food that will have to stand up to all the fuss. For the most part it does—from perfectly seared steaks and local prime rib to delights like a poached lobster salad or blue crab cake starters. This is a splurge, so plan accordingly, then sit back and enjoy.

Village Pizza, 4266 Corrales Rd., Corrales, NM 87048; (505) 898-0045; villagepizzacorrales.com; Pizza; $. I'll admit it: Village Pizza was one of my first favorite places around town. I lived nearby and was on a bit of a budget; here was a comfortable spot with an all-you-can-eat buffet of handmade pizza—how could one go wrong? Thankfully, the place still holds up, even though the restaurant scene has changed over the years. The back patio is the best place to eat in warm temperatures, with shade trees and lots of local chatter from regulars. The buffet's still available during lunch and Monday and Tuesday evenings, but ordering your own pizza works just fine; their crust is medium thick with not much char, but it can hold tons of toppings as required for some of the specialty combinations. You can fold your pizza in half and have a calzone, or just nosh on their salad bar—after a slice of the meat lover's pizza, that might not seem like a bad strategy.

Western View Diner, 6411 W. Central Ave., West Side, Albuquerque, NM 87105; (505) 836-2200; Diner; $. Soft spots in our hearts are reserved for places like Western View—it's out at the edge of nowhere, exactly the place travelers would stop while driving the Route 66 corridor. The freeway has removed all traffic, and the folks who go to Western View love it for all its charms: the staff that serve up coffee with a smile, the kitchen that makes meat loaf like it's going out of style, and the cityscape stretched out to the twinkly east. The food is straightforward—this is a dive, after all—but you never feel for a moment that the milk shake or the mashed potatoes and gravy are second-rate. That's real ice cream, those are perfect hash browns, and the thinly frosted chocolate layer cake was probably made by someone's aunt before getting sliced up in front of your ogling eyes and eager fork.

Landmarks

Casa de Benavidez, 8032 Fourth St. NW, Los Ranchos, NM 87114; (505) 898-3311; casadebenavidez.com; New Mexican; $$. Paul and Rita Benavidez started their little restaurant called El Mexicano about a mile down the road from here more than 50 years ago. Over time they became well known for good home-style food and their famous sopaipilla burger, and in the early 1980s an older location—literally—was found. They moved into a 100-year-old structure composed of cut mud blocks rather than adobe bricks—a true historic landmark. This location allowed patio dining and tons more room inside, so that regulars could keep coming and bring all of their friends for the dining journey. Charred salsa starts each meal, and you'd better get that burger: The juicy patty stacked between flaky sopaipillas is a heavenly combination. While *carne adovada* and green chile enchiladas are always an option, the pork short ribs are highly recommended for their tenderness and spice, even if pricey. The Benavidez menu falls on the slightly higher end of the New Mexican pricing spectrum but still well short of **El Pinto** (p. 227), and with the comfortable patio and view of the Sandias, you could say this is a lovely alternative.

Circle T Drive-In, 523 S. Main St., Belen, NM 87002; (505) 864-4135; fb.me/circletburgers; Burgers; $. It may seem to be just an ordinary or run-down burger joint in a small town, but inside the Circle T is years of history, not to mention years of seasoning on that flattop where green chile cheeseburgers are made every single day. Watch for the big fiberglass teenager icon sign with a red T and a burger in one hand, and you have arrived. Gil Tabet opened the place in 1958 as the nation's love affair with drive-thru burgers was just getting started, and his family still runs it to this day. The basics are all you need: burgers in ⅙-, ¼-, and ½-pound sizes; thin-cut fries like other famous burger joints; and milk shakes made with hard ice cream rather than soft-serve. The green chile added to burgers is flaming hot and the reason why this spot is included on the state's Green Chile Cheeseburger Trail. Add to Circle T's many attractions the fact that this diner destination is the closest restaurant to the Belen Rail Runner train station, and you have a recipe for continued growth and happy commuters.

El Camino Dining Room, 6800 Fourth St. NW, Los Ranchos, NM 87107; (505) 344-0448; New Mexican; $$. The oldest restaurant on Fourth is not the bustling **Sadie's New Mexican** (p. 231), nor that shrine to meat **Mr. Powdrell's Barbeque House** (p. 223), nor even 50-year-old **Casa de Benavidez** (p. 220). Rather, it is a more unobtrusive little hangout called El Camino. Directly out of the '50s—1950 to be exact—El Camino has an original sign out front, one of the most striking and lovely signs in all of Albuquerque. The owners celebrated the 60th anniversary with not much fanfare, but that suits this laid-back neighborhood just fine. The food details are this: The pancakes are diner heaven, and the *huevos rancheros* rise to greatness under spicy green chile and perfectly cooked pinto beans. Burgers pile on the piquant green (chopped or strips, your choice) and fill up the plate with round home fries. I just feel comfortable in this place—the old pueblo style against the diner decor makes for a pleasant getaway lunch.

Grandma Warner's K & I Diner, 2500 Broadway Blvd. SE, South Valley, Albuquerque, NM 87102; (505) 243-1881; Diner; $. Whether you refer to this institution as Grandma Warner's or just the K & I, it does not change the appeal of the timeworn favorite. Start with the decor: The walls are nearly covered in kitchen paraphernalia from decades and generations past—milk bottles, coffee cans, whisks, spoons, all for your eyes to soak up. Speaking of soaking up, I recommend that you base your K & I meal on fluffy carbohydrates, such as the Grandma's Biscuits platter with hash browns, white gravy, and two tender biscuits filled with eggs, cheese, and meat. This is the "mick muffin" of your dreams. When it comes to pancakes, these are nicely hearty with the addition of cornmeal. I often just order one plate-size cake with a side of *carne adovada* to make a bizarre breakfast burrito. In a non-breakfast mood? Make sure you witness the K & I's claim to fame: the Travis. This is a literal food-challenge kind of platter (*Man v. Food* taped a spot here in 2010) wherein a 7-pound burrito is smothered in french fries. It will cost you about $20 if you don't finish it in an hour. Good luck with that.

Monte Carlo Steakhouse, 3916 W. Central Ave., South Valley, Albuquerque, NM 87105; (505) 831-2444; Steaks; $$. Locals love the Monte Carlo because it doesn't flinch at being what it is—a retro/nostalgic steak house fronted by a dive liquor store. Forty years in, business is only picking up, partly thanks to a spot on a national food TV show, but mostly because they serve excellent steaks and prime rib. The second-generation ownership is Greek (a common situation in the Albuquerque restaurant scene), which explains the presence of a Greek appetizer plate on the menu. Enjoy tangy imported feta, peppers, olives, and dolmas. If it is Thursday night, you can move on to the showstopper prime rib special for a slab of warm pink deliciousness with ample horseradish to smear on each bite; by Friday night they might all be gone. All of the steaks are done expertly as well—the doneness you order is the doneness you'll receive, and each steak is cut by hand every day. Other menu items include a green chile cheeseburger and roasted Greek chicken that is great, even when most folks just care about those steaks.

Mr. Powdrell's Barbeque House, 5209 Fourth St. NW, North Valley, Albuquerque, NM 87107; (505) 345-8086; mrpowdrellsbbq .com; Barbecue; $$. **Pete Powdrell brought the most enduring taste of the South to Albuquerque. In the 50 years since Powdrell's opened in a historic house on Fourth Street, barbecue culture has expanded to bring other excellent examples, but for the history behind the smoke ring, go to Powdrell's to start your quest. Cozy barely describes the atmosphere, with built-in china cabinets still in place and dining tables dotted throughout small rooms. Starters include buttered mushrooms and deep-fried chicken wings with genuinely spicy glaze. Don't get too far into noshing before you receive your meat: brisket already fallen apart, glazed ribs in normal pork or Flintstone-size beef, and smoky chicken by the piece or quarter-bird. Even sides are delectable—crunchy fried okra and corn bread served as thick iron-skillet rounds ready for a butter bath. Pete Powdrell is no longer around, but he'd be proud indeed of the devotion his legacy still garners. The still-delicious but way less lovely Southeast location is at 11301 E. Central Ave., Albuquerque, NM 87123; (505) 298-6766.

Perea's Tijuana Bar, 4590 Corrales Rd., Corrales, NM 87048; (505) 898-2442; New Mexican, $$. During Prohibition a honeymooning couple visited a Mexican cantina called the Tijuana Bar, and vowed that their own bar after the silliness of Prohibition would be called just that. Here we are, generations later, and the business is run by T. C. Perea and family members, all happy to cook something you'd have in mom's house. That is, if mom's house was a 200-year-old historic building made from earthen block. In any case, you must have the traditional enchilada plate (complete with fried egg on top), with perfect whole beans and bright red chile with nice medium heat on the tongue. For Santa Fe fare, there is a rather good Frito pie with either ground beef or *carne adovada,* and the *adovada* itself makes a fine plate with more of those beans. And, talk about mom's food—Perea's is one of the few restaurants anywhere that serves enchilada casserole, the staple of home cooks all over the state but rarely seen in professional kitchens. It sings with chicken and green and is truly New Mexico's answer to lasagna. *Molto bueno!*

Pete's Cafe, 105 N. First St., Belen, NM 87002; (505) 864-4811; New Mexican; $$. Several years after the Second World War, Pete Torres and wife Eligia opened a cafe across the street from a recently closed Harvey House restaurant. They succeeded in picking up those existing rail-passenger customers, though restaurants were a new career for them. Over time New Mexican foods were added to the menu, and locals increasingly ate here in addition to the train folks. More than 60 years in, Pete's still draws a good crowd for breakfast and lunch, even if some folks say the quality has slightly declined since Eligia passed away. The rellenos are crispy and breaded rather than battered, giving them resilience against any chile sauce you'd like to drown them in. The red chile here is rustic: Seeds and an unsieved texture mean you experience every bit of the chile pod— this has a wonderful effect when made into *carne adovada*. On the green chile front, it is HOT. Get it on *huevos rancheros* or just a nice bowl with some beans, and the words *"Harvey House"* will fade from your lips.

All Chile, All the Time

El Bruno's Restaurante y Cantina, 8806 Fourth St. NW, North Valley, Albuquerque, NM 87114; (505) 897-0444; elbrunos.com; New Mexican; $$. For many years road-trippers would talk about this amazing place to eat in Cuba, admonishing anyone who would listen that this New Mexican restaurant halfway between Albuquerque and Farmington was fabulous. That place is El Bruno's, and it has its true home in Cuba, NM, but in 2010 Albuquerque was blessed with their first outpost. The preferred chile color here is red, a tempestuous hue with spice in spades. Drench it over enchiladas or a plate of *carne adovada,* or just eat it in a bowl, as I love to do. The sprawling layout of the restaurant makes intimate meals possible in tiny booths or tucked-away tables, and you might want some "alone time" with their guacamole after it's prepared in front of you with only the add-ins you desire. The Herrera family has embraced Albuquerque while keeping the quality up in Cuba—try out both locations and enjoy some of the best New Mexican on the planet.

El Modelo, 1715 Second St. SW, South Valley, Albuquerque, NM 87102; (505) 227-8213; New Mexican; $. Some of us are lucky enough to get our tamales from a family member, but for the rest of us, there's El Modelo. Christmas Eve day is a masa holiday, the day that hundreds of locals head just south of downtown to pick up their order of steamed porky bliss. For weeks the extended family and extra help have been cranking out tamales to fill the orders, but once the holiday is over, the tamale production continues on its normal schedule. The underpriced and oversize hunks are the best in the city (and I hope so—the family has been perfecting the formula since 1929), but you'll still understand those who order burritos or even something with green chile, just for a change of pace. No formal dining area is offered—you'll eat your tamale standing up and be darn happy about it, or have a seat at a picnic table outside. Just one trip and you'll mark your calendar to order tamales in December.

El Pinto, 10500 Fourth St. NW, North Valley, Albuquerque, NM 87114; (505) 898-1771; elpinto.com; New Mexican; $$. No one exists too long in this state without knowing about El Pinto ("the spot")—this is where out-of-town guests are taken and families have reunions. The large interior space doesn't do justice to the two patio areas that can hold hundreds more. This high-volume restaurant started tiny 50 years ago, but brothers Jim and John Thomas took over from their parents in the '90s and made El Pinto a well-oiled machine that serves outstanding New Mexican foods and bottles salsa by the truckload (see sidebar). My recommendations are to skip the buffet and order whatever looks appealing from the menu, and also to ask for the hot salsa at your table—trust me.

El Pinto Salsa & the "Salsa Twins"

Jim and John Thomas are towering powerhouses when it comes to local chile and the flow of chile products in the state and nationwide. How so? They have created a company that started at El Pinto restaurant and became a massive salsa and chile sauce production endeavor, and they do it with single-minded (dual-minded?) vision.

Since the age of three they have adored food and building things. They particularly loved the things that their grandmother cooked from New Mexico traditions, and they use her recipes to this day. Their mother, Consuelo, convinced her husband to give up engineering and open a restaurant in 1962 in Albuquerque's North Valley, calling it "the spot"—El Pinto. When Jim and John were kids there was always stuff to do to help out when they finished school, so they grew up around everything food and restaurant business—it is in their blood. For many years they worked in capacities from dishwasher to landscaping help, until their parents retired and the twin sons took over. Expansion followed, bringing the capacity up to 450 inside and 1,000 when the patios are considered, making El Pinto the largest restaurant in the state.

New Mexican plates are big enough to share (and priced to match, unfortunately), but the enchilada combo plate and the stuffed sopaipillas are not to be missed. Nor is the crazy tasty biscochito-based tiramisu called *levante*. Just thinking about it makes me levitate a little.

In 2000 the bottling enterprise was begun, starting in the restaurant's kitchen with relatively small batches.  Their salsa is delicious, and over the course of several years, supply dwindled in the face of demand. Larger-capacity salsa hardware was clearly required; co-packers were considered and then rejected. The huge packing facility behind the restaurant was completed a few years ago and now makes 2,000 cases per day. That's a lot of capsaicin love. Each variety of salsa and sauce starts with green chiles and adds tomatoes, spices, and jalapeños (if needed for heat), then everything is put together in a machine that you can think of as the "great salsa combobulator," packed into jars, and quick-pasteurized. Flavors range from chipotle salsa to mild green chile sauce to *HOT* enchilada sauce; those heat ratings are for locals—the hot is really, really incendiary.

The reach of the operation is such that El Pinto salsa can be found at the grocery store in my hometown of 5,000—in Wisconsin. That's a fantastic achievement and a wonderful convenience when I visit for the holidays and start craving a bit of New Mexico warmth. Learn more at elpinto.com.

Garcia's Kitchen, 1113 Fourth St. NW, North Valley, Albuquerque, NM 87102; (505) 242-1199; garciaskitchen.com; Mexican/New Mexican; $. Since 1975 Garcia's has been an easy choice when faced with the prospect of breakfast (or lunch) and other nearby options just don't sound appealing. You go to Garcia's to return to the Albuquerque of decades ago, when folks who ate at diners were genial and hardworking and on their short break before heading back to their job. The red chile is flavorful but not too hot, and during the breakfast hours the egg and chile platters are quite tasty. Their food is not what you'd describe as "amazing" or "mind-blowing"—it is simple cafe New Mexican served with efficiency in dining rooms oozing with good cheer and community. And that is what makes a great go-to restaurant. You never have to go far to find one of the seven Garcia's all over town: 6961 Taylor Ranch Rd. NW, #B, Westside, Albuquerque, NM 87120, (505) 899-7960; 1736 W. Central Ave., Downtown, Albuquerque, NM 87104, (505) 842-0273; 4917 Fourth St. NW, North Valley, Albuquerque, NM 87102, (505) 341-4594; 2924 San Mateo Blvd. NE, Northeast Heights, Albuquerque, NM 87123, (505) 888-3488; 8518 Indian School NE, Northeast Heights, Albuquerque, NM 87110, (505) 292-5505; and 3601 Juan Tabo Blvd. NE, Northeast Heights, Albuquerque, NM 87111, (505) 275-5812.

Mary & Tito's Cafe, 2711 Fourth St. NW, North Valley, Albuquerque, NM 87107; (505) 344-6266; maryandtitos.com; New Mexican; $. If you really love red chile, you have only scratched the surface of what is possible until you have had Mary & Tito's red, which tastes of the earth and is like a peppery blanket of fire. With nearly 50 years of restaurant experience, Mary Gonzales still presides over the dining room every day, keeping an eye on regular customers and serving as cashier. Tito has been gone a long time, but diners pay tribute to him every time they order his incomparable food, especially the red chile dishes. The adoration is not heard only by the ears of fans—in 2010 Mary & Tito's was awarded a James Beard Foundation America's Classics honor, for restaurants "with timeless appeal, beloved in their regions." Mary sat down with me for an interview a while back, and not only did I hear stories about the restaurant's beginnings, I heard her verbal recipe for the famous red chile. Hint: It's really, really simple. Other than that, stick your butt on one of her lovely diner seats and order up some *carne adovada* or simply a whole bowl and see what the fuss is about, and tell Mary she's a treasure.

Sadie's New Mexican, 6230 Fourth St. NW, Los Ranchos, NM 87107; (505) 345-5339; sadiesofnewmexico.com; New Mexican; $$. With no disrespect intended, Sadie's is the Cheesecake Factory of Albuquerque. Let me explain. Sadie's is the place that everyone adores on weekend nights, where the service is good, the portions are Americanized, and the wait times are horrific. That being said, if you have to have a vibrating coaster kind of experience, wouldn't you rather have homespun New Mexican rather than big-chain formulated cuisine? Indeed. So, start with the nice and spicy salsa while you read the novel of a menu, or just order what Sadie's does best: enchiladas with whatever meat your heart desires, piled on the plate with beans that should be their own attraction. Only order the Roberto Special if you have a bottomless pit growling away, or a love of leftovers: Its pile of hamburger patty, beans, potatoes, and *queso* is a feat of sloppily delicious New Mexican. While the

Fourth Street location is full of character, it's also a bit louder than the new spot up in the Heights, at 15 Hotel Circle NE, Northeast Heights, Albuquerque, NM 87123; (505) 296-6940.

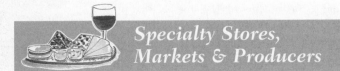

Specialty Stores, Markets & Producers

The Fruit Basket, 6343 Fourth St. NW, Los Ranchos, NM 87107; (505) 344-0885; Grocery. This place stumbled into my awareness one day when I was waiting for a table at **Sophia's Place** (p. 212) and wandering the nearby parking lot. I saw roasted chiles, cantaloupes, and apples, and I walked right in and bought more food than I could eat, but never had a second thought about it. The store employees were happy to be around so much fresh produce, stacking avocados high and scooping roasted chiles into ziplock bags to sell for a few bucks each. It's like a farmers' market but less hipster and available year-round. Delightful! Find them also at 8405 Fourth St. NW, Los Ranchos, NM 87114, (505) 898-7367; and 3821 12th St. NW, Albuquerque, NM 87107, (505) 345-3942.

Joe S. Sausage, 3846 Rio Grande Blvd. NW, North Valley, Albuquerque, NM 87107; (505) 688-0445; joessausage.com; Sausages. There isn't a ton to say about Joe S. Sausage, other than he makes everything from scratch in his tiny little processing facility and wins tons of awards. Varieties include Spicy Southern

Italian with Green Chile, CrazyHott Italian Sausage, Jamaican Jerk Sausage, Garlic Habanero Hot Link, Curry Sausage, Lamb Sausage, Maple Blueberry Sausage, and Hungarian Kolbasz. His website mentions how much he is committed to this craft, giving instructions on how to contact him for a "sausage emergency."

Keller's Farm Stores, 6100 Coors Blvd. NW, #H, West Side, Albuquerque, NM 87120; (505) 898-6121; kellersfarmstores.com; Butcher/Grocery. Walking into a store and taking a number is strange around here—many of us have unpleasant memories of the DMV rather than yummy delis and the like. Grab a number to order from the deli case, from meats to cheeses. My first reason to shop here was the cheese—a great selection at prices that knock most of the highbrow places out of the whey. Meats are a huge draw, from holiday birds and natural meats without hormones (many of these are raised on the family's farm in Colorado) to bacon and sausage cured in-house. The "normal" grocery selection is minimal but will get you by in a pinch, whether you need cream for coffee or pasta to serve with your meat order. One of their best services is assembling complete meals for all of the holiday seasons—no need to spend all day cooking for your guests (or buy a premade meal from a chain) when you can give them something delicious and local. Also serving the east side at 2912 Eubank Blvd. NE, Northeast Heights, Albuquerque, NM 87112; (505) 294-1427.

Pro's Ranch Market, 4201 W. Central Ave., West Side, Albuquerque, NM 87105; (505) 833-1765; prosranch.com; Grocery/ World Market. It took until 2008 for Albuquerque to have the Mexican equivalent of **Talin Market** (p. 195)—Pro's is a huge, boisterous, and friendly market where people from all over town come for the south-of-the-border supplies and the delicious short-order food. Channel your inner Mexican grandma and go to Pro's to get tortillas, canned chipotles, fajita meat, or whole chickens for stewing—whatever strikes your fancy. The produce is insanely cheap (which may unfortunately reflect harvesting conditions; this is worth more research) and stacked up meticulously by the staff. If you don't want to blow your budget, eat at the short-order picnic area before shopping. Feast on tamales, tacos, fresh tortillas, and a nice salsa bar for applying liberal condiments. Finish with a freshly spun smoothie, and now you're ready to get groceries with an unhungry stomach.

St. James Tearoom, 320 Osuna Rd. NE, North Valley, Albuquerque, NM 87107; (505) 242-3752; stjamestearoom.com; Tea. Tea was the perfect antidote to the tech-fueled panic of the end of the millennium: a full English-style tearoom with white gloves and tasty finger-foods and ladies who actually wore hats and lace. St. James Tearoom filled a niche Albuquerque didn't know existed, and owner Mary Alice Higbie, trained in tea protocol and master of Japanese porcelain, has done steady work in the relaxing afternoon business ever since. I visited with girlfriends not long after it opened and marveled at the attention to every detail, from tea-pouring etiquette to the tiered presentation of edibles. A rotating menu features about a dozen small bites, paired with tea in courses. The monthly changeover makes return visits exciting— one month you might have classic miniature beef Wellingtons and cucumber sandwiches, the next your plate has skewered lamb and lime mousse tart. Gender is invisible here: While the proper decor might imply femininity, really what it represents is luxury and relaxation. Feature events are held at intervals to encourage the tea-shy to have a gander—even special evenings with wine from local producers.

Yiayia Maria's, 740 Rankin Rd. NE, North Valley, Albuquerque, NM 87107; (505) 923-3210; yiayiamaria.com; Sweets. Baklava can be a contentious pastry, a minefield of personal interpretations and family recipes. Should the layers be thick or thin? Should there be butter in the honey syrup? Should the dough be made by hand and never, ever bought? These concerns will likely melt away when you taste really great baklava like from Yiayia Maria's, as I did at the local Greek Festival. Until then I hadn't heard of this talented little company, named after the grandmother who provided the recipe over 50 years ago. Now if I have a baklava craving, Yiayia's is handy, making it both delicious and dangerous.

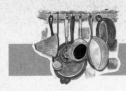

Los Poblanos Historic Inn & Organic Farm, 4803 Rio Grande Blvd. NW, North Valley, Los Ranchos de Albuquerque, NM 87107; (505) 344-9297; lospoblanos.com/events-calendar/cooking-classes. Make no mistake, this is seriously fancy cooking instruction, but the guidance is given by Jonathan Perno, one of the best and most experienced chefs in town. Drawing on his experience from many high-end establishments, he shows small groups how to do essential techniques, like break down and prepare a whole chicken, or how to make basic sauces. Take several of his classes, and your next dinner party will be an event to remember.

Southwest Cooking with Jane Butel, PO Box 2162, Corrales, NM 87048; (505) 243-2622; info@janebutelcooking.com; janebutel.com. Jane is a long-avowed cook and local fixture in the cooking education arena. She's published fantastic books over the last half century; a recent favorite of mine is 2006's *Real Women Eat Chiles*. Her classes are held in her own kitchen in the village of Corrales, as well as all over the city for weekend events or group demonstrations. It seems pretty solid to trust a woman who has been working with New Mexican cuisine for nearly six decades.

Taos

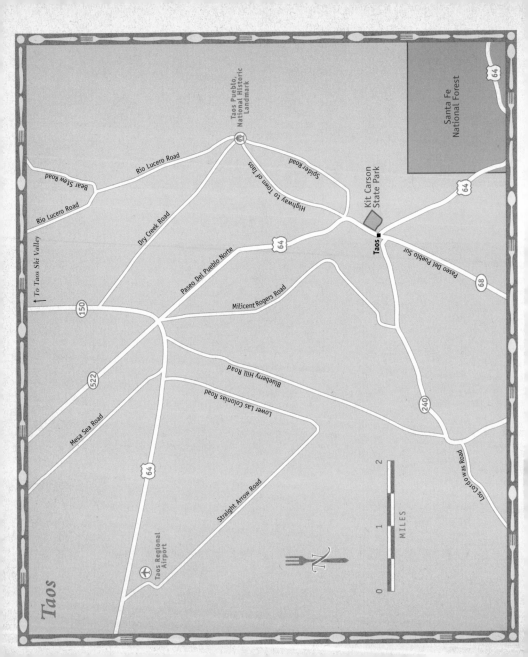

Taos

Preconceived notions abound when it comes to Taos: It's isolated and proud, the altitude makes for chilly weather, there's not a lot to do but see galleries or go skiing, it's a bastion of New Agers and crunchy types, the light shimmers and there is a hum. All of these are true—mostly. The small-town feel and relatively affordable real estate, coupled with a world-class ski resort, make Taos a city that is teeming with artists and creative types and an economy greatly assisted by tourist expenditures, both on the skiing and the gourmet food. The light is frankly stunning and something you have to see, whether it's a view of town from the southern approach or the Taos Gorge Bridge over the Rio Grande about 10 miles west of town. As to the "Taos hum," well . . . it might depend on how strong your coffee was in the morning.

This proud enclave of fewer than 10,000 residents has a rich state history due to location and the presence of several Native tribes. Some recent history centers around Christopher "Kit" Carson. It was Colonel Carson who resettled thousands of Native Americans to southeastern New Mexico, fed them military rations, and inadvertently contributed to the invention of fry bread—a distinction in the food world, even if a dubious one. The park that bears his name is a nice stroll between visits to galleries or the delicious cafes that are strewn all over town. Taos doesn't have a particular dish or food they call their own, but that doesn't stop the progress of creative chefs and bakers, all fighting to make sure their food tastes good at 8,000 feet.

Getting Around

Taos is approximately 90 minutes from Santa Fe, through the towns of Pojoaque and Española on NM 68. After following the Rio Grande for a while, you'll pop out onto the sweeping plain that contains the whole of the county and the base of the towering Wheeler Peak mountain group.

Getting around Taos is simple—the main artery is called Paseo del Pueblo, with "Norte" and "Sur" designating the north and south sides of town. Most attractions are along this street or just a few blocks away. North of town about 8 miles on NM 150 is the hamlet of Arroyo Seco (home to Taos Cow); another 10 miles to the end of the same highway is the Taos Ski Valley and a few notable dining destinations.

Foodie Faves

Antonio's, 122 Dona Luz St., Taos, NM 87571; (575) 751-4800; antoniosoftaos.com; Mexican; $$. Just off the Plaza you'll find a few delicious spots that do quite well without serving New Mexican cuisine; at Antonio's you'll find cuisine from farther south—south of the border, that is. Antonio's does sneak in crowd pleasers like fish-and-chips and burgers using locally raised yak. Ponder that and order the tableside guacamole, realizing that every guacamole should be made fresh to order: The squeeze of lime, the garlic, the salt—everything is vibrantly potent. Pair green on green by ordering the roasted poblanos in corn soup, or enjoy a proper Cesar salad—remember, it was invented in Tijuana, not Italy as most menus 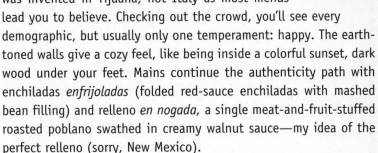 lead you to believe. Checking out the crowd, you'll see every demographic, but usually only one temperament: happy. The earth-toned walls give a cozy feel, like being inside a colorful sunset, dark wood under your feet. Mains continue the authenticity path with enchiladas *enfrijoladas* (folded red-sauce enchiladas with mashed bean filling) and relleno *en nogada,* a single meat-and-fruit-stuffed roasted poblano swathed in creamy walnut sauce—my idea of the perfect relleno (sorry, New Mexico).

Bent Street Cafe & Deli, 120 Bent St., in the John Dunn House Shops, Taos, NM 87571; (575) 758-5787; Cafe/Deli/Sandwiches; $$. You can hunt for the perfect spots to eat all over Taos—and, of course, they exist. But sometimes you're shopping in the cute little walkway of the John Dunn shops and decide right then and there that you're hungry, and **Graham's Grille** (p. 249) has a line. Bent Street it is, and you won't regret the choice. Their daily specials

Taos Ski Valley

Let's face it, there are certainly locals that live in Taos. There are artists and businesspeople and students and so on. There are day-trip visitors from Santa Fe or elsewhere in the state. And then, there are the skiers. For more months out of the year than you might think, the slopes are the place to go, all day, until your eyes are hurting and the last call on the lifts is sounded. Only some of those skiers stay up in the Village—but while up there, it is good to know that there is food on hand, from coffee to fine dining.

Those who head up in the morning and back down at night can take advantage of edibles during all hours, from espresso when arriving to cocktails or brewskis in the evening. This is but a few of the options—find everything in detail on the official website: skitaos.org.

Black Diamond Espresso, *122 Sutton Place, Taos Ski Valley, NM 87525; (575) 770-3122; Coffee, $.* I'm partial to coffee spots that exist in inclement locations. There, the owner knows full well that the more inconvenient the environment, the more a great cup of coffee is appreciated. At the bottom of the slopes up in the Taos Ski Valley, get "the fastest lift on the mountain" in the form of shots, Americanos, macchiatos, and beyond. They make excellent hot chocolate, much to the delight of the many kids that come up here to ski with the family. You'll be impressed enough with the quality that you'll drop the 50 cents to buy a sticker and proudly slap it on your favorite mug or laptop.

Rhoda's, *at the base of Lift 1, Taos Ski Valley, NM 87525;* *(575) 776-2005; skitaos.org/content/dining; American,* $$. Rhoda's includes some variety for those "trapped" on the mountain for a week or more: international nights, Saturday prime rib, and build-your-own breakfast at their daily buffet. Evenings you'll get to marvel at the idea that cocktails grow in the wild at the Martini Tree Bar, with a light menu and delivery service late nights in the Valley.

Tim's Stray Dog Cantina, *105 Sutton Place, Taos Ski Valley, NM 87525; (575) 776-2894; straydogtsv.com; Pub/American;* $$. There are a few fine-dining spots in the Taos Ski Valley tucked into high-end hotels, but Tim's fills a need for something laid-back and local. This is a place where you can have a beer and burger and tell real or fabricated skiing tales before retiring for the evening. While their cocktail list tends toward the touristy, the food is nicely inventive, using local flavors with borrowed presentations. Take the Suzie Sushi, a chicken-stuffed chile relleno cut and served like a sushi roll—cute and delicious. Enchiladas come as chicken or mole pork; tacos are steak or ahi tuna for a bit of trendy flair. I love their Local Loco, a take on Hawaii's rice-hamburger-gravy pileup called Loco Moco, where the twist is green chile sauce giving gravy the heave-ho. Weekends add breakfast hours, when the menu is equally hearty if a bit less creative.

are worth hearing (or reading on the board), for they might include something neat like a green chile spinach tamale. Otherwise, the sandwich list is massive, using fresh deli meats in enough combinations for any sandwich lover—how about a turkey, cranberry, and cream cheese? Breakfasts show off one of my favorite treats (and weaknesses): homemade granola.

Byzantium, 112 Camino de las Placitas, Taos, NM 87571; (575) 751-0805; Eclectic; $$. Forestry is tough work—both literally and sometimes breaking into the trade at all. Skot Kirschbaum tried to start his forestry career in Taos but fell back on cooking when the job prospects were slim way back in 1994. Since then he's maintained open doors at his mostly one-man show called Byzantium. I couldn't crack the code that connects the feel of the place with the name—it is bizarre, or sort of Moroccan? It turns out that no, it's just plain good. Kirschbaum cooks simple food that he likes and caters to his customers one-on-one, with just a single chef in the kitchen most nights. He makes some mean braised ribs with pineapple-chipotle glaze and homemade corn bread, but then there are sesame dumplings with chicken and  ginger; there is no location to this cuisine, only quality. Skot is famous for his pork loin, but I'd vote for the chicken curry served Korean-style in a sizzling hot pot with rice—lovely.

Caffe Renato, 133 Paseo del Pueblo Norte, Taos, NM 87571; (575) 758-0244; Italian; $$. I went by this place, next door to the Taos Inn, a bunch of times before the positive buzz started luring me in. The patio lined with trees and chatty diners is enough to get a person in the door, and the menu typically seals the deal: Northern Italian pastas and meats highlight dinner, while lunch is more panini-oriented with build-your-own combos and even a take-out lunch option for hitting the slopes or trails. Reading down the menu, I stopped dead at Hot Steak Salad—how could that not be good? Those opposed to steak should instead look toward Chicken & Gorgonzola, available as a salad or panini. Even though the low-carb thing is nearly gone, you can still specify "Atkins-friendly" on nearly anything and have your bread-free wishes granted. That kind of service brings locals back over and over again.

The Coffee Spot, 900 Paseo del Pueblo Norte, Taos, NM 87571; (575) 758-8556; Coffee/Cafe; $. From all things hot and brewed to sandwiches, breakfast platters, and even eggs Benedict, the Coffee Spot wants to be a go-to breakfast place. They've invented a few lattes with chile that will warm you up two ways, and every price is simplified by including tax. Locals bring their own mugs and save 50 cents—great deal!

Dragonfly Cafe, 402 Paseo del Pueblo Norte, Taos, NM 87571; (575) 737-5859; dragonflytaos.com; Bakery/Cafe; $$. There isn't a single person in Taos who doesn't like the Dragonfly—it is on the recommended list of locals, visitors, foodies, and curmudgeons alike. In addition to the locally sourced ingredients, staff that bounce from table to table like they might actually have wings, and killer pastries (such as the famous almond croissant), Dragonfly does not suffer from the chill that permeates many local shops in winter. The reason is evident as you walk up to the front door and smell the smoke: a roaring central fireplace throwing off BTUs to the hipsters in T-shirts and knit hats. Once a beverage is on its way to your table, you'll have to make menu choices, like lamb gyros for lunch or Moroccan chicken in the evening hours, but their raw kale salad has all of my kale-addict alarms going off—I could eat that alone, two of them. Brunch on the weekends pairs wicked strong coffee and a refreshingly shortened menu from granola to Eggs Dragonfly, poached eggs on corn bread with black-eyed peas and Southern greens.

El Gamal, 112 Dona Luz, Taos, NM 87571; (575) 613-0311; Middle Eastern/Vegetarian; $$. Most of the components that we associate with Middle Eastern food are already vegetarian: hummus, falafel, lentils, eggplant, and so on. El Gamal takes the flavors of that spice-laden region and swaps the meat for even more variety in the dishes. Here you'll find thick-as-paste *labnah* (homemade spreadable cheese), a standard but flawless baba ghanoush, and housemade pita a fluffy half-inch thick. The space is cavernous and can seem chilly, but an array of soups helps immensely: My favorite was the lentil with feta, but I've heard reports of an infrequent special yogurt soup with cucumber, dill, and raisins—wow!

El Meze, 1017 Paseo del Pueblo Norte, Taos, NM 87571; (575) 751-3337; elmeze.com; Spanish/New Mexican/Fine Dining; $$$. Let's not beat around the bush: Ask anyone which restaurant to visit in Taos for "one fancy dinner," and they'll say El Meze. Here's why: Chef Fred Muller returned to cooking in Taos in 2008 after the wildly acclaimed Fred's Place came and went in the '90s. With El Meze he brings back his Southern training and love of local ingredients, landing a James Beard nomination for 2012—clearly the man knows what he is doing. Let him show you with his menu: sage-buttermilk fried sweetbreads, fried green olives with blue cheese, a buffalo tamale with green chile and Spanish cheese, and a unique poblano relleno with chèvre and romesco sauce. When he's cooking with local ingredients—trout, mushrooms, corn—his passion comes through. One of the most famous plates is simply called Mushrooms on Toast, but, of course, it's not popular because of the blunt name—those mushrooms were probably foraged in the hills around town. Give El Meze a shot and you'll nod with approval, even before you have a finale of mini cardamom donuts.

Eske's Brew Pub & Eatery, 106 Des Georges Lane, Taos, NM 87571; (575) 758-1517; eskesbrewpub.com; American/Pub; $$. When visitors head to **The Gorge** (p. 248), locals head to Eske's—a little bit grittier, a little less fancy is the comfortable atmosphere at Eske's after 20 years of serving Taos. Live music fans will find much to love here: Check the schedule to find the lineup, but first take a peek at the menu and I bet you'll find exactly the thing you're craving. From burgers using grass-fed beef to burritos to green chile stew and a sizable vegetarian collection, everyone can be happy here. Even rotating specials are intriguing—every week there is a sushi night (!) and another evening dedicated to world cuisines. Eske's other claim to fame is the beer they brew on-site and tap for your sudsy pleasure. Bottoms up!

Five Star Burgers, 1032 Paseo del Pueblo Sur, Taos, NM 87571; (575) 758-8484; 5starburgers.com; Burgers; $. The ascendance of the gourmet burger is a welcome trend to most people. Even those who have never been to California have heard of In-N-Out, and the ones who have gone, well—they are far less likely to ever have a conventional drive-thru burger again. When Bob Gontram decided to bring that sensibility to New Mexico, Taos was the start of a high-quality yet still fast-food burger joint. Two years of doing it right with Harris Ranch meats and delectable salads, it was time to grow. Ultimately an expansion would grow the Five Star Burgers to three, first on Albuquerque's east side, and then putting down roots in Denver.

The Gorge Bar & Grill, 103 East Plaza, #1, Taos, NM 87571; (575) 758-8866; gorgebarandgrill.com; American/Pub; $$. This landing spot for quality cocktails and burgers worth raving about is almost too convenient—situated right on the Plaza, with a wide patio overlooking the goings-on. Even dining inside seems to have good energy, with everyone talking about the bison sliders and who will order them. And someone should, trust me. They come three in a row, often literally attached, on properly squishy buns—even if the meat is not steamed, as slider snobs would insist—with caramelized onions spilling onto the plate from their slippery position. Piquancy is bumped by a slice of jalapeño, though it hardly registers to locals. Oysters are on offer (usually) and should not be feared despite the desert location: Most come in from the same suppliers, on the same ice, all over the country. Cocktails are particularly good, like a gin, lemon, and cucumber creation tasting like slightly boozy lemonade. Midafternooners, check out the happy hour specials to save a few bucks for coffee in the morning.

Graham's Grille, 106 Paseo del Pueblo Norte, Taos, NM 87571; (575) 751-1350; grahamstaos.com; Cafe/Eclectic; $$$. Lesley Fay is the ebullient chef and inspiration for the menu at this lauded dining destination. She started with a relatively simple cafe lineup and breathed character and quality into every corner, from entrees to garnish. The "new American" menu covers the gamut from fancy mac and cheese to burgers to tamale pie, with decadent desserts to match the sportiest metabolisms around. Reservations are highly recommended, as walking in to find a table can be tricky, even during brunch. You'll be rewarded in rum sticky buns, eggs Benedict with chorizo, and rellenos—blue-corn-crusted rellenos, that is. They're filling and cheese-laden but still crunchy enough to hold up to a generous application of salsa. Pair that with a handmade tamale and whole black beans, and it will get you through a day of skiing or shopping.

Guadalajara Grill, 822 Paseo del Pueblo Norte, Taos, NM 87571; (575) 737-0816; guadalajaragrilltaos.com; Mexican; $$. "Let's do the Guad." That's a phrase you'll hear pretty often when locals and seasoned tourists choose their casual dinner destination. "The Guad" is ridiculously popular, much of that owing to authentic Mexican dishes that don't skimp on spices and do fill the belly. Seafood is a common base in the menu items, with many shrimp combinations, from garlic-sautéed to plump taco filling to shrimp cocktail in the spicy traditional style. Steaks and fajitas address red meat cravings; I adore the fresh guacamole and the handy salsa bar to add to any entree. The only dish that seems to not live up to the promise is soggy chiles rellenos—a New Mexican dish almost out of place on this menu. Also on the south side at 1384 Paseo del Pueblo Sur, Taos, NM 87571; (575) 751-0063.

Gutiz, 812B Paseo del Pueblo Norte, Taos, NM 87571; (575) 758-1226; gutiztaos.com; Spanish/French/Cafe; $$. Look for the rooster to know you've arrived at this breakfast and lunch ode to continental Europe, with its focus on both fresh ingredients and well-preserved accompaniments. Any light meal can and should start with a side of andouille sausage (or a chocolate croissant in the morning hours) to whet your palate. One of the best things on the menu is the Taoseño, a warm pile of beans, rice, green chile, and fried eggs—comfort to the nth degree and a nice reinterpretation of *huevos rancheros*. Sandwiches include the standards: *croque monsieur*, grilled brie with apple, and onward to chicken and grilled steak. At the end you'll still find it hard to resist things like flourless chocolate cake or lemon tarts, even after having a light and refreshing beet salad. The back patio is often busy, for good reason: The sun is powerful at this elevation and even winter days can be cozy with those beams hitting your back.

La Cueva Cafe, 135 Paseo del Pueblo Sur, Taos, NM 87571; (575) 758-7001; New Mexican/Mexican; $. Formerly known as Rellenos Cafe, this literal hole-in-the-wall is still serving reasonably priced fare to diners in the know. True to the old name, the chiles rellenos are crisp and are even prepared gluten-free by default—a great option if you have dietary restrictions. Tortilla soup is hearty with chicken and avocados, and all New Mexicans welcome the inclusion of Frito pie—our version of "trashy" comfort. It tickles me that they offer a Caesar salad; after all, this creation was born in Tijuana despite the subsequent adoption by Italian restaurants. The tiny room holds just a smattering of tables and can be a little dim, but it doesn't seem to matter when you can get a tasty plate of shrimp enchiladas for under 10 bucks.

The Love Apple, 803 Paseo del Pueblo Norte, Taos, NM 87571; (575) 751-0050; theloveapple.net; Eclectic/Organic/Local; $$.

It took months before I finally made it to this favorite of every single person whose dining opinion I trust; now I just want to gas up the car every weekend to come back. Open just six dinners per week, the reservation book fills fast with regulars and newbies like myself. You'll find an intimate space, candle and Christmas light lit, with an equal mix of couples and families there to dine. No tableside bread is offered—you will order either the hand-made flour tortillas or the yellow and blue corn breads and realize that paying for great bread is vastly preferable to receiving free mediocre stuff. Flavored butters and garnishes perk up the wonderful breads; a contrasting starter of grilled venison sausage adds depth to this appetizing array. Vegetable lovers of all kinds fare well here—a small plate of baked squash with local egg and mushrooms reminds me that so many foods are amazing when prepared with care, and a raw beet and citrus salad sends a huge shout-out to the red root's fans. (See Chef Andrea Meyer's **Raw Beet Salad** recipe on p. 300.) Shredded pork stew is of the traditional type without much New Mexican spiciness, but the corn cake floating on top is excellent. Wines by the glass are limited; look to a well-composed craft beer list for pairing nirvana. I would do the Love Apple a disservice by not mentioning the desserts—the goat's milk panna cotta is so delicate, it shudders at an approaching spoon, and house-made ice creams are on hand to serve alone or as a la mode.

Mante's Chow Cart, 402 Paseo del Pueblo Sur, Taos, NM 87571; (575) 758-3632; Mexican/American; $. Mante's has a great business model: Serve the seasonal tourists who come to Taos to shop when they are not on the slopes (or while their friends are on the slopes), but never forget the locals—the ones that were there since the beginning, when Mante's was a converted delivery truck lobbing burritos at avid fans through a tiny window. Now it still has a window, but it has taken a more permanent form, as a drive-thru fixture with beloved burritos that have first names: the Susie and the Lucero. The Trujillo is memorable enough that it has stood witness to at least one marriage proposal. Now that's devotion.

Pizaños, 23 NM 150, El Prado, NM 87529; (575) 776-1050; taospizza.com; Pizza; $. High altitude does a number on things that need yeast to rise, so it was a little intriguing to hear that two guys from Utica, NY, came out here to make New York–style pizza. You want to wish them good luck, but perhaps have a thought in the back of your head that it couldn't possibly work out. These very words are here because Pizños is a success, both in local acclaim and their ability to produce pizza crusts with no thin-air issues. The owners pronounce the name PIE-zan-yos, adding a little grin to go along with their slices and specialty pies. Using top-notch ingredients means that a few of those fancified concoctions hit above the $20 mark, but when you consider that a single entree at a decent restaurant is right around that price and a pizza will easily feed two . . . sounds like a good deal, then! A kids' menu and local beer make it relaxing for the whole family.

Plaza Cafe, 108 South Plaza, Taos, NM 87571; (575) 758-7498; lafondataos.com; New Mexican; $$. Taos's La Fonda hotel has no connection to Santa Fe's instantiation, but the refinement is similar if not more elevated here in the city of extremes. Those not staying in the rarefied hotel rooms can still partake of deep wood accents and high-backed chairs at the not-so-casual ground-floor restaurant. An abbreviated menu keeps the New Mexican foods simple and what you'd expect—with a twist or two. One of the twists brings in a favorite comfort food from its origins in Tucson: the chimichanga, ably fried as it should be. However, I'd rather you order the lovely chicken tortilla soup or handmade tamales before moving on to any other menu twists. A sopaipilla sundae is fine and all, but the chipotle chocolate cake bends expectations just enough to be worthwhile. Newly added alcoves have parties of two sitting on cushions behind semitranslucent curtains, giving the feel of the Middle East, but when that relleno arrives, so will reality.

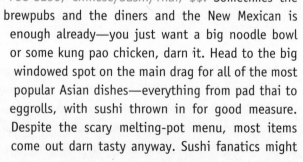

Song's Asian Restaurant, 703 Paseo del Pueblo Sur, Taos, NM 87571; (575) 758-3256; Chinese/Sushi/Thai; $$. Sometimes the brewpubs and the diners and the New Mexican is enough already—you just want a big noodle bowl or some kung pao chicken, darn it. Head to the big windowed spot on the main drag for all of the most popular Asian dishes—everything from pad thai to eggrolls, with sushi thrown in for good measure. Despite the scary melting-pot menu, most items come out darn tasty anyway. Sushi fanatics might only find the offerings a bridge until they can visit a proper sashimi shop, but the rest of the party will find what they need, even the vegetarians.

Taos Cow Ice Cream Co., 485 Hwy. 150, Arroyo Seco, NM 87529; (575) 776-5640; Frozen/Cafe; $. North of Taos a few miles, this outpost of frozen treats draws in spring and summer crowds for unique flavors and a down-home vibe. Since having frozen goodies is not enough in this tiny town—you might have forgotten to bring along traveling snacks, after all—a small menu has you covered, from deli sandwiches to hot items like breakfast tacos and pancakes. Visit them on the way to hiking spots—they'll pack a lunch for you if that's handy for your day's plans. The ice cream is often packaged for use at other shops around the state, so you might see the brand when you're buying chocolates at Theobroma or other ice-cream shops.

Taos Diner, 908 Paseo del Pueblo Norte, Taos, NM 87571; (575) 758-2374; taosdiner.com; New Mexican/Diner/Organic/Local; $. First things first: The parking lot is full of pickup trucks. When Taos Diner says that they are "where the locals eat," it appears that they mean every bit. Tables are packed with hungry bellies of all ages, apparel, and skin tone from pale to sunburnt to deep leather. Despite the popularity with bargain-seekers, Taos Diner still strives to prepare everything in-house and use mostly organic ingredients. You can get a grass-fed burger with trendy (but still delicious)

ROAD TRIP TO & FROM TAOS:
CHILE & DIVERSIONS

There are two ways to get to Taos (and no, one isn't spiritual—both of our routes here are on highways). There's the usual route through Española on NM 68 up the river valley, or you can take what is known as "the high road" and see a myriad of historic sites and galleries while tasting some of the most revered chile in the region.

The occasion: a weekend trip to Taos for Saturday-evening dinner and an overnight stay. Employing both routes to make a loop, you can see the best of both byways. Head up the NM 68 route early Saturday and plan on lunching along the way. Enter the hamlet of Embudo and decide: BBQ or not? Rustic or refined? Brisket burrito or grass-fed organic burger? For the former answers, look for a teeny shack on the south side of the road labeled Sugar's BBQ, *1799 NM 68, Velarde, NM 87582; (505) 852-0604; Burgers/Barbecue; $.* Prepare to have your required daily allowance of brisket. Sugar the bulldog is now memorialized on the wall, watching over the huge green chile cheeseburgers and the fat brisket burritos with chile and little to no filler. For the latter group of answers, on the north side of the road after crossing the river is Embudo Station, *1101 NM 68, Embudo, NM 87531; (505) 852-4707; embudostation.com; Burgers/Organic; $$.* Step into a gourmet establishment, menued up with local produce and a short burger list, all organic with devoted fans.

On Sunday, after a leisurely walk around the Plaza it's time to head back via the high road. Head out south from Taos and turn onto NM 3 or 518 toward Chimayó. Meander until you reach NM 75 and turn west toward Peñasco. In this little village is a spot called Sugar Nymphs Bistro (*15046 NM 75, Peñasco, NM 87553; (575) 587-0311; sugarnymphs.com; American/Organic; $*), known for homey upscale food like salads and meat loaf. You should know that I have had the best scone of my life plucked warm off the baking pan from Sugar Nymphs. Don't get overfull—the prize is yet to come (alternatively, have lunch at Sugar Nymphs and do gallery hopping before dinner in Chimayó).

Take NM 76 after Peñasco and wind through a few towns before reaching Chimayó. Take the southerly turn on CR 98 to get to a restaurant serving wonderful and potent red chile: Rancho de Chimayó, *300 CR 98, Chimayó, NM 87522; (505) 984-2100; ranchodechimayo.com; New Mexican; $$.* Order whatever you want, just get red chile. The chile served here is a specially selected crop from Hatch, but don't let that dissuade your local aspirations. The locally grown Chimayó strain of chile is revered, protected, and only currently grown by individual families—those roadside stands advertising local red chile are probably not what they seem, unfortunately. You'll still enjoy the restaurant and its wonderfully labyrinthine rooms.

To finish, pop back up to NM 76 and head west to Española, then south to Santa Fe.

sweet potato fries, or a brilliant "Cobbwich," piling all the requisite Cobb salad ingredients between bread. The penny-pincher menu starts the deals off with $4 for an egg, home fries, and homemade biscuit. Beat that, drive-thru! A little bit south of the Plaza is the other location: Taos Diner II, 216B Paseo del Pueblo Sur, Taos, NM 87571; (575) 751-1989.

Taos Pizza Out Back, 712 Paseo del Pueblo Norte, Taos, NM 87571; (575) 758-3112; taospizzaoutback.com; Pizza; $$. More than a dozen years of "best pizza in Taos" should tell you something about this spot, just north of town in a near-shack behind a residential building (hence the name). But inside, the stove is warming and the pizzas are being fired while you make some tough decisions. Not only will you have to shove your way past gourmet salads that would pass muster in any fine-dining restaurant, the pastry case beckons at the front, and the other tables probably have pies that catch your eye. First-timers might as well have the landmark Southwest pizza with our locally mandated green chile followed by smoked cheese, garlic, feta, and basil pesto. Sounds weird, but just trust me. Slices of every kind of pie can be had for $5 to $8, which seems high for a slice, but their size makes them about the same acreage as a "personal" pizza at other places. I'm not complaining—it works.

Doc Martin's, 125 Paseo del Pueblo Norte, Taos, NM 87571; (575) 758-1977; taosinn.com; New Mexican/Steak; $$$. I think a place gets to be called a landmark after 75 years, and Doc Martin's is that spot you have to visit to get a real feel for this city of significance along the old commerce trails of the state. It feels like someone's den: Sunken and dark, leaving the sense that smoking only stopped indoors in recent memory—you can easily picture folks puffing on cigars while tipping a cocktail. Not your typical steak house is how the menu goes—starters of rattlesnake sausage and grilled apple salad should make that clear. Entrees span from a juicy elk burger to blue-corn-battered chiles rellenos to, of course, a New York steak occupying the priciest slot on the whole list. Come and hang out at Doc Martin's, or pop next door to the Adobe for live entertainment and even more delicious bar food, and savor this spot steeped in history.

Lambert's of Taos, 309 Paseo del Pueblo Sur, Taos, NM 87571; (575) 758-1009; lambertsoftaos.com; Eclectic/Fine Dining; $$$. A city as small as Taos oughtn't to have restaurants as good as Lambert's, but there it is, and you ought to go. Start with the cocktails list, and if you don't have moral objections to whiskey or cherries, get Zeke's Manhattan with marinated—not mara-schino—cherries that are so decadent, it's hard not to ask for a bowl of them for dessert. But we'll get to dessert in a bit. First up is the bread bowl with a side dish of roasted garlic—over the top and nicely unusual. There are delectable small plates, tender lamb tacos, and mild but savory green chile stew. Beet fans must order the most stereotypical salad of the last 10 years: roasted beet with goat cheese. The thing is, these are delicate beet slices with tart dressing and blobs of local goat cheese—you can taste every bit of detail. Entrees are chops and chicken and lamb—whatever strikes your fancy—but save a smidgen of room for the house-churned ice cream, on its own or as a hot fudge sundae.

Michael's Kitchen, 304 Paseo del Pueblo Norte, Taos, NM 87571; (575) 758-4178; michaelskitchen.com; Cafe/Bakery/New Mexican; $. Reliable, reputable, and reasonable—when you are talking about a wildly popular diner that everyone, their mom, and their neighbors go to, you're talking about Michael's. Early morning through most of the day, this spot is ready to serve up unpretentious plates of Americana, sometimes with a line to get inside, but ample seating keeps grumbling stomachs at bay. Michael's has the added benefit of being one of the first to open its doors each morning—at 7 a.m.—providing a guaranteed early-riser crowd ready for pancakes to fuel their ski runs. A menu staple are the center-cut pork chops, served with eggs at breakfast or as a plate at dinner and loved for their Flintstone size. The whole "Spanish" section of the menu brings out all the New Mexican entrees, including the deliciously inventive enchiladas smothered in guacamole—*¡Muy bueno!*

Don't forget the massive bakery case before you leave—but it will be hard to pass it by, no matter what you just ate.

Orlando's New Mexico Cafe, 1114 Don Juan Valdez Lane, Taos, NM 87571; (575) 751-1450; orlandostaos.com; New Mexican; $$. I have to smile when I see Orlando's artwork and advertisements—the drawn Día de los Muertos skeleton with his mustache and sandals is happy and, to my mind, hungry for some northern New Mexican grub. Only a few variations from "normal" local foods appear, like shrimp tacos or a chili sauce of a more Tex-Mex orientation. Otherwise, everything is perfectly appropriate, from blue corn enchiladas (egg on top as required) to chiles rellenos and tamales tender enough to make you wonder how they hold a shape at all. If the chile is tingling your tongue more than you'd prefer, douse it with a *cerveza* and soldier on, happy and sweating. For years when I've asked folks from all over which restaurant comes to mind when they think of Taos, Orlando's is always in the top three, and it's easy to see why.

Specialty Stores, Markets & Producers

Caffe Tazza, 122 Kit Carson Rd., Taos, NM 87571; (575) 758-8706; Coffee/Cafe. There's extensive room to kick back and spread out in this established adobe structure protected from the sun. In the winter it can seem a little cool, but summer renders these dim alcoves a refreshing escape. Coffees and espressos start out the menu, but a light food selection is on hand for real noshing: salads, sandwiches, and a few warm things like quesadillas. Ice cream and smoothies are the preferred way to drink your meal if the trails are calling.

Cid's Food Market, 623 Paseo del Pueblo Norte, Taos, NM 87571; (575) 758-1148; cidsfoodmarket.com; Grocery. This friendly shop a mile north of central Taos might seem out of the way if you're walking around the Plaza area, but it makes perfect sense when returning to the vacation rental after a day on the slopes. You can pick up coffee, produce, and whatever raw ingredients you'll need to cook a rejuvenating dinner for the gang. In Cid's refreshingly large store, you can get most of the strange-label things you might only expect in the "big city," from lip balm to dog food. Cid's hours are 8 a.m. to 8 p.m., making things easy for anyone out all day and needing dinner fixings—but not on Sundays.

Coffee Cats, 124F Bent St., Taos, NM 87571; (575) 758-0606; Coffee. This shop has tasty little pastries and every coffee drink you can dream up, from chai to espresso in flavor combinations that make black coffee drinkers wince. To each their own, right? The Taos quirkiness comes alive when you are offered to add a rock to your drink for a buck. Yes, really—drop any of 20-plus rock varieties into your beverage to change its energy and your mood: bloodstone for courage, citrine for abundance, and so on. The "rock bar" is a great way to experience a little Taos energy, whether or not the rock changes your day.

Mondo Kultur, 622 Paseo del Pueblo Sur, Taos, NM 87571; (575) 751-7712; Bagels/ Coffee. This is a twin business of Mondo Video and Kultur Cafe, the latter serving up delicious coffee blends and—here's a perk—real New York bagels flown in from the Big Apple. The owners' New York history gave them enough desire to bring in the good stuff, and all of Taos is happy for it. It's a welcome and toothsome breakfast to slug black coffee with a buttered and toasted "everything" bagel, figuring out the rest of the day. Ample power outlets, free Wi-Fi, and reasonably late hours means this is a fantastic place to hang out and keep the buzz flowing.

World Cup, 102 Paseo del Pueblo Norte, #A, Taos, NM 87571; (575) 737-5299; Coffee. Of note is that World Cup is one of the earliest cups of coffee you can find near the Taos plaza on weekends. That being said, they know their java and will make you one of the best Americanos in the state so that you can start your day with a caffeinated spring in your step. The tiny space is all about coffee—only a couple of pastries are offered as sustenance (brought over from Dragonfly), but this coffee is pretty sustaining on its own.

Learn to Cook

Cooking Studio Taos, (575) 776-2665; cookingstudiotaos.com. Chef Chris Maher has taken his James Beard Award–winning talent and given it life in the kitchens and cooking skills of others by creating an enterprise of classes, events, and catering services. He ran the locally beloved (and many-starred) restaurant Momentitos de la Vida until 2005 before stepping back. His next leap was a new direction with teaching and making packaged dips and salsas under the Caleb & Milo label. Many of the classes are single session and draw from Maher's international experience—one week will be Cajun, the next Brazilian, the next Indian, and so on.

Food Trucks & Carts

Before the Korean sliders and the cake pops, there were tacos: lots and lots of tacos. The food truck phenomenon that has percolated up into foodie culture over the last decade has roots in the Mexican taco trucks of many cities. These mobile street-food slingers, often brightly festooned RVs with converted kitchens, tended to corral themselves in small groups in open parking lot spaces, creating an impromptu food court of sorts. Cities that had any decent-size Mexican population usually had a food truck contingent—whether or not the rest of the dining public noticed it. Walk up to the window, order a taco, hand over your dollar—that was the formula. Try another window and another flavor, then have a seat at communal tables and apply condiments at will. I've done this in Oakland, Denver, and even Yuma, where the near-border location meant everything was wonderful.

And then, the foodie truck explosion happened, fueled by the newly hip Twitter which allowed owners to let their followers know on an hour-by-hour basis where they were parked. The trend incubated and spread to the Bay Area, Los Angeles, Austin, and Portland, OR, to name a few places. These new trucks take advantage of quick sales and curious clientele to offer delicious but often truly bizarre flavor combinations—Kogi BBQ in Los Angeles made their name with Korean tacos, and it only got weirder from there.

In New Mexico those old-school trucks have always existed, many in Albuquerque's South Valley, but a few would set up a spot along far eastern Central Avenue near Wyoming or Eubank or along the Zuni corridor. Once the national trend was under way, nouveau trucks began to appear in our neck of the woods, both gourmet shops and down-home BBQ carts.

Here is a small roundup of the local players, with a caveat: Call ahead or check for a daily Twitter feed (if available) to make sure your favorite spot is going to be around. And bring cash, just in case.

Santa Fe & Taos

Antojitos Mexicanos Judith, Siler Road and Rufina Street, Santa Fe, NM; Mexican. You won't believe how cute this little truck is, with hand-painted cartoon depictions of the menu, until you saunter up to place an order. Then a fistful of street food heads your way from the window, and, cute or not, you devour your handheld food with wild abandon. Shrimp tacos are one of the most popular choices.

Chicago Dog Express, 600 Cerrillos Rd., Santa Fe, NM (permanent location); (505) 984-2798; Hot Dogs. Visitors to Santa Fe from the Windy City have been known to career off their trajectory when they spot this dog shack along Cerrillos Road. It would be like a New Mexican seeing a "chile relleno" shack in Iowa—you'd have to stop, right? The poppy seed bun might not be steamed as required by Chicago tradition, but sometimes you just want to reminisce, and you can do that just fine here.

Chivita Colombiana, Hopewell Street at Sixth Street, Santa Fe, NM; Mexican. A big smiling face adorns the side of this truck that purveys a mean bowl of *menudo* and handheld favorites like chorizo burritos and *torta* sandwiches. Lunch is the popular time and can be crowded, so have a backup plan if the lines are more than you bargained for.

El Chile Toreado, 950 Cordova Rd. near St. Francis Drive, Santa Fe, NM; (505) 500-0033; Mexican. Looking like a tiny house, the pitched roof of El Chile Toreado shelters some amazing and authentic Mexican foods, from burritos to tongue tacos. Red and green chile is also offered, as this is, after all, New Mexico.

El Molero Fajitas, E. San Francisco Street at Lincoln Avenue, Santa Fe, NM; New Mexican. Start with the fajitas, the namesake of this little pink and blue walk-up cart. But you'll wind up with a heck of a tamale if today's the day that the red chile chicken tamales are hot off the steamer pot.

Great Noodles, 120 Bent St. (in the John Dunn House Shops walkway), Taos, NM; (575) 613-5372; nullvegan@excite.com; Eclectic/Asian. You know a cart has a devoted fan base when 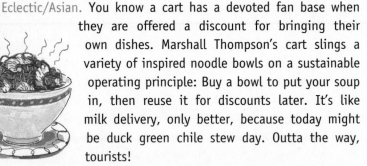 they are offered a discount for bringing their own dishes. Marshall Thompson's cart slings a variety of inspired noodle bowls on a sustainable operating principle: Buy a bowl to put your soup in, then reuse it for discounts later. It's like milk delivery, only better, because today might be duck green chile stew day. Outta the way, tourists!

La Fuente Burger, 2810 Cerrillos Rd. (in front of Jackalope), Santa Fe, NM; (505) 470-0939; Burgers/New Mexican. If a tiny menu means that you can do a few things really well, this is the spot. The smothered La Fuente burger is what most folks order, but they marry crunchy with hearty in a *chicharrones* burrito for the pork fans out there (and I know you're out there).

Le Pod, 502 Old Santa Fe Trail, Santa Fe, NM; (505) 501-0069; lepodsantafe.com; lepodsantafe@yahoo.com; French. This shiny

Airstream trailer is a shrine to casual French fare, from crepes to paninis to vegetarian sandwiches, with a side of comforting gratin potatoes. Chef Jean-Luc will be on hand with a smile and your delicious lunch, every weekday from 11 a.m. to 4 p.m.

Leonel's Fresh Tamales, 519 Paseo del Pueblo Sur (in the Super Save parking lot), Taos, NM; (575) 751-2801; New Mexican. The sign in front of Leonel's says UNTIL THEY'RE GONE! and I can't tell you how many times I've gone by with the chairs folded up and everyone on their way because the awesome tamales have ended their daily run. Rumor has it the burritos are excellent, but for now, I'm too smitten with the namesake menu item.

Roque's Carnitas, on the Santa Fe Plaza, Santa Fe, NM; New Mexican. It's almost not fair to proclaim Roque's "trendy"—this cart has been a Plaza fixture for many years, with all the benefits and drawbacks of popularity: lines, happy diners, and closing up shop when the food runs out. Despite that, it is worth at least one visit to see what the fuss is about. Roque's opens around noon every day except Tues.

Slurp, 444 Galisteo St., Santa Fe, NM; (505) 690-5994; @slurp santafe; Vegetarian/Sandwiches. Cooking exactly what they want, the Slurp food trailer has specials that change with the mood: paella, Spanish tortillas, Caribbean black beans, tandoori chicken paninis—all mouthwatering and beloved by customers. Weekdays from 7 a.m. to 3 p.m. is the window of tasty opportunity.

Albuquerque

Food trucks dart all over the Duke City, clumping together or setting up their own spots along streets or in parking lots. A good half dozen or more make a weekly gathering at Talin World Market every Wednesday from 10 a.m. to 3 p.m. This is a great spot to try several trucks at once. Find ongoing events and news by following the Twitter accounts @ABQFoodTrucks and @DukeCityTrucks.

Alison's Homestyle Cooking, (505) 280-9823; @AlisonsHSC; New Mexican. Just look for the yellow truck to know you're at Alison's, a spot for traditional New Mexican fare, from burritos to Frito pie. It is probably the only truck around with a hand-carved wooden door on the rig.

Big John's BBQ, (505) 203-1539; on.fb.me/ bigjohnsbbq; Barbecue. Since 1972 John has cultivated his smoking technique, bringing the usuals to your plate: chicken, ribs, brisket, and enormous turkey legs with brown, crispy skin. Big John's is almost always parked at Montgomery and Carlisle, but call ahead regardless.

Bill's BBQ, (505) 362-0412; hallieporter_2@msn.com; Barbecue. Bill Porter has a huge operation: His full-size RV tows behind it a masterful little red smoker where his meats acquire their appropriate smoke rings and perfect flavor. He parks all over, including outside of Santa Fe—call to find out the current status, and enjoy!

The Burger Basket, (505) 241-9823; theburgerbasket@live.com; @theburger basket; Burgers. For many months this truck has made it a habit to park outside **La Cumbre Brewing Company** (p. 289) to serve up bun-encased nosh to beer fans who need a meal to pair  with their brew. A towering burger is called the Big G Basket Buster, with fried chiles and enough meat to induce spontaneous mooing.

The Chopping Block, (505) 280-1153; thechoppingblockcatering .com; shaypatchell@msn.com; American/Fusion. Start with fish tacos on soft corn tortillas for fresh and almost messy but perfect five-bite fare. Then have a slider or two in Asian-fusion flavors, like shredded pork with Thai sauce and red peppers.

Firenze Mobile Wood Fired Pizza, (505) 730-7492; firenze mobilepizza.com; Pizza. Putting a really good oven in a food truck is a fantastic idea—pizza needs heat and a ton of it, and Firenze delivers on that promise with organic toppings and blistered crusts. They park around town on a weekly schedule; check their website or give Steven and Felicia a call.

Good Food Eat Here, (505) 604-9924; tobywhite@yahoo.com; Vegetarian/Local. The truck is green, the food is green and vibrant, and hopefully you will feel the same way after eating the tasty offerings from this vegan-friendly truck with curries, cookies, guacamole, and even raw falafel.

JoJo's Salsa Machine, (505) 688-8937; jojossalsamachine @gmail.com; @jojosmachine. Tamales and burgers come out of this white truck with the enormous blue Zia symbol. They have enough downtown visits to proclaim that the late-night-crowd favorite is the Rattlesnake Burger with BBQ sauce and grilled sweet onions.

Make My Lunch, (505) 450-9507; makemylunchcallie.com; @make mylunch; Sandwiches/Organic. Callie and her sister assemble quick and healthy food from as many local ingredients as they can, serving it up from their truck or as a delivery service around town.

Oz Patisserie, (505) 659-6452; ozpatisserie.com; @OzPatisserie; Desserts. People who know their desserts say that Gary's pastries are some of the best in town—that's fodder for your sweet tooth. There will be a smile on your face as you sample his perfectly portioned crème brûlée or red velvet moon pies or sweet corn panna cotta or magic bars or . . .

Roxy's Bistro on Wheels, (505) 620-1830; roxysbistroonwheels .com; @roxysbistro. Allow your brain to linger on the phrase *green chile wafflewiches*. Then set out to find the Roxy's truck and experience nirvana firsthand. Wafflewich skeptics can settle for some green chile mac and cheese instead.

The Seasonal Palate, (505) 934-3866; theseasonalpalate.com; @seasonalpalate; Asian/Fusion. Far from the über-casual chic of many food truck owners, Kim wears her chef whites and turns out well-executed fare like green curry, handmade falafel, and seafood po'boys (her Seattle training comes through). She is often parked in Placitas or at the weekly Talin roundup.

Zingaro, (505) 715-2225; thezingaro.com; @BigRedZingaro; Burgers/American. Watching Zingaro's Twitter feed is dizzying— they are all over town, wherever the wind blows and customers will show up. I'd show up at their window for the Kristine Burger with blue cheese and a fried egg—decadence!

Cocktails & Hops & Grapes, Oh My

It is easy to think that drinkers tend to be all-or-nothing in their refinement when it comes to beverage, but the hard line that seems to separate the "six-pack with the game" gal from the "tiny sips from the absinthe glass" guy—it just doesn't exist. The spectrum is vast, from vinophiles to home bartenders to beer geeks. Drinking preferences mirror food palates more than you might think—many of us are quite omnivorous when it comes to our alcohol, as long as it's good.

Nearly 80 years after Prohibition was repealed, the state of appreciation for fine alcoholic beverages is excellent, resulting in a cocktail and craft beer resurgence. In New Mexico the last 10 years have seen at least a doubling of craft brewers, while the number of distillers has jumped from one to three. All are creating libations with both talent and local ingredients and letting us, the drinkers, take notice of the fruits of their labor and savor the delicious variety, one sip at a time.

Distilleries

Don Quixote Distillery, 18057 NM 84/285, Pojoaque, NM 87506 (tasting room); (505) 695-0817; dqdistillery.com. The sole distiller in the state for a good decade, Ron and Olha Dolin's Don Quixote Distillery makes a myriad of spirits using local botanicals and old methods to craft some amazing bottles. Ron's chemical tinkering met its match in Olha's Ukrainian distilling heritage, and the two have been crafting since meeting in 1999. Visit their Pojoaque tasting room (right off NM 84/285) and start with the five-item sampler, picking your own lineup or allowing them to hear your preferences and guide your choices. Brandy fans will rejoice, for there are at least three varieties, from the multilayered Spirit of Santa Fe to Qalvados, a cleaner apple-only variation. Same goes for port, with a mellow white Portuguese or their bracing tawny cherry with the silky thickness often associated with port. Bourbon and vodka lovers are covered, too—Don Quixote makes both spirits with blue corn for an earthy taste you can't get just from wheat. Buy right from their tasting room for handy gifting or for your own stock.

BITTER END BITTERS & SWEET BILL YORK

Bill York, proprietor and creator of Bitter End Bitters, is extremely hyperactive, though you won't see it immediately. After you chat with him a bit and he decides you're not going to dive off a cliff when he talks business, off he'll go into cocktailing and the craft of steeping bitters. They started out as digestive aids or tonics—mostly something that tasted "medicine-y" and had some herbal benefits, though many drew their relief from the alcoholic base. Over time they started to be treated like spices. Think of it this way: When cooking food, you add whole or ground spices. That's kind of inconvenient and icky when you are "cooking" a beverage, and that's where an herbal tincture is perfect.

Bill started with an orange bitters recipe, and once that turned out just fine, the research began, yielding not a lot of competition in the unique flavors market. So he set to work filling that niche. (A few more companies do the same thing, but market saturation doesn't seem to have happened.) He started with five flavors—Mexican Mole, Thai, Jamaican Jerk, Moroccan, and Memphis Barbeque—and

KGB Spirits, 183 County Rd 41, Alcalde, NM 87511; (505) 852-0083; call to inquire about availability in retail shops. On the way to Taos is a tiny bump of an enclave called Alcalde, with a few homes, a school, that sort of thing. Oh, and also New Mexico's newest distillery: KGB Spirits. They've set up a few small stills in the last five years and are producing all manner of small-batch stuff. The Los Luceros Hacienda Gin's profile leads with juniper (which New Mexicans know well) and then gets complicated quickly with

recently added Chesapeake Bay and Curry. That first flavor, Mexican Mole, took trial and error and consultation with real mole recipes before realizing that upping the chile level was key when the tonic is so small in volume. Even the Mexican Mole with tons of ingredients gets everything listed on the label to keep potential allergy sufferers aware.

I'd like to say that every bartender in town and many in the state are using Bitter End; there are only a few, but word of mouth is growing, especially from patrons who have cocktails using Bitter End and then start chatting it up when they visit other places. I saw a vial of Mexican Mole sitting on the bar at one of the trendiest places in Austin, TX—a great sign in a cocktail-obsessed city like that. Locally you can buy them at Susan's Fine Wine & Spirits (p. 97) or have one of the expert bartenders craft a cocktail at the Secreto Bar & Loggia at the Hotel St. Francis (p. 286). I'll vouch for the quality of Secreto's—my favorite in Santa Fe this year.

Learn more at bitterendbitters.com.

floral notes and enough depth of flavor to drink straight. Another clear spirit is the Vodka Viracocha, potato-based and well regarded by the local vodka experts (of which I am not one). They bottle a three-year Taos Lightning Rye that was originally sourced outside the state, but local production is coming around as KGB becomes rooted in this area. Their full lineup continues to grow, and the local spirit aficionados are happy indeed.

Santa Fe Spirits, 7505 Mallard Way, Santa Fe, NM 87507 (tasting room); (505) 467-8892; santafespirits.com. Englishman Colin Keegan founded Santa Fe Spirits in 2010 after a conversation with local craft brewer (and hobbyist distiller) Nick Jones over some hard apple cider. The question was how to take the next step and begin producing local brandy. Many conversations later, Keegan found his distiller. The company had something ready to sell in early 2011, with a spirit new to most local folks: a white whiskey called Silver Coyote. The un-aged spirit with malted barley flavor has none of the hue that comes from barrel-aging. It will reside on shelves next to vodkas and white tequilas, but is still whiskey-like in flavor. The longer life-cycle Scotch-style spirits are aging on schedule, to be ready beginning in late 2012. Give the unadulterated white whiskey a go and cool your heels, until Keegan and Jones have had time to properly "adulterate it," as they say. What about the apple brandy, the brainstorm product that started the whole company? Good news: The first batch is already in stores, made with apples from Tesuque and blended and aged for the right flavor profile. Try everything in their new tasting room.

Cocktail Lounges & Wine Bars

When it comes to having a drink, there are the restaurants that have full bars and might be able to pour a good glass or have a great bartender—those places will be noted in the content of that restaurant's listing. But then there's everything else: brewpubs, wine bars, cocktail lounges, you name it. Any place that draws people in for the libations and might also happen to serve food—this is their section.

Adobe Bar at the Taos Inn, 125 Paseo del Pueblo Norte, Taos, NM 87571; (575) 758-2233; taosinn.com. Margaritas are a universally appealing cocktail, not unlike pizza's place in the food world: Even when just average, both are still pretty tasty. Unfortunately, a great margarita that makes you stand up and say "Wow!" is often hard to find. Except, that is, at the Adobe Bar, where the margaritas are deadly strong and the right balance of puckery lime and quality tequila. Take a seat in the bar's lounge area and enjoy some of the best entertainment in Taos—they've been showing off musicians almost as long as the 75 years the bar has been open. The only margarita to order is the famous Cowboy Buddha with Herradura Silver and only fresh lime juice—no mix. Consider affordable snacks from the bar menu before you leap into the cocktails; happy hour specials of nachos and other bar foods are better than at your average pub.

Agave Lounge at the Eldorado Hotel, 309 W. San Francisco St., Santa Fe, NM 87501; (505) 995-4545; agaveloungesantafe .com. The featured ingredient should be easy to guess at the Agave Lounge inside the Eldorado Hotel. Tequila flights, premium cocktails (often with premium pricing), and a refreshing happy hour (along with a reverse happy hour after 10:30 p.m.) allows locals to escape the usual down-home Santa Fe bar scene. Done up in deep colors and low lighting, the mood evokes big-city swank, for better and for worse. But all that considered, this is a fine escape, especially when you'd like to go out and wear that fancy black outfit instead of jeans and boots.

Apothecary Lounge on the roof of the Hotel Parq Central, 806 E. Central Ave., Albuquerque, NM 87102; (505) 242-0040; hotelparqcentral.com. Albuquerque is not Los Angeles, nor is it Phoenix, but we get to play a little bit of that luxury angle when sitting on the roof of the Hotel Parq Central near downtown in the warm evening air, cocktail in hand. The hotel bar is called the Apothecary Lounge to evoke some of the history of the building as a sanatorium and hospital—back in the day when many spirits were considered medicinal by doctors, not just drinkers. When there is

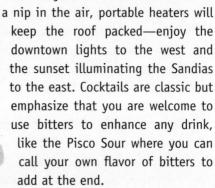

a nip in the air, portable heaters will keep the roof packed—enjoy the downtown lights to the west and the sunset illuminating the Sandias to the east. Cocktails are classic but emphasize that you are welcome to use bitters to enhance any drink, like the Pisco Sour where you can call your own flavor of bitters to add at the end.

Artichoke Cafe, 424 Central Ave. SE, Albuquerque, NM 87102; (505) 243-0200; artichokecafe.com. The Artichoke Cafe has always offered a fine selection of wines and small plates in their wine bar area, curated for years by Stewart Dorris. When the full liquor license came through and Stew was already over manning the kitchen at **Farina Pizzeria** (p. 111), it was time for Artichoke to offer full cocktails and a more focused classy bar experience. Even with the refinement, there is still an afternoon weekday happy hour with a few bucks off everything, from the daily select cocktail to aperitifs and a house cheese plate. The cocktail list offers specialties from bartender Robert Lemberger like a Pepino Chilaca with chipotle vodka, agave, and cucumber and a fuchsia Prickly Pear Mojito that is thankfully not as sweet as it appears.

Dragon Room Bar, 406 Old Santa Fe Trail, Santa Fe, NM 87501; (505) 983-7712; thepinkadobe.com/dragonroom.php. I had my first Silver Coin margarita at this hipster bar associate to **The Pink Adobe** (p. 82), the Dragon Room. Other drinks followed, but of prime importance is the fantastic bar food, from nachos with lamb to a two-fisted sloppy burger that dares teeter toward unctuous but remains wonderful as a hangover prevention device.

Scalo Il Bar, 3500 E. Central Ave., Albuquerque, NM 87106; (505) 255-8781; scalonobhill.com. Adjoining **Scalo Northern Italian Grill** (p. 176), one of the favored Italian restaurants in town, Il Bar

Margaritas Worth Their Salt in Santa Fe

A lot of folks will claim that you can't not have a margarita with your big ol' plate of New Mexican food. Whether you agree or prefer a few great margaritas spaced out over the seasons, it seems like a good idea to know where you can get a reliably good salted concoction. Some are stronger, some are weaker, but all should use fresh lime juice and no premade mixes. One important note: The local brand Santa Fe Mixes is used in many bars and restaurants, and while still a mix, they use only fruit juices and cane sugar—no artificial colors or high-fructose corn syrup. If you've ever had a prickly pear margarita, it's probably with this mix—and it's pretty good.

In the City Different of Santa Fe, finding a good margarita is like finding a *ristra*—if you're not in sight of one, walk around the corner and there you go. Generally the local spots are going to be doing it with fresh ingredients, but there are some notables if you're planning a margarita tour. A disclaimer: This is a much saner idea with 10 people who each sip from one or two drinks at each spot, and walking from place to place. This list is not an itinerary.

We might as well start with Maria's New Mexican Kitchen (p. 89) just because, well, they're legendary. Dozens of tequilas and hundreds of margarita combinations, all of them using fresh citrus and triple sec, will get your palate set. Then go old-school with the coiner of the Silver Coin designation, El Farol on Canyon Road (p.

78). It goes to show that serving Spanish food doesn't detract from serving Mexican liquors. A few doors up you'll find Geronimo (p. 78) shaking theirs with Don Julio Blanco and fresh fruit juices, and across the street at The Compound's (p. 40) bar, they serve a signature version with Sauza Silver and blood orange liqueur.

On Old Santa Fe Trail, the old-school Pink Adobe (p. 82) and Dragon Room (p. 281) serve my favorite Silver Coin in town—not overly sweet but packing a big punch with Herradura Silver. Back on the Plaza you'll find margarita love at Coyote Cafe (p. 76) under bartender Quinn Stephenson with his Señorita topped with lime foam, and they get more interesting from there. Downscale on the fancy meter is many locals' absolute favorite margarita joint, The Shed (p. 90). Six different Silvers are available—you could have one every day for a week and compare notes. Patio fiends should hop up to the Ore House (p. 80) to try one of their house margaritas and watch the Plaza in the evening.

After dark the best place to be anywhere near the Plaza that won't be crawling with folks wanting neon pink cocktails is Del Charro (p. 42), one of the "local secrets" of great bar food and almost perfect drinks. Feast your eyes and wallet on the house margarita with Jose Cuervo (ho hum) and tequila-marinated lime (neat!) for 6 bucks (yow!).

gives the nod to those who appreciate a great cocktail even before deciding on dinner. Mixologist Ben Williams is a guy with many inventions up his sleeve and the cocktail awards to prove it (see his **Mariposa Cocktail** recipe on p. 324). His lavender honey martini took top honors in a vodka mixology competition, and gets extra credit for using local ingredients—the North Valley has a huge lavender season. Weekends are a draw with a Bloody Mary bar that will quickly become the only buffet you ever want to see again. The bar menu is restrained and refined, using much of Scalo's Italian small-plate creations. Winter cocktails don't get much sweeter than Ben's take on our state cookie with a warm, creamy Biscochito, using half-and-half, Tia Maria liqueur, and white Sambuca for the licorice flavor. Yep, it's a warm liquid cookie. With alcohol. Santa is jealous.

Low 'n Slow Lowrider Bar in the Hotel Chimayó, 125 Washington Ave., Santa Fe, NM 87501; (505) 988-4900; hotelchi mayo.com. The Hotel Chimayó has a great name going for it—with the best chile variety on the planet on its masthead, you can't go wrong. Furthering that, the hotel has recently renovated a nightlife hangout called the Low 'n Slow Lowrider Bar, complete with car-seat chairs and hubcaps galore. It's fantastic that one of the bartenders explains his name by saying, "Frido. Like the pie but with a D." From that noble introduction you'll get to try cocktails like La Musica, evoking the energetic tunes coming from vibrantly upholstered low-riders, with grape vodka, pomegranate liqueur, lemon, and Tuaca.

Less punchy but more potent is the Vato Loco, a tempting mix of bourbon, Campari, sweet vermouth, apples, and cinnamon. Sounds wonderful.

The Matador, 116 W. San Francisco St., Santa Fe, NM 87501; (505) 984-5050. For the most comfortable and anti-upscale-foofery kind of bar, you need to go underground. Really. Just off the Plaza on San Francisco there's a staircase between the sidewalk and the building with a sign attached to the wall that simply says THE MATADOR with an arrow pointing *down*. At the bottom of those stairs you will enter the best dive bar around. No old-time kind of place, the Matador often has a DJ spinning modern tracks or just playing old punk music. Bring your cash and leave any apprehensions at the door—this place is awesome.

Q Ultra Bar in the Hotel Albuquerque, 800 Rio Grande Blvd. NW, Albuquerque, NM 87104; (505) 225-5928; qbarabq.com. An on-again, off-again nickname for Albuquerque is "the Q," or just "Q," so a few places take advantage of that when selecting a business name, including the downtown cocktail lounge Q Ultra Bar. Known for their trendy clientele and fruit-based drinks, they've won a local award for a blueberry mojito, as well as awards for best high-end lounge. Another favorite is a plum martini with Pearl plum vodka, Chambord, orange and grapefruit juices, and basil. Looking to polish your high-roller shine? Try the Top Shelf Margarita for a cool 50 bucks that uses Gran Patron Platinum as its base.

I couldn't say if it comes out with fanfare or with a sly wink and a nod, but this place is about being seen, so the former sounds likely. A short bar-food menu features mini burgers, lobster rolls, and an old-school shrimp cocktail.

Secreto Bar & Loggia in the Hotel St. Francis, 210 Don Gaspar Ave., Santa Fe, NM 87501; (505) 983-5700; hotelstfrancis .com. No stranger to good cocktails, the city of Santa Fe treasures its outstanding mixologists, and in the last few years not many have reached the level of Chris Milligan at the Hotel St. Francis's Secreto Bar & Loggia. For local cocktail excellence, this is the guy. He writes (*santafebarman.com*), he creates, he constantly dreams up tweaks to formulas to end up with a cocktail that is just a little bit better (see his **Ragin' Cajun Cocktail** recipe on p. 323). The Spicy Secreto with St. Germain, cucumber, lime, and jalapeño wins on bold flavor and popularity. I long for the Dry Martini, done in the pre-Prohibition style with bitters and more vermouth than current trends. Noshes also have a historic nod, with a three-cheese crostini that follows the path of Franciscan monks from Italy to Spain to New Mexico, and twin tamales in red pork and green veggie.

Slate Street Cafe Wine Loft, 515 Slate Ave. NW, Albuquerque, NM 87102; (505) 243-2210; slatestreetcafe.com/wineloft. Downtown has plenty of bars of all types, from pool hall to "marketplace" to band venue. For a mellower vibe, just north of downtown, you can escape to an upstairs refuge for a bit of the vine in Slate Street Cafe's Wine Loft. While the restaurant downstairs (p. 120) also serves wine, the Wine Loft is singly dedicated to owner Myra Ghattas's love of grapes in their next life, and is open five nights a week until 9 or 10 p.m. Myra's a certified sommelier and crafts the wine list and pairings for each person and for their monthly tasting event. It's the perfect almost-weekend break when one of the tastings comes around the last Thursday of the month (followed by a repeat the next Tuesday): Sample three wines in a theme, and have a few bite-size noshes that pair perfectly.

Staab House Lounge at La Posada, 330 E. Palace Ave., Santa Fe, NM 87501; (505) 986-0000; laposada.rockresorts.com. Boy howdy, you can't throw a tamale without hitting a high-end hotel around the Plaza, can you? Next in line is the swanky-pants La Posada de Santa Fe with tiny casita rooms that are, in all seriousness, really wonderful—when someone else is picking up the tab. What you don't know is that the bar at the hotel is open to all comers, despite needing to walk through several rooms and a reception area, and it is refined and a respite, just like the hotel. Flanked by a long hallway and several anterooms, the Staab House Lounge is the place you'd meet Hemingway for a cocktail, or your most intimate friend at one of the corner tables or across the hall in library-like sitting rooms. It oozes class and seems to have earned it, with a liquor list to envy and competent bartenders. See you there.

Zinc Cellar Bar, 3009 E. Central Ave., Albuquerque, NM 87106; (505) 254-9462; zincabq.com. Walk in the doors at **Zinc Wine Bar**

& Bistro (p. 172) and head for the stairs—down to the cellar—for happy hour heaven in the Zinc Cellar Bar. Specials every day of the week mean that you can enjoy happy hour goodies designed to make you linger over another well-crafted cocktail: roasted garlic crostini, tenderloin tacos, or house-made chips. In the cool, dry evenings, the ABQ Apple cocktail sounds like a lovely homage to hot cider: vanilla-infused bourbon with apple liqueur and baked-apple bitters. The first cocktail I had at the Cellar was a French 75, so that remains my favorite. You can't go wrong when combining gin and bubbly champagne, of course.

Breweries & Taprooms

For those new to craft beer, the best place to get started is in a taproom—the staff will take care of your preferences and have you sample a variety to guide your experience, usually for a nominal charge (or even free). Luckily we have a nice variety of taprooms to explore, all over the region. See a larger list here: nmbeer.org/breweries.

Chama River Brewing Company Micro Bar, 106 Second St. SW, Albuquerque, NM 87103; (505) 842-8329; chamariverbrewery .com. This is the intimate downtown spot to hit when you want to sample Chama River's fantastic brews without trekking over to their full restaurant and its overwhelming crowds. Brewer Justin Hamilton has worked with the best brewmasters in Albuquerque and makes a mean Belgian porter in his 3 Dog Night, a national award winner. For the hop fiends, Jackalope IPA is up your alley, or keep things mellow with the Rio Lodo brown ale. At both the downtown taproom and the Chama River restaurant, samples are encouraged to help you find the perfect fit.

IVB Canteen, Il Vicino Brewing Company, 2381 Aztec Rd. NE, Albuquerque, NM 87107; (505) 881-2737; ilvicino.com/brewery. **IVB** gets big props for serving my favorite mustard in the world—locally made Lusty Monk. It comes as a dip/spread with their signature snack, the brilliant Beer Sponge: two hot and soft pretzels. When you're just in to sample some brews, you need little more than nice carbs to soak it up. Try their famous IPA, or go even darker with one of their stouts. Seasonally crafted beers are always on hand—just ask the taproom expert, and they'll find something you'll love.

La Cumbre Brewing Company, 3313 Girard Blvd. NE, Albuquerque, NM; (505) 872-0225; lacumbrebrewing.com. **One of** the newer darlings on the craft beer scene, La Cumbre has won fans, and fast. Their Bavarian brews are crowd favorites, and both their IPA and stout have already won awards. Look for this brand to only gain momentum in the next few years. Food on hand is sandwiches brought in from a local deli, and often there is a handy food truck parked outside.

Marble Brewery, 111 Marble Ave. NW, Albuquerque, NM 87102; (505) 243-2739; marblebrewery.com. Founded in 2008 as a new venture by the owners of **Chama River Brewing Company** (p. 288), Marble Brewery parked itself in downtown Albuquerque with an on-site tasting room and small eatery. Within two years the awards were flowing in, including a spot on *Draft Magazine*'s Top 25 Beers of 2010 for their From the Wood beer. Just about every beer fanatic in town has good things to say about Marble, from their brewing talent to their visual appeal—they took the "marble" concept and ran with it, creating everything from luminous pop-out logos for the beers to huge spherical tap pulls. As the selection is refined, brewmaster Ted Rice's experience shows through and gives residents another reason to sip their suds.

Nexus Brewery, 4730 Pan American Frwy. East, Ste. D, Albuquerque, NM 87109; (505) 242-4100; nexusbrewery.com. Nexus opened this brewpub and restaurant in 2011, a tucked-away spot just off I-25—the first trip out to the place can be tricky, but the rewards arrive soon after you choose a seat inside or out on the patio. Good beer has a way of seducing even the most hesitant tasters, as was dis-covered with a starter of White Ale to tickle and refresh the taste buds with orange and coriander flavors. Advanced sippers will jump on their hoppy American IPA, but the whole party will want to order from a tasty menu that includes fish tacos and fried chicken.

Santa Fe Brewing Company Tap Room, 35 Fire Place, Santa Fe, NM 87508; (505) 424-3333; santafebrewing.com. The oldest brewery in New Mexico, Santa Fe Brewing Company makes more than a dozen varieties, from pale ales to a seasonal Oktoberfest lager. With massive distribution statewide and beyond, this brewery's reach is wide, but the company is still small and friendly. With two tasting rooms in Santa Fe, you can pick your favorite variety six days a week. The State Pen Porter wins award after award (recently the 2012 Best of the Rockies/Southwest Region Winter Tasting at the US Beer Tasting Championships), due partly to deep chocolate notes but also to the whole drinking experience, likened to "a velvet sofa in solitary." Find their newly opened second tap room minutes from downtown Santa Fe in the neighborhood of Eldorado at 7 Caliente Rd., Unit A9, Santa Fe, NM 87508; (505) 466-6938.

Second Street Brewery, 1814 Second St., Santa Fe, NM 87505; (505) 982-3030; secondstreetbrewery.com. Here's a compliment to ponder: When a dozen craft brewers were asked, "What is the beer you drink by choice?" the local favorite was Rod's Best Bitter from Second Street Brewery. That's like talking to a group of different smartphone designers and finding out a bunch of them personally use a particular Nokia. Rod is Rod Tweet, brewmaster and general talent when it comes to formulating craft beer. At either of their brewpubs you can narrow down your tastes, from their nice Red Ale to the Extra Special Bitter—my personal favorite for hitting bitter

BEER: IT'S ALL IN THE CRAFT

Microbrew and craft—what's in these names, and should they mean something to beer drinkers? Basically craft beer is anything made in smaller batches, produced and sold in tiny amounts relative to the corporate beer makers. Growth nationally is about 15 percent, compared to negative 1 percent for mass-market beer, and new breweries open all the time.

Craft beer is of particular note in New Mexico, where fans of beer grow by the day and breweries blossom all over the state (not to mention inside many garages, where home brewers get their start). The state was home to more than 30 breweries in 2012, at least double the number of just over five years ago. Previously a handful of small crafters dominated, like Chama River's award-winning bottles and the reliably drinkable offerings from Il Vicino. Spend a few minutes on a search engine, and you'll find local groups like the ABQ Beer Geeks or the Dukes of Ale.

Are you new to craft beers and what sets them apart? Not to worry: Everyone was a novice at some point. Beer has flavors that can

notes without much hop flavor. Their second location is right at the farmers' market: 1607 Paseo de Peralta, Santa Fe, NM 87501.

Sierra Blanca Brewing Company at ABQ Brewpub, 6601 Uptown Blvd., Albuquerque, NM 87110; (505) 884-1116; abqbrewpub.com. In terms of local brewers, this one does a lot of volume, producing popular labels like their Outlaw Lager, baseball-themed

be as interesting as good wine, and that can even convert previous "wine snobs" into avid craft beer drinkers—if more folks appreciate great beer, it is better for all of us. Here's a short and sweet primer of styles and basic flavors used by American brewers:

Ales: With strong malty/grainy overtones, ales can have aggressive bitterness from strong hops; they often have extra flavors layered in such as chocolate, fruit, or coffee. When a friend orders an IPA (India Pale Ale), they are in the "ale-iest" of ales.

Lagers: With a crisp flavor, much "cleaner" than ales, lagers can smell almost grassy (in a good way); they are often described as refreshing. Many German or Vienna-style beers are lagers.

Specialty: The sky's the limit with specialty beers—they don't have to be wheat or yeast based, and therefore malty or hoppy flavors can be muted. Fruit, honey, pumpkin, and green chile are all variations; seasonal items like Oktoberfest or Christmas ales fall in this category as well.

Isotopes Slammin' Amber, and Alien Amber Ale (with an alien head on the bottle for good measure). With wide distribution, their suds can be found all over the state—including their flagship bar, ABQ Brewpub—and in select flavors regionally. They even make a chile-infused beer called Pancho Verde Chile Cerveza which is fun to taste, even if not a connoisseur's top pick.

Taos Ale House, 401 Paseo del Pueblo Norte, Taos, NM 87571; (575) 758-5522; taosalehouse.com. This new little spot doesn't directly compete with the few brewpubs in town—there is only a small bar-oriented menu—but it indeed gives beer lovers another place to sample tiny-batch beer. Skiers and locals alike adore hanging out at a place like this after a day on the mountain or around town. Owner Jesse Cook built the hardwood tap bar and crafts the beer, too—his Unprincipled IPA is always popular, but seasonal varieties are what keep folks coming back, from wheat beers to pale ales timed for the changing weather.

Tractor Brewing Company Tap Room, 118 Tulane Dr. SE, Albuquerque, NM 87106; (505) 433-5654; getplowed.com. Made in Los Lunas but tapped to recent acclaim right in Nob Hill, Tractor is winning fans quickly as a no-fuss alternative to Kelly's and Il Vicino, both of which serve food and can get really crowded. A new brewer came on board in 2010, changing Tractor's game from "just OK" to "wow, these are nice!" Beer geeks love the Doppelbock when on tap, but you can't take it home—zoning forbids growlers, unfortunately. Nob Hill residents can take the website domain to heart and then stumble home if necessary, or soak it up at the food truck that often parks right outside.

Turtle Mountain Brewing Company, 905 36th Place SE, Rio Rancho, NM 87124; (505) 994-9497; turtlemountainbrewing.com. Rio Rancho can seem like a lonely place for drinks—just one wine-maker and one brewer so far in the town (they're also the same person, making the talent nicely replicated). But oh, what a nice brew Turtle Mountain makes. Under the gentle guidance of owner Nico Ortiz, head brewer Mark Matheson creates memorable beers like the super-bitter Big Toe Barleywine and the far more mellow yet rich Milkshake Stout. Pretty much everything is good here—that's a craft drinker's opinion.

Wineries & Tasting Rooms

All of the wineries below have tasting rooms, with that location listed if different from the actual winery. Most tasting rooms are open daily, often lunchtime to late afternoon, but always call ahead to confirm tasting room hours. Many wineries and their wares are locally famous, while a few have nationwide distribution and fans (Vivác and Gruet come to mind). For a statewide list that is always updated, see the New Mexico Wine Growers Association website: nmwine.com.

Acequia Vineyards & Winery, 240 Reclining Acres, Corrales, NM 87048; (505) 264-1656. Known for their Red Tail Hawk Zinfandel, vintner Al Knight also loves their newest addition: Leon Millot Rosé.

Anasazi Fields, Inc., 26 Camino de los Pueblitos, Placitas, NM 87043; (505) 867-3062; anasazifieldswinery .com. Fruit wines are the specialty here, from New Mexico Peach to Placitas Wild Cherry, either straight up or blended with grape wines to keep the sweetness under control and refined.

Black Mesa Winery, 1502 NM 68, Velarde, NM 87582; (505) 852-2820; blackmesawinery.com. Black Mesa is famous for their Black Beauty dessert wine, with red wine's natural cherry notes and a chocolate infusion to push it over the edge.

Casa Abril Vineyards & Winery, 1 Camino Abril, Algodones, NM; (505) 771-0208; casaabrilvineyards.com. Between Albuquerque and Santa Fe you'll find this Spanish-Argentinean-leaning winery with award-winning Tempranillo and Malbec grapes, including a nice Tempranillo Rosé.

Casa Rondeña Winery, 733 Chavez Rd. NW, Los Ranchos de Albuquerque, NM 87107; (505) 344-5911; casarondena.com. Local vinophiles love their Viognier, and they produce a bottle called 1629, a blend of Tempranillo, Syrah, and Cabernet Sauvignon that celebrates the year of the first grapevine plantings in the US—in New Mexico!

Estrella Del Norte Vineyards & Santa Fe Vineyards, 106 N. Shining Sun, Santa Fe, NM 87506; (505) 455-2826;

estrelladelnortevineyard.com. Offering frequent wine-pairing dinners with a local chef, these wineries also win national awards, notably for Estrella Del Norte's Pinot Noir and Santa Fe Vineyard's Malvasia Bianca.

Gruet Winery, 8400 Pan American Frwy. NE, Albuquerque, NM 87113; (505) 821-0055; gruetwinery.com. Serious credentials come with the Gruet family: They started out making champagne in France in the '50s, before moving to New Mexico and using the same grapes to make the best sparkling wine you can buy (to be champagne it must come from the Champagne region of France—other than that, the production is the same at Gruet).

La Chiripada, 3 miles up NM 75 off NM 68, Taos, NM 87571; (575) 579-4437; lachiripada.com. Fruity whites like Viognier win this winery awards, but they also make a deep Cabernet Sauvignon that the vintner recommends for meaty dinners.

Matheson Wine Company, 103 Rio Rancho Blvd., B3, Rio Rancho, NM 87124; (505) 350-6557; mathesonwines.com. If you live in Rio Rancho and want to buy local wine, this is it. Good thing the vintner Mark Matheson knows what he is doing and makes darn fine blends—I love the Rio Cuvee.

Milagro Vineyards, 985 W. Ella Dr., Corrales, NM 87048; (505) 898-3998; milagrovineyardsandwinery.com. The Cabernet Franc is beloved by some of the best wine experts in town, and Milagro does right by their Merlot as well. You can find their wines at dozens of restaurants around the area—perfect for trying out with your favorite food.

St. Clair Bistro, 901 Rio Grande Blvd. NW, Albuquerque, NM 87104; (505) 243-9916; stclairwinery.com. This winery does well with sweeter wines, so those looking for a fantastic Gewürztraminer should look no further than their award-winning bottle.

Vino del Corazon, 235 Don Gaspar Ave., Ste. 6, Santa Fe, NM 87501; (505) 216-9469; vinodelcorazon.com. Wine from the heart is this couple's operating goal, and they've found fans around the country with their reserve Merlot that seems to pick up a hint of chile from merely growing in this spicy state.

Vivác Winery, 2075 NM 68, Dixon, NM 87531; (505) 579-4441; vivacwinery.com. *Wine Enthusiast* gave Vivác's 2008 Syrah 88 points, a rare feat for New Mexican wines and something to be proud of. Try their Diavolo, a blend of Bordeaux that can carry strong meat dishes or even chocolate pairings with ease.

Recipes

Raw Beet Salad

Chef Andrea Meyer describes this salad—why it is a favorite becomes clear:

"I always have a raw beet salad on our menu for three reasons: Raw beets are loaded with vitamins and minerals, are totally delicious, and local beets are available nearly all year-round. This winter version is topped with avocados, South Texas Ruby grapefruit, fresh mint, and lime vinaigrette. This refreshing salad's sweetness comes from the beets."

Serves 4

Salad

4 local beets, peeled and grated (raw)

1 Ruby grapefruit, cut into supremes (sections between the pith)

1 avocado, halved and sliced

4 stems fresh mint, stem removed and thinly sliced

Fresh Lime Vinaigrette

1½ cups olive oil

¼ cup brown rice vinegar

1 tablespoon minced garlic

1 tablespoon honey

Zest of 2 limes

Juice of 6 limes

1 tablespoon finely chopped fresh mint

1 tablespoon finely chopped shallot

Freshly ground black pepper

Dressing: *Puree all the vinaigrette ingredients in a blender or food processor until emulsified. Adjust with salt, pepper, and honey to your liking.*

Assembly: *Toss the grated beets with ¾ of the dressing and place the grapefruit and sliced avocado atop the beets on each plate. Sprinkle liberally with the fresh mint. Top with a splash of remaining dressing and a sprinkle of black pepper.*

Courtesy of Chef Andrea Meyer of The Love Apple (p. 251).

Romesco

Jay Wulf's Greenside Cafe upped the ante for dining options in the East Mountains when it opened in 2007. For well over a decade Jay's cooking (and business acumen) had contributed to the casual upscale scene at spots like Range Cafe (p. 211), Standard Diner (p. 121), and Gecko's Bar & Tapas (p. 146). He fled the "big city" cooking life in Albuquerque to be closer to home and offer the same sensibilities to a community that often gets burned out on Chinese, pizza, burgers, and barbecue. He churns his own ice cream as well as prepares gourmet meatloaf alongside spicy peanut udon noodles, not to mention killer breakfast treats.

This deceptively simple appetizer brings lightness to your dip repertoire with peppers and lemony olive oil flavors. Often served in Spain as a spread for breads, it can just as easily stand duty as a pasta sauce—the texture is like a rough marinara, but the taste is far more interesting.

Makes approximately 1½ cups

- **4 roasted and peeled red bell peppers (instructions below, or use jarred)**
- **¼ cup bread crumbs**
- **¼ cup sliced almonds, toasted in a dry pan until barely browned**
- **3 cloves garlic, peeled and smashed**
- **2 tablespoons lemon juice**
- **¼ cup excellent olive oil of your choice**
- **Salt and pepper**

To roast the peppers: *Core the peppers into halves and take out the seeds. Line a pan with foil and preheat your broiler. Put the peppers on the foil, skin side up, pressing them down so they almost lie flat. Broil until skins are almost* completely black—10 minutes or more. Remove to a plastic ziplock bag and let them steam for 10 minutes. Now, peel off the black skin and you're done!

To make the romesco: Put the peppers, bread crumbs, almonds, garlic, and lemon juice in a food processor and pulse for 1–2 seconds, making a lovely "BRRRRP!" sound. Keep pulsing until the texture is a little bit chunky—not as smooth as hummus. Add the olive oil and pulse just briefly to combine everything. Now taste and add salt: If you are serving with plain bread, use more salt, but if serving with salted chips, use less.

Serve at room temperature or slightly warmed with any bread or dippable delivery system.

Courtesy of Owner & Chef Jay Wulf of Greenside Cafe (p. 146).

Roasted Beet Soup

This soup will change your life. I have seen several beet skeptics do a 180 on their opinion of the lowly red root after tasting this crimson bowl. It didn't turn me into a beet lover—I was already on the beet bandwagon when I first tried Jennifer's soup many years ago at her previous restaurant, Graze, and it still nearly blew my mind. The simple ingredients conspire to make a whole when brought together; the flavors are set off at the very end by garnishes that tingle your tongue and complement the earthy beet qualities. Co-owner, co-chef, and co-genius Nelle's suggested garnish ideas follow the recipe, but my favorites are sour cream, toasted walnuts, or a drizzle of the best olive oil you can find.

Makes 2 quarts

- ¼ cup unsalted butter
- 1 carrot, peeled and chopped
- 1 stalk celery, chopped
- ½ medium yellow onion, chopped
- ½ small jalapeño
- 2 cloves garlic

- Kosher salt and freshly ground black pepper
- 3 cups chopped roasted beets (roast in their jackets, then peel and chop)
- 3 cups (approximately) vegetable stock

Melt the butter in a soup pot. Add the carrots, celery, onion, jalapeño, and garlic and sauté until translucent and soft. Season with salt and pepper, tasting as you go. Add the beets. Cover with vegetable stock and simmer for at least 30 minutes. Let the soup cool slightly, then puree. Adjust seasoning with salt and pepper.

Garnish Ideas: croutons, chopped parsley, sour cream, flavorful olive oil, beurre noisette, toasted nuts, grated cheese.

Courtesy of Nelle Bauer and Jennifer James of Jennifer James 101 (p. 152).

Thai Rice Balls

Rob Connoley creates everything from sandwiches at lunch to 12-course tasting menus featuring hand-foraged ingredients and molecular gastronomy techniques. He often finds that because his skills are adaptable, requests for vegan dishes come in frequently. These little snacks are the result of one of those requests. Don't be put off by the steps—each is quick and straightforward. This is a great recipe that is delicious to all and looks pretty on the plate with pureed mango or on a salad.

Serves 4

Cashew Cheese

2 cups cashew pieces

2 tablespoons Thai red curry paste

2 inches fresh lemongrass, outer layer removed, and chopped

1 inch fresh ginger, roughly chopped

½ cup boiling water

Salt to taste

In a food processor, combine the cashews, curry paste, lemongrass, and ginger. Process just enough to keep rough. Add the water and process until moist but not runny. Taste and adjust salt. Cover and chill for 30 minutes or overnight.

Assembling the Rice Balls

½ cup leftover cooked rice (any kind)

½ cup grated coconut

½ cup panko bread crumbs

½ cup flour

2 eggs, whisked (vegan: 2 tablespoons baking powder, 2 tablespoons water, and 1 tablespoon oil, whisked)

Combine the rice, coconut, and panko in a bowl. In two separate bowls, hold the flour and the eggs. Roll the chilled cashew cheese into golf-ball-size portions, then coat in flour, then egg, and finally the rice mixture. Gently reshape into desired size without compacting outer coating. Chill for 30 minutes or more.

Sauce and Final Cooking Steps

¼ cup fish sauce (vegan: use vegetarian fish sauce—yes, it exists!)

2 tablespoons palm sugar (or brown sugar)

1 tablespoon cayenne pepper

¼ cup rice wine vinegar

Frying oil of choice (peanut or coconut works well), heated to just below smoke point

Combine all the sauce ingredients well.

Deep-fry the rice balls until golden brown. Finish with a squirt of the fish sauce mixture. Great by themselves (Rob likes to serve with a mango puree as a main course) or on a bed of salad greens.

Courtesy of Owner & Chef Rob Connoley of the Curious Kumquat (p. 118).

Tea Egg Salad Sandwich

Tea eggs are a daily staple in China, available from street vendors on nearly every corner for pennies, yet they are almost unheard of around here. Brian Clark is helping to change that at Kung Fu Cowboy Tea Cafe, his spot in the Northeast Heights for tea geeks and those who love homemade cafe food. The lovely coloring on tea eggs is created by cracking the shells of hard-boiled eggs and then soaking them in a strong-brewed tea for several days. The patterns are lovely and the eggs take on some tea flavor (which, of course, you can vary by using different teas, but the base should be a black tea, not herbal).

Makes 2 sandwiches plus 2 extra tea eggs

For Tea Eggs

2½ quarts cool water, divided

2 tablespoons Lapsang Souchong Chinese black tea

6 large eggs

Make the tea: *Bring 1 quart water to a boil, add tea, and steep 8–10 minutes. Strain steeped tea into a container. Cool to room temperature.*

Make the eggs: *Place the eggs and 1½ quarts water in a pot; bring to high heat and then down to a bare simmer (stage when tiny bubbles are breaking the surface steadily). Immediately shut off the burner and wait at least 10 minutes. Chill the cooked eggs under cool running water with shell on. On a hard surface, gently roll the eggs with the palm of your hand, cracking the eggshell uniformly, being careful not to break the egg itself. You are not removing the shells, just cracking them.*

Place the cracked hard-boiled eggs in the chilled tea. Cover the container and refrigerate for at least 24 hours (can be refrigerated up to 72 hours).

Preparing Tea Egg Salad

4 brined tea eggs
2 Roma tomatos

1 tablespoon mayonnaise, or more as needed

Peel the brined tea eggs (eggs will be delightfully marbled from tea, with a light smoky taste). Remove the core from the tomatoes and slice in half through the center (not lengthwise), then cut the tomato half into a medium-size dice. Place the peeled eggs and diced tomato in a bowl and add 1 tablespoon mayonnaise. Mix and break the eggs with a spoon until the mayo and tomato are well incorporated. The egg whites and yolks should be broken into the approximate size of the diced tomato. Do not overmix. Mayo should be enough to barely hold the salad together; add an additional small amount of mayo if needed to accomplish this.

Preparing Honey Mustard

¼ cup honey
¼ cup yellow mustard
2 tablespoons Dijon mustard
½ teaspoon lemon juice

½ teaspoon apple cider vinegar
Pinch of salt and cracked black pepper

Combine all the ingredients.

Preparing the Sandwiches

4 slices rye bread
Honey mustard dressing
Tea egg salad

4 slices cucumber
2 large pieces red- or green-leaf
lettuce

Lightly toast the rye bread. Drizzle each slice with honey mustard. Stack the tea egg salad, cucumber, and lettuce on two slices of rye bread, and finish the sandwiches with the other slices of bread. Slice the sandwiches on a diagonal.

Tea egg salad is also wonderful when used on top of a mixed green salad with fresh veggies and balsamic vinaigrette.

Courtesy of Owner Brian Clark of Kung Fu Cowboy Tea Cafe (p. 154).

New Mexican Mole

While New Mexican cuisine dominates the restaurant scene in this state, places like Epazote offer mainland Mexican at a level that is revelatory, rather than having chimichangas or smothered platters. Seafood, fresh corn, peppers, and nut-based sauces are major focal points for this hidden gem a few blocks from the Santa Fe Plaza.

Mole really just means "concoction," a sauce comprised of many spices laboriously combined, then thickened with nut flour or bread. There are dozens of varieties all over Mexico; the most well known is mole poblano, a dark brown chocolate-tinged elixir. Chef Fernando Olea takes the traditional mole compositions and serves them in rotation, a few at a time, along with his own creation utilizing local New Mexican ingredients to create a delicious fusion of flavors. This particular recipe was created by Chef Olea in commemoration of Santa Fe's 400th anniversary.

Note: Chef Olea uses regional ingredients to celebrate New Mexico—substitute what is local to you if possible.

Makes approximately 3 cups

½ cup fresh Española Valley apricots

½ cup northern New Mexican piñon nuts

¾ cup Las Cruces pecans

1 stick Mexican cinnamon

4 cloves

⅓ cup sesame seeds

¼ teaspoon cumin seeds

1 teaspoon anise seeds

½ cup butter

¼ cup chopped Española Valley onion

½ cup chopped Española Valley garlic

4–6 dried Chimayó red chile pods, stems and seeds removed

3 ounces white chocolate
½ cup chicken bouillon

½ teaspoon white pepper
Salt to taste

Wash the apricots and remove the pits.

Heat a pan over medium heat for about 2 minutes. Lightly toast the piñon nuts and pecans. Then add the cinnamon, cloves, and sesame, cumin, and anise seeds, stirring constantly until lightly golden.

Place the butter in a separate pan over medium-high heat and add the chopped onion, garlic, and red chile. Sauté until clear and soft, 3–5 minutes.

In a food processor or blender, process all the ingredients (including apricots) until very smooth, adding water if necessary. Place the blended ingredients in a large saucepan; bring to a boil and lower heat. Simmer 60 minutes, stirring often. Add white pepper and salt to taste.

Serve the mole with a strong red meat, such as New Mexico lamb. (Talus Wind Ranch produces spectacular lamb. It can be found along with other local ranchers' meats at the Santa Fe farmers' market.)

Courtesy of Owner & Chef Fernando Olea of Epazote (p. 43).

Grandma Tita's Red Posole

Posole is a traditional dish throughout the winter holidays in northern New Mexico. It is a rich and hearty dish that sticks to your ribs and warms you up from the inside out. This recipe is from Roberto Cordova's grandmother Tita; the whole family enjoyed it every year during the coldest months of the season. Roberto stresses that the best ingredients can make the dish even better, so note the suppliers if you live nearby and try to obtain from them.

Makes 2 quarts

Posole

1 pound posole, fresh or frozen (preferred supplier is Casados Farms)

1 yellow onion, quartered

1 teaspoon salt

Pork

2 pounds pork shoulder

2–4 cloves garlic, minced

1 teaspoon cumin

1 bay leaf

1 yellow onion, finely chopped

1 teaspoon salt, or to taste

Chile

6–8 chile pods (preferred supplier is Wagner Farms in Corrales)

2 cups hot broth (from the cooked pork)

Prepare the posole: *Soak the posole overnight. Drain and rinse posole, then place it in a cooking pot and cover with water; use approximately 2 parts water to 1 part posole. Add the onion and salt. Bring to a boil on the stove, then lower* heat and simmer until posole has started to "bloom," about 1½–2 hours. The posole will swell and start to resemble popcorn, but will still be chewy.

Prepare the pork: Place the pork shoulder in another pot and cover with water. Add the remaining ingredients. Bring to a boil and then cook over medium heat until tender and falling off the bone. Remove meat from broth and let cool. Remove meat from bones and pull apart into small pieces; set aside.

Prepare the chile: Place the rinsed chile pods, stems removed, in about 2 cups of hot broth (from the cooked pork) and let them soak about 20 minutes or until soft. (Note: Remove the seeds if you want a milder chile.) Place broth and chile pods in a blender and blend until smooth.

When the posole is at the chewy point, add the pork, chile, and any remaining broth to the posole and let it finish cooking (total cooking time about 4–6 hours). Stir the posole mixture periodically, adding hot water if necessary; do not allow it to dry out. Taste and adjust salt and pepper. The key to a successful posole is watching for it to finish "blooming." Posole is fully cooked when it has completely opened and is tender when chewed.

Serve in a bowl and place garnish on the table so that each person can do their own. Garnish may include sliced limes, chopped cilantro, finely chopped onion, oregano, cubed avocado, or grated cheese.

Courtesy of Owner Roberto Cordova of Casa Chimayó (p. 85).

Roasted Pork Belly

Pork belly is a tricky thing: Cook it not long enough and you have a big fatty mess; cook it too long and the meat left after the fat renders out can be tough (not to mention tiny). Shibumi Ramenya chef and owner Eric Stapleman makes several diners per week (sometimes per night) swoon over his slow-roasted pork belly that uses a few spices, coupled with a long slow roast, to achieve tender porkiness. He serves some of the pork in his Tonkatsu, a rich ramen soup, and some is reserved for small-plate presentation.

Find the pork online or ask your favorite butcher for a recommendation. As for the spices, both can be found at Asian markets or gourmet shops. The ichimi togarashi is dried red pepper flakes, while the sansyo pepper is a greenish ground leaf that has a strange heat unlike other peppers or even wasabi.

Makes roughly 1 quart if diced or shredded; serves 6

2 pounds center-cut untrimmed Kurobuta (Berkshire) pork belly

½ cup soy sauce

⅓ cup kosher salt

⅓ cup white sugar

⅓ cup light brown sugar

½ teaspoon ichimi togarashi

½ teaspoon sansyo pepper

½ teaspoon ground white pepper

Cut the pork belly in half lengthwise against the grain and place in a baking pan. Add the soy sauce and rub firmly over the pork belly to coat evenly. Let it rest in the fridge for 30 minutes.

Mix the salt, white sugar, light brown sugar, togarashi, sansyo pepper, and ground white pepper in a mixing bowl to incorporate evenly.

Remove the pork belly from the fridge and sprinkle with the dry ingredients, turning the pork gently to coat evenly. Place plastic wrap directly on the pork belly to prevent oxidation and then place plastic wrap over the entire baking dish. Refrigerate overnight.

Preheat oven to 220°F. Place the pork belly in a perforated pan placed inside another baking pan, making sure there is enough space between the perforated pan and the baking pan in order to render pork fat properly (basically you are leaving room for the fat to run out). Cover with plastic wrap and then with aluminum foil. Bake for approximately 4 hours until pork is tender. Check the pork with a paring knife (you should feel little resistance), then finish uncovered for 20 minutes.

If you have a smoker, you can pre-smoke with fruitwood (cherry or apple) for 1 hour at low temperature prior to baking and then reduce baking time by 30 minutes.

Serve any gosh-darned way you'd like. It's rich, so pairing with something sharp or acidic is not a bad idea.

Courtesy of Owner & Chef Eric Stapleman of Shibumi Ramenya (p. 62).

Veal Piccata

As old as the hills, getting a good veal piccata in Italy is probably like shootin' fish in a barrel. Scalo's had this dish on their menu intermittently as diners rediscover the classic, year after year. Current chef Garrick Mendoza says that it is a best-of-both-worlds recipe—extremely simple for the home cook and delicious as well. Start with some good veal from a butcher you like and choose a good white wine—one that you would drink with dinner. The rest is a slam dunk.

Serves 2

- **6 ounces spaghettini or angel hair pasta**
- **2 veal cutlets**
- **½ cup flour seasoned with 1 teaspoon salt and ½ teaspoon pepper**
- **Oil (vegetable or olive—not extra virgin)**

- **⅓ cup white wine**
- **⅓ chicken stock**
- **2 tablespoons lemon juice**
- **2 tablespoons capers**
- **1 tablespoon finely chopped parsley**
- **1 tablespoon butter**
- **Salt and pepper to taste**

Cook the pasta according to package directions while cooking veal.

Cover the cutlets with plastic wrap and pound thin using a meat pounder or small mallet. Coat in the seasoned flour; shake off excess.

Preheat ½ inch of oil in a large skillet; do not allow to smoke. Drape the cutlets into the pan (this avoids splashing oil), then wiggle the pan to let the oil come up over the edges of the meat. Cook until browned on one side, flip to other side, and cook until browning begins.

Remove the cutlets from the pan to a plate or cutting board. Pour off the oil, then add the white wine to the pan and deglaze by scraping up bits from the pan as the wine cooks. Add the chicken stock, lemon juice, capers, and parsley and keep cooking until reduced by half. Add the butter and whisk quickly—the sauce will thicken slightly. Add salt and pepper to taste.

Serve the veal over the pasta, pour the sauce over it, and garnish with additional parsley.

Courtesy of Chef Garrick Mendoza of Scalo Northern Italian Grill (p. 176).

Frog Legs Provençale

As Christophe, the effervescent owner of P'tit Louis, explains, this is about as classic as you can get for French bistro cooking. Much of what makes his restaurant great is the ability to take simple dishes and win people over—people who don't like pâté, think mussels are strange, or, in this case, consider frog legs to be really out there. As a bonus, you can win over eggplant doubters in the same dish with this perfectly crafted ratatouille.

Serves 4

Ratatouille

2 zucchini	2 tablespoons olive oil
2 yellow squashes	1 cup white wine
1 eggplant	3 bay leaves
1 yellow onion	1 sprig thyme
1 head garlic	Salt and white pepper to taste
10 Roma tomatoes	Cayenne pepper to taste

Preheat oven to 325°F.

Chop the unpeeled zucchini, yellow squashes, and eggplant and the peeled onion into 1-inch pieces. Peel all of the garlic and thinly slice half of the cloves. Blanch the tomatoes in boiling water for 20 seconds and then peel. Dice the tomatoes.

Heat the olive oil in a large oven-safe skillet. Add the onion and sauté until beginning to soften, then add the zucchini, yellow squashes, and eggplant. Sauté until the veggies start to soften. Add the white wine and burn off all the alcohol. Add all of the garlic (sliced and whole) to the vegetables. Add the tomatoes, bay leaves, and thyme to the mixture. Season with salt, white pepper, and cayenne pepper to taste.

Cover the ratatouille with parchment paper or foil and bake in the oven for 2 hours.

Frog Legs

Frog legs, 8 medium pairs (Asian markets or fishmongers are good sources)

Flour, seasoned with salt and white pepper (for dusting the frog legs)

8 tablespoons olive oil

4 cloves chopped garlic

8 sprigs chopped parsley

4 tablespoons butter

Dredge the frog legs in the seasoned flour.

Using the largest pan you have to avoid crowding the legs (cook in two batches if necessary, keeping first batch warm in oven while preparing second batch), bring the olive oil to high temperature in a nonstick pan. Sear the frog legs on one side, flip them over, and turn down the heat to medium. Sprinkle with garlic, parsley, and butter; cover and cook for 5 minutes.

Serve the frog legs over warm ratatouille. Et voila!

Courtesy of Owner Christophe Descarpentries of P'tit Louis Bistro (p. 117).

Apple Crostata

The chef at Trattoria Nostrani, Nelli Maltezos, says that this recipe is the first "pie" she's ever loved. A former pie-hater, she couldn't see how pie on the menu would sell, until experimenting with apples one fall. Finding a great crust and handling the apples with care, she hit upon the magical formula and says, "When I had my first taste of it, I immediately saw the appreciation others had for pie." Just like that, she was hooked, but only for her pie. Nelli further notes, "I believe the quality suffers if the crostata sits overnight, so we make them fresh every day. If we sell out, great; if not, our chef gets the first right of refusal, then we open them up to the staff."

Serves 10

Crust

1½ cups all-purpose flour
2 tablespoons sugar
¼ teaspoon salt
Zest of ½ lemon

5 ounces (10 tablespoons) butter, cut into small cubes and well chilled
Scant ¼ cup chilled white dessert wine

In the bowl of a food processor, combine the flour, sugar, and salt. Pulse the ingredients for 5 seconds; repeat twice more. Add the zest and butter. Pulse for approximately 10 seconds or until the butter cubes become the size of small peas. With the motor running, add the dessert wine. Pulse until the dough just comes together.

Place the dough on your work surface and form it into a disk. Wrap the disk in plastic and refrigerate for at least 1 hour.

Filling

1 cup white sugar	⅔ cup water
½ cup brown sugar	1 Rome Beauty apple
Zest of 1 lemon	1 McIntosh apple
1 vanilla bean, split and scraped	1 Jonathan apple
1 tablespoon vanilla extract	1 Honeycrisp apple
2 tablespoons chestnut honey	¼ cup applesauce
Pinch of salt	1 tablespoon cornstarch
	1 Granny Smith apple

In a very large sauté pan, add the two kinds of sugar, lemon zest, vanilla bean, vanilla extract, honey, salt, and water. Place the pan on the stovetop over medium heat.

Peel all of the red apples. Add the peels from two of the apples to the pan; discard remaining peels. Cook the liquid until it turns into the thickness of maple syrup, approximately 10 minutes.

In the meantime, core all of the red apples and cut in half. Cut each half into ¼-inch slices. Toss the apple slices with the applesauce and cornstarch. Set aside.

Strain the syrup to remove the vanilla bean and apple peels. Return the syrup to the sauté pan and bring to a boil. Add the red apple slices and cook for 2 minutes. While the red apples are cooking, peel, core, and slice the Granny Smith apple.

Remove the apple mixture from the stove. Transfer the entire mix to a bowl. Fold the raw Granny Smith apple slices into the cooked apples. Allow the apples to cool completely.

Assembly of Crostata

2 tablespoons butter, at room temperature

1 egg, whisked with 1 tablespoon cream

3 tablespoons sugar

Preheat oven to 350°F.

Pull the dough from the refrigerator. Lightly flour your work surface. Unwrap the dough and roll it out into a circle approximately 12–13 inches in diameter. Spread ½ tablespoon butter onto the surface of the dough and refrigerate for a few minutes.

Strain the apples from the syrup. Place the syrup back on the stovetop over low heat. Reduce the syrup by one-third. Remove from heat and set aside.

Pull the dough from the refrigerator and pile the apples tightly into the center of the dough. Allow for a 1½-inch overhang of dough. Dot the top with the remaining butter. Fold the dough up and around the apple mixture.

Brush the dough with the egg wash and sprinkle with sugar. Transfer the crostata to a parchment-lined sheet pan and bake for 20 minutes. Remove the crostata from the oven and brush the crust completely with the reserved syrup. Return the crostata to the oven for an additional 25 minutes.

Remove the crostata from the oven and allow to cool slightly. Slice into wedges and serve warm or cool.

Courtesy of Chef Nelli Maltezos of Trattoria Nostrani (p. 69).

Ragin' Cajun Cocktail

Chris Milligan is Santa Fe's go-to guy when you want a classic cocktail done right or a truly unique formula—he will create a cocktail for you on the spot once you give him a few clues to preferences and mood. This style is called "bespoke" and is not unlike omakase at a sushi bar. When Chris uses local ingredients, as he does here with Bill York's Bitter End Bitters, the drink goes from interesting to really special.

1 ½ ounces Jamaican rum
2 ounces peach nectar
½ ounce lime juice
½ ounce simple syrup

5 drops Bitter End Jamaican Jerk bitters
Ginger beer

Pour all the ingredients except the ginger beer in a mixing glass. Shake with ice and strain into an ice-filled glass. Top with ginger beer. Garnish with a peach slice and a cherry.

Courtesy of Chris Milligan of Secreto Bar & Loggia at the Hotel St. Francis (p. 286).

Mariposa Cocktail

Ben Williams likes this icy cold drink as an alternative to a margarita—he says the margarita is not the most popular cocktail south of the border. They instead prefer a white tequila and grapefruit soda mix and call it the Paloma, which makes me think of a nicely tart mimosa. He created a drink reminiscent of the Paloma, perfect for spring and summer sipping. It has the Southwestern kick of tequila but extra oomph with the botanical liqueur St. Germain and an extra punch of grapefruit juice. When he serves it, tiny shards of ice still play in the pink pool—this is a refreshing drink in any season.

1¼ ounces Patron Silver   ¼ lime, squeezed
¾ ounce St. Germain   Crushed or shaved ice
¾ ounce red grapefruit juice

Add all the ingredients to a cocktail shaker and vigorously shake. Strain into a martini glass. Garnish with a red grapefruit wedge.

Courtesy of Mixologist Ben Williams of Scalo Il Bar (p. 281).

Appendices

Appendix A: Eateries by Cuisine

Tune-Up Cafe, 71

Appendix B:
Dishes, Specialties
& Specialty Foods

Alcohol (Package)
Jubilation Wine & Spirits, 189
Kelly Liquors, 189
Kokoman Fine Wine & Liquor, 95
Susan's Fine Wine & Spirits, 97

Bagels
Mondo Kultur, 263
New York Deli, 54

Bowl of Chile, Green (Best of)
B & E Burritos, 118
Casa Chimayó, 85
Cocina Azul, 110
El Farolito, 38
Frontier Restaurant, The, 138

Horseman's Haven, 88
Mary & Tito's Cafe, 230
Perea's New Mexican, 184
Silvano's New Mexican, 185

Bowl of Chile, Red (Best of)
Barelas Coffee House, 127
Cecilia's Cafe, 130
Cocina Azul, 110
Duran's Central Pharmacy, 131
El Bruno's Restaurante y
    Cantina, 226
Mary & Tito's Cafe, 230
Rancho de Chimayó, 257
Sadie's New Mexican, 231
Shed Creative Cooking, The, 90

San Antonio General Store, 129
Whoo's Donuts, 98
Yiayia Maria's, 235

Frito Pie
Five & Dime General Store on
  Santa Fe Plaza, 94

Frozen
Alotta Gelato, 119
Chillz Frozen Custard, 187
Chocolate Cartel, 187
Ecco Espresso & Gelato, 93
Taos Cow Ice Cream Co., 255

Gluten-Free Options (Always Inquire!)
Andiamo!, 32
Antonio's, 240
Body Cafe, 36
Cube, The, 144
Dragonfly Cafe, 245
El Farol, 78
El Meze, 247
El Pinto, 227
Five Star Burgers, 248
Flying Star Cafe, 134

Graham's Grille, 249
Greenside Cafe, 146
Gutiz, 250
Harry's Roadhouse, 44
Il Piatto, 45
Il Vicino, 182
Indigo Crow Cafe, 206
Jambo Cafe, 46
Joe's, 46
Just a Bite, 189
Kung Fu Cowboy Tea Cafe, 154
Love Apple, The, 251
Museum Hill Cafe, 53
New York Deli, 54
Paisano's, 157
Rio Chama Steakhouse, 59
Scalo Northern Italian Grill, 176
Seasons Rotisserie & Grill, 126
Shed Creative Cooking, The, 90
Slate Street Cafe, 120
Sophia's Place, 212
St. James Tearoom, 234
Taos Diner, 255
Taos Pizza Out Back, 258
Tomme, 69
Tree House Pastry Shop &
  Cafe, 70

Index